Italian Fascism's Forgotten LGBT Victims

Italian Fascism's Forgotten LGBT Victims

Asylums and Internment, 1922–1943

Gabriella Romano

BLOOMSBURY ACADEMIC
LONDON • NEW YORK • OXFORD • NEW DELHI • SYDNEY

BLOOMSBURY ACADEMIC
Bloomsbury Publishing Plc, 50 Bedford Square, London, WC1B 3DP, UK
Bloomsbury Publishing Inc, 1385 Broadway, New York, NY 10018, USA
Bloomsbury Publishing Ireland, 29 Earlsfort Terrace, Dublin 2, D02 AY28, Ireland

BLOOMSBURY, BLOOMSBURY ACADEMIC and the Diana logo are trademarks of
Bloomsbury Publishing Plc

First published in Great Britain 2024
Paperback edition published 2025

A catalogue record for this book is available from the British Library.

A catalog record for this book is available from the Library of Congress.

ISBN: HB: 978-1-3503-7708-0
PB: 978-1-3503-7709-7
ePDF: 978-1-3503-7710-3
eBook: 978-1-3503-7711-0

Typeset by Newgen KnowledgeWorks Pvt. Ltd., Chennai, India

For product safety related questions contact productsafety@bloomsbury.com.

To find out more about our authors and books visit www.bloomsbury.com
and sign up for our newsletters.

To Emma

Contents

Preface

This book represents the conclusive phase of a research that I started in the mid-1990s. My aim was that of documenting the repression of LGBT lives under Mussolini. At the time, little had been written or recorded on this topic, and I embarked on a series of oral history projects over the following two decades.

The persecution of LGBT people in Italy under Mussolini has often been denied or belittled because it took place in a hidden and subtle way. My research aimed at demonstrating how the repressive system against LGBT people operated effectively and efficiently, albeit without specific laws or public statements. It relied on instilling fear and mistrust in people, so that they would act in a self-censored manner, and it created a climate of violence that pushed people underground.

This book expands the question of the persecution of LGBT people during the fascist regime in Italy by adding the use of psychiatry as a tool of repression, a subject that has not been investigated until now. My research draws together the substantial archival record of patients, doctors and the fascist authorities to reconstruct this highly complex and intricate behind-the-scenes 'dialogue' and to document one of the ways in which the regime repressed LGBT lives. The archival materials I consulted have barely been investigated from this specific perspective.

My research fills a gap in the history of psychiatry, as most historians until now have focused mainly on the decades between the end of the nineteenth and the beginning of the twentieth century, or on the 1970s and 1980s, when asylums where abolished with the introduction of the so-called 'Basaglia Law' (Law n. 180 of 13 May 1978). It also sheds light on how the fascist regime operated, by adopting a different analytical perspective. Finally, it adds a segment to the historiography on homosexuality in Italy and reconstructs the lives of many LGBT people.

Most importantly, it reinstates that, despite the repression, the unjustified arrests, the possibility of being sent to an isolated and remote island or of being interned in an asylum, LGBT Italians still found ways to live their lives as they intended to. They met, socialized, fell in love, had sexual affairs and lived in steady relationships, effectively contesting pressure from relatives, authorities and security forces. This book is a tribute to their undeterred courage and a celebration of their *Resistenza*.

Acknowledgements

I wish to thank the following people for their help with archival and bibliographical research: Pompeo Martelli, Gianna Capannolo, Vera Fusco, Ivo Ferrier and Paolo Verdini at the Santa Maria della Pietà Archives in Rome, Francesca Fiori at the Florence State Archives, Roberto Leonetti and Elena Cabras at the San Salvi Archives, Anna Salvini and Leonardo Pasquini at USL Toscana Centro, Salvatore Ritrovato and Oreste Bianco at the Girifalco Asylum Archives, Maria Cristina Labanti at the Biblioteca Biomedica of Bologna University, Stefano Salesi of the Biblioteca Medica Statale di Roma and Roberto Faleri of the Biblioteca Area Medico-Farmaco-Biologica of Siena University. I also thank the helpful and competent staff of the Wellcome Trust Library in London.

I am particularly grateful to my PhD supervisor, Sean Brady, and to Emma Sandon for the encouragement, the discussions and the advice. In addition, I would also like to thank, in alphabetical order, Claudio Ascoli, Joanna Bourke, Matt Cook, Giovanni Dall'Orto, Vinzia Fiorino, Kate Franklin, Oscar Greco, Leonardo Musci, Daniel Pick, Lucy Ryall, Chandak Sengoopta, Francesco Ventrella and Joseph Viscomi.

This research was made possible thanks to a Wellcome Trust grant that fully funded my MRes and my PhD at Birkbeck College, University of London.

Abbreviations

ASL It stands for Azienda Sanitaria Nazionale, equivalent to the NHS in the United Kingdom. Sometimes it is mentioned as USL, which stands for Unità Sanitaria Nazionale

FSA Florence State Archives

GAA Girifalco Asylum Archives

o.d.s. *Ordine di Servizio* (Order to Staff on how to carry out their duties)

PNF *Partito Nazionale Fascista* (Fascist National Party)

SMPA Santa Maria della Pietà Archives

SSA San Salvi Archives

Glossary

Atto di Notorietà: an official declaration, where ordinary citizens officially declared their opinion on another's mental health status. Signed in the presence of a notary or a local authority representative, it constituted additional legal proof that a person was in need of internment.

Carabinieri: the Italian military police force (*Polizia* being the civil police force).

Confino: punishment consisting of a forced period of residence in a remote location, usually an island or a village in the south of Italy.

Diario: usually a term that indicates a diary, memoirs and personal recollections; in asylums it applied to daily reports, often written by nurses.

Ergotherapy: a form of therapy that consisted of imposed working activities, widely used in asylums of the past. Discipline, a lack of idleness and a sense of achievement were thought to be beneficial and to improve, or even cure, mental health conditions.

Fascistizzazione: the process of imposition of fascist rules and rituals that was meant to transform and substitute the structure and functioning of Italian schools and institutions.

Follia morale: moral madness.

Libretto: a small book or the poetic text of an opera; in asylums, the term was used to describe pamphlets containing instructions to staff.

Logorrhoea: a condition where a person cannot refrain from talking, often to themselves.

Modula Informativa: the form GPs were asked to fill out and send to asylum psychiatrists when one of their patients was interned. Today, the feminine *Modula* is obsolete.

No-restraint:	a term that in psychiatry refers to an approach to patients that does not utilize methods of coerced restraint, such as straitjackets.
Pederast/y:	terms that, during Fascism, were used as synonyms of homosexual/ity.
Prefettura:	an institution that represents the State at a local level, coordinates the police forces and is in charge of public order. It is therefore in dialogue with both the Ministry of the Interior and with the police. Its chief is the *Prefetto*.
Pretura:	Magistrates Court.
Saffismo:	a euphemism for lesbianism.
Ventennio:	the twenty years Mussolini was in power.

Introduction

'Until now there has been no specific research in Italy on the use of psychiatric internment as a tool of social control of homosexuality.' In 2017, Giovanni Dall'Orto, one of the first Italian historians to investigate the history of homosexuality in Italy, lamented this historiographical gap.[1] The idea that homosexuality in Italy was repressed historically through psychiatry is widespread, but in the absence of a systematic study of the documentation of psychiatric hospitals, data is sketchy and often contradictory.

This book investigates the attitudes, theories and medical practice of Italian psychiatry with regard to homosexuality during the fascist regime in Italy. The research identifies continuities between the fascist era and the past, namely, in the persistence of degeneration and eugenic theories from the late nineteenth century and the beginning of the twentieth century, and emphasizes changes that took place in psychiatric thinking on deviancy, perversion and sexual inversion in the years between 1922 and 1943. It also reveals that psychiatry became, often reluctantly, a tool for the repression of homosexuality during Fascism. Psychiatric care was used by ordinary citizens, usually relatives of homosexuals, and by the security forces as an alternative to punishment and imprisonment.

The history of psychiatry and homosexuality in Italy

To understand how psychiatry pathologized homosexuality, we need to analyse the existing literature on the subject. Prior to 2000, barely any scholar addressed issues concerning homosexuality, psychiatry and sexology. The few articles to analyse the subject tended to focus on the end of the nineteenth and the beginning of the twentieth centuries. One, by Nerina Milletti, draws on articles published by the *Archivio di psichiatria, antropologia criminale e scienze penali per servire allo studio dell'uomo alienato e delinquente*, a journal founded by

Cesare Lombroso in 1880, whose name changed in 1909 to become *Archivio di antropologia criminale, psichiatria, medicina legale e scienze affini*.[2] Milletti's research covers the years from 1880 to 1949, but tends to privilege the first part of the period. It provides a reconstruction of how lesbianism was analysed by Italian psychiatrists and criminal anthropologists, such as Cesare Lombroso (1835–1909), Giovan Battista Cosimo Moraglia, Luigi Bianchi, Pasquale Penta (1859–1904), Alfredo D'Urso and Mario Carrara (1866–1937), in those crucial years that anticipated future theories such as the connection between homosexuality and criminality or between endocrinology and sexual behaviour.[3] Milletti's study pays special attention to book reviews of the time, demonstrating which foreign psychiatrists, endocrinologists and forensic anthropologists were considered worthy of mention and which theories circulated in Italy. The fact that she considers the period as a whole, without singling out the Mussolini years, suggests that she sees more continuity than discontinuity with the preceding decades.

Much more recently, my own research into the case of a man interned in 1928 in the Collegno asylum, near Turin, because of his 'homosexual tendencies', focuses on psychiatry and homosexuality during the regime.[4] Expanding from this case, my study examines the persecution of homosexuality during Fascism. It highlights how the rhetoric of the regime pushed stereotypes of masculinity to the extreme and how this came to justify the marginalization of anybody perceived as 'different'. The findings of my research offer evidence that internment of homosexuals was the joint effort of families and the security forces, while psychiatry seemed to accept only half-heartedly its role of social control imposed from above.

Other relatively recent studies, which I refer to later in this chapter, touch upon the topic of psychiatry during the fascist regime in Italy, although most of them do not specifically analyse it in depth.[5] In the reconstruction of the history of a specific mental health institution, these studies analyse the chosen institution's patient files and mention cases of homosexuality. As I explain later, only a few focus on the fascist regime or include the *Ventennio* in their analysis.[6]

Several publications have appeared on the connections between homosexuality and psychiatry between the 1920s and the 1940s in other European countries. Outside Italy, this subject has recently attracted unprecedented interest. Although this book does not aim to be a transnational comparative study, such publications are useful for reflection and contextualization, especially in the absence of a scholarly field in Italy. Two studies focusing on Spain are relevant to this research because of the parallels between two countries under a dictatorship whose years partially overlap. Furthermore, during the *Ventennio*, the twenty years Mussolini was in power, there was a strong connection through theory between Italian psychiatrists and psychiatrists of the Hispano–Portuguese region, such as Gregorio Marañon (1887–1960) and Egas Moniz (1874–1955). The co-authored book by Richard Cleminson and Francisco Vasquez Garcia includes a chapter on the connection between sexological theories and the repression of homosexuality in Spain in the years 1915–39.[7] The second study, by Alvar Martinez-Vidal and Antoni Adam Donat, addresses homosexuality and psychiatry specifically during Franco's regime.[8] Their research was presented at an international conference held in December 2008 at Bergen University together with another paper, by Runar Jordåen, on homosexuality in forensic psychiatry in Norway between 1930 and 1945, also relevant to my research.[9] Studies on homosexuality during Nazism and on psychiatry and homosexuality in twentieth-century Germany are clearly central to this research, given the strong connection between the two dictatorships and the influence that the German psychiatric school had on its Italian counterpart.[10] Other scholars' work, such as Malick Briki's writing on sexology in Europe,[11] Janet Weston's study on sexual deviance in Great Britain[12] and Ira Roldugina's essays on LGBT history in Russia, adds interesting aspects to this research.[13]

The history of Italian psychiatry: The interwar period

It is essential to frame the debate on how psychiatry dealt with homosexuality during the regime in a broader context, and this research examines the historiography of psychiatry during the fascist regime, to give this wider picture. However, this subject too suffers from lack of investigation. 'Extremely out of focus and distant' were the words used in 1989 by historian Ferruccio Giacanelli to describe the state of historical research on psychiatry for the interwar period in Italy.[14] He asserts that the historiography of Italian psychiatry as a whole experienced, or rather suffered from, multiple *lacunae*, and the interwar period was almost forgotten in this regard until recently. Giacanelli wonders whether this scholarly gap, which he calls an 'historiographical "void"', was due to the difficulties in analysis and reconstruction of a period that was still too close and painful to re-elaborate.[15] He laments that Italian psychiatry in the fascist period was frequently dismissed as an insignificant phase, characterized by backwardness, isolation and provincialism. He insists that this description is too reductive and would make the remarkable developments in psychiatric theory and practice after the Second World War inexplicable. He emphasizes the need to take a close look at its transformation between the Liberal State (1861–1922) and the end of Fascism, urging historians to concentrate on themes and currents of thought and practice, rather than focusing on the biographies of famous psychiatrists.

The same year, and in the same collection of essays, Giorgio Bignami agrees with Giacanelli.[16] He concludes his article on the merging of neurological and psychiatric university teaching during Fascism, voicing concern that the era of the dictatorship is still completely under-researched. He too identifies the need to understand the relevance of the *Ventennio*, in terms of psychiatry, with the belief that this era influenced theory and practice in the following decades.

It is no coincidence that this historiographical gap was noticed after new legislation on psychiatric internment and care was introduced in Italy. These laws were approved as a result of the movement led by psychiatrist and campaigner Franco Basaglia (1924–1980).[17] In 1978, Law 180 (the so-called Basaglia Law) abolished mental health hospitals in Italy.[18] This did not happen overnight: it was the final step in a long process that started in the late 1960s and included public debates, political demonstrations, sit-ins, conferences and publications. Basaglia, his wife Franca Ongaro (1928–2005) and the group of psychiatrists who worked with them started a movement across the whole country, which drew the attention of politicians, media and public opinion. In the wave of the 1968 and 1977 student and feminist movements, marginalized and liminal worlds became fundamentally important. The critical debates on psychiatric care questioned society and its mechanisms of power and oppression, and were a social lever in this time of profound change in social attitudes. Asylums were identified as central to the debate on civil liberties. They epitomized *bourgeois* society and the brutal persecution enacted on 'others', especially towards rebellious and nonconforming people, who were by this time regarded as victims of the system. Psychiatry became synonymous with oppression in Italy. It symbolized the supremacy of rationality and convention over irrationality and spontaneity, the imposition of rigid laws and meaningless discipline on free individuals. It is no coincidence that the beginning of the LGBT movement in Italy is traditionally said to coincide with a demonstration by F.U.O.R.I.! (Fronte Unitario Omosessuale Rivoluzionario Italiano) activists outside a psychiatrists' congress in San Remo in 1972.[19]

This new focus on psychiatry also led to an interest in its past. Giacanelli, Bignami and others showed that historical research until then had concentrated mainly on the period from the end of the nineteenth century to the beginning of the twentieth. Anything after the 1920s and before the 1980s had been merged into an indistinct lapse of time to become an undistinguished period of backwardness and cruelty. In 1991, only a couple of years after Giacanelli's and Bignami's critique, Patrizia Guarnieri examined the history of Italian psychiatry as a whole and published the first comprehensive bibliographical monograph, which listed, year by year, everything that had been written on the subject from 1864 to 1990.[20] Her work gives tangible proof that the historiography of Italian psychiatry had huge gaps, in terms of chronology and content, and was written from a nationalist and uncritical point of view. It concentrated, Guarnieri argues, on a few historical periods, identified as 'glorious' for the country, and was anchored to old-fashioned methodological approaches. In her extensive introductory essay, Guarnieri divides books on Italian psychiatry into roughly three categories. The first consists of the more traditional historical works documenting the period from the Renaissance to the beginning of the twentieth century. She emphasizes that these were written mostly by practitioners. The consequent lack of distance from the subject would explain their strong nationalistic approach and positive perspective. In other words, the history of Italian psychiatry had been recounted largely by those who were eager to tell a story of constant improvement. By the 1920s, the fascist regime had inherited this tradition. In a dictatorship that made it compulsory to Italianize even foreign names, the history of psychiatry was written with an even clearer intention of underlining the relevance of results obtained by Italian psychiatrists of the past.

The second category identified by Guarnieri is biography. Mostly hagiographic in tone, biographies reconstructed and celebrated, often rather emphatically, the life and work of mainly Italian eminent practitioners, from Vincenzo Chiarugi (1759–1820) – generally considered the founder of psychiatry in Italy – onwards. This second category of publications also revealed the nationalistic pride at its roots. The author includes the autobiographies of psychiatrists in this category, or rather memoirs for publication, a literary genre in its own right in Italy. The lack of distance between the author and its subject means that the majority of these publications lack objectivity. In particular, survivors of Fascism, like survivors of all dictatorships, tend to self-censor their memories, as has been observed in several differing circumstances.[21] The implication that they might not have opposed the regime makes them cautious, and they are also wary of younger generations judging them negatively. Keeping in mind its limits, this autobiographical writing did constitute an interesting source for the purposes of this research.[22]

Finally, the third category of publications on psychiatry identified by Guarnieri is the history of mental health institutions. For centuries, the institution's discipline and rules were considered the main and most effective psychiatric cure. As a result, the history of Italian psychiatry and the histories of its institutions often overlap. This last category has seen the greatest development in Italy in recent years, as asylum archives became accessible to the public.[23] Yet this genre of research has also tended to focus on the historical period before Fascism.

In addition, Guarnieri draws attention to the fact that historical analysis of Italian psychiatry seems to have stopped at the first two decades of the twentieth century. Undoubtedly, the period immediately prior to Fascism has traditionally been the most celebrated at an international level because of its impact on European psychiatry and criminal anthropology. The golden age of Italian psychiatry, the 'luminous pause',[24] coincided with the publications and activities of criminal anthropologist Cesare Lombroso and his followers. It is still the most studied period in the history of Italian psychiatry and the history of its institutions to this day, together with eugenics, which directly informed and shaped the psychiatric theory and practice of the time. Studies on this crucial period for psychiatry in Italy, from the end of the nineteenth century to the beginning of the twentieth century, are essential if we want to understand subsequent theory and practice. They constitute a body of work that explains what the *Ventennio* psychiatrists studied and read as well as their background. Most Italian psychiatrists operating in the 1920s and 1930s started their professional training in earlier decades, and almost all of them paid tribute to their predecessors, eager to be placed within a certain strand of the tradition. However, as Guarnieri underlines, to concentrate only on the period considered to be the most glorious and internationally praised is in itself another aspect of a nationalist approach.

The four decades that preceded the fascist regime have attracted the largest body of research, followed by studies on the Basaglia Movement in the late 1970s and 1980s. Publications on the period 1880s–1920s include monographs on eugenics and on the Lombrosian school,[25] the history of nineteenth- to early-twentieth-century psychiatry[26] and specific studies on sexology and sexuality in Italy, and more broadly in Europe.[27]

Guarnieri's bibliography has been integrated and updated by another bibliography by Matteo Fiorani, published in 2010, who shows how the Basaglia Movement translated into an increased interest in the history of psychiatry and how to some extent certain *lacunae* have been partially filled in recent years. It would take me astray to comment on it in detail, but this accurate publication constitutes an essential point of reference for this research.[28]

Another group of publications relevant to this research, which could be added to Guarnieri's classification, consists of studies on the history of the legal and administrative aspects of psychiatry. Their focus is the complex political and theoretical process that led to the approval of the internment law, Law n. 36, in 1904, which remained in force during the regime and was never amended. Historians such as Romano Canosa, Michael Donnelly, Franco Silvano and Ada Lonni show how Fascism extended pre-existing legislation, simply by no more than bending it to its needs.[29] Law n. 36/1904 reduced psychiatry to a mere function of social control. Although it gave more power to psychiatrists, and especially to asylum directors, from the start it was perceived by most professionals as reductive of a doctor's scientific and medical role. This discontent was inherited by psychiatrists in the fascist years, who continued contesting several aspects of the law and proposed several amendments. Almost everybody who touches on the subject of Italian psychiatry, its history and methods mentions how this controversial law had an impact on it and shaped its practice. Identifying continuity with the past, Canosa, Donnelly, Silvano and Lonni unanimously underline the fact that Fascism never considered it necessary to alter the 1904 law, as it was sufficiently ambiguous to allow different interpretations and therefore to accommodate the fascist dictatorship's repressive needs. All historians dealing with the history of Italian psychiatry and its institutions draw attention to its Article 1, the most problematic, which stated that a person should be interned when s/he caused public scandal, an aspect that was thoroughly exploited by the regime.

When analysing Italian interwar psychiatry, most historians are eager to underline continuity with the Lombroso era rather than innovation. Romano Canosa, one of the most authoritative historians of law and psychiatry in Italy, warns that it would be a mistake to ascribe to Fascism certain trends or influences on subsequent psychiatric thought and practice.[30] He emphasizes that, despite a supposed interaction between psychiatry and the regime in handling social problems and in giving more authority to a neurological/medical approach, there was very little input from psychiatrists when the Rocco Code of laws was drafted and discussed.[31] In addition, according to Canosa, 'constitutionalist' theories had little impact on routine psychiatric practice, and neurology was also given priority in countries where a long-lasting fascist dictatorship had never taken place, such as France.[32] His pronouncements made younger scholars cautious in their attempts to identify some of the peculiarities of psychiatry under Fascism. This, together with the already mentioned evident self-censoring process from psychiatrists who lived through the *Ventennio*, contributes to explain the absence of historiography on psychiatry during the fascist regime.[33]

It was not until 2008 that an entire monograph was published on the 'difficult' subject of psychiatry and Fascism. Paolo Francesco Peloso's book starts with the reconstruction of a single episode, the killing of a nurse in the early days of the regime, which he sees as emblematic of how violence entered the psychiatric system, becoming an integral part of it, under Mussolini.[34] Peloso then illustrates the organization of mental health institutions and retraces the career and thought of some of the most influential psychiatrists of those years. Stressing that psychiatry was indebted to the theories of previous decades, he interprets the dictatorship period as a moment of suspension between two major eras, a sort of limbo. He synthesizes this concept in the following way:

> Psychiatry at the beginning of the twentieth century no longer believes in 'moral' treatment, nor does it yet believe in the new 'moral' treatment, which will be psychoanalysis: it believes in chemical and physical treatment, which is not completely available yet.[35]

Within the general context characterized by conformism and hostility towards new thinking, Peloso traces instances in which psychology was pioneered by some Italian professionals, despite the fact that during the regime its teaching was relegated to the Faculties of Literature and Philosophy. He interprets this drastic exclusion from the syllabuses of university Faculties of Medicine to be a consequence of ideas that were already in circulation before Fascism. A substantial part of the book centres on eugenics in Italy, showing how under Mussolini Italian psychiatrists developed these theories further, laying the ground for theories of racial supremacy and colonialism.[36] Peloso then shifts his focus and style. Talking about the war period, he briefly sketches a few biographies of psychiatrists involved in the *Resistenza*. He includes topics such as the use of asylums during the war, the consequences of the conflict in terms of the population's mental health and how psychiatry addressed the problem of war-related traumas at the time. Peloso's writing deals with many issues, using a variety of approaches (biographical, theoretical, historical). He tries to give shape to psychiatry during the *Ventennio*, a subject that had never been analysed systematically. For the purpose of this research, his book is a fundamental point of reference, although homosexuality is mentioned only once.

Peloso's book was preceded by an article by Massimo Moraglio, a scholar who has written extensively on the history of mental health institutions in Italy, focusing mainly on Piedmont.[37] He is one of the first historians to point out that psychiatric debate in Italy continued during the fascist regime, despite its rigid censorship, and sometimes showed innovative elements. He also emphasizes that, from the introduction of the 1904 internment law onwards, a heated and constant exchange of views took place among psychiatrists on the legal aspects of the mental health system, which continued throughout the dictatorship. Moraglio underlines that even Arturo Donaggio (1868–1942), one of the staunchest supporters of the regime among psychiatrists, expressed hopes for a reform of the law in 1933, which proves the independence of thought of psychiatrists, even at the height of the dictatorship. The debate on how to amend the 1904 law forced the entire psychiatric profession to analyse the meaning and methods of its work, from 'no-restraint' techniques to pharmacological therapies and psychoanalysis, in line with the rest of Europe. This debate demonstrates resistance to the regime's censorship and provincialism. In addition, Moraglio recognizes other signs of vitality in the *Ventennio* psychiatric scenario. Among them, he mentions that several professional associations and psychiatric journals started during Mussolini's dictatorship, regular congresses took place where all the modern trends of the discipline were discussed, the Italian psychiatric system was constantly criticized from within and its practices were severely scrutinized by professionals. An emphasis was placed on prevention which, although tainted by eugenics theories, can be viewed as another step towards a modern approach to mental health care. Moraglio insists that we no longer consider the fascist period as a monolithic bloc but instead highlights the different currents of thought and practice within it.

A third decisive contribution to the historiography of psychiatry during Fascism comes in 2009, when Valeria Babini writes a chapter of her book on the history of twentieth-century Italian psychiatry on the *Ventennio*.[38] She too points to the fact that during Fascism Italian psychiatry went through an important phase of re-elaboration and was certainly far from being idle or silent. Babini focuses on the rejection of psychoanalysis during the fascist regime, when the so-called 'organicist' approach to mental illness was favoured. Italian psychiatrists looked for somatic, genetic and pathological causes of mental illness and saw little scientific certainty in the new psychoanalytical theories. Babini analyses the key steps in the psychiatric profession's processes of distancing itself from psychoanalysis. Italian successes in endocrinology, combined with a nationalistic spirit, created fertile ground for psychiatric theories that saw chemistry, endocrinology, serology and clinical observation as most important. Babini too underlines that the 1923 Gentile University Reform took psychology away from all Faculties of Medicine throughout the country. Psychology remained in the philosophical and literary programmes of studies. The teaching of psychiatry and neurology everywhere merged, except at the universities of Milan and Rome where they remained separate. In agreement with historians of psychiatry, Babini judges this merger as a regressive step, emphasizing that separation of disciplines always means greater specialization, therefore more scientific progress.

Babini also describes the available cures at the time and points out that there was a general feeling of demoralization among psychiatrists who were aware of the inadequacies in this sector. She indicates that, to overcome this widespread feeling of defeat, Italian psychiatrists enthusiastically adopted shock methods, such as malariotherapy or insulin-induced coma, on a vast scale. It is not a coincidence, she writes, that electro-shock treatment was invented by an Italian psychiatrist, Ugo Cerletti, in 1938 and that psychosurgery found fertile terrain in Italy. Most importantly, she argues that research and debate on all available therapies continued throughout the 1930s and had tangible consequences for successive decades. The years of the regime, she concludes, must be regarded as a laboratory for testing new ideas and for discussing new and old practices.

An additional original contribution to the reconstruction of psychiatric theory and practice under Fascism comes from Zbigniew Kotowicz, who studied the history of psychosurgery in Europe.[39] He demonstrates how psychosurgery attracted interest in Italy in the 1930s, where it was quickly deployed on a greater scale than in most European countries. He documents the tough criticism it raised among contemporaries, together with the enthusiastic praise it sometimes obtained, both nationally and internationally, and how it was central to psychiatric debate. In fact, Kotowicz shows that its applications became a peculiarity of Italian psychiatry. His publications shed light on a relatively unknown aspect of psychiatric practice in Italy and fill another 'historiographical void'.

A decisive attempt to fill the *lacuna* comes in 2016, when a book by Mariopaolo Dario, Giovanni Del Missier, Ester Stocco and Luana Testa retraces the history of Italian psychiatry and psychotherapy and dedicates an entire chapter to the interwar period.[40] This publication brings to light some very important aspects. In it, the authors rightly stress that the Rocco Code of Laws (1930) imposed that internment would figure in a person's criminal record, a clear tribute to the Lombrosian theories that linked degeneration and mental illness to criminality. However, the authors are keen to highlight that during the dictatorship there was a considerable plurality of opinions in the psychiatric theory debate, aptly illustrated by the varied positions that could find a voice in the *Enciclopedia Italiana* published by Treccani.[41] Fascism was a period of transition, in the world of psychiatry, which meant debate and elaboration of new ideas, not just backwardness. They draw attention to the decisive shift of mentality that took place in those years, when the word 'asylum' started to be replaced by the more appropriate psychiatric hospital, and when *dispensari*, home visits and home care were given real impulse. In addition, in the authors' view, some negative aspects have been traditionally ascribed to Fascism, while in some cases this is historically not correct. For instance, the merging of neurology and psychiatry, often described as an identifying element of the *Ventennio* and judged to be a sign of involution, was already in place in the Positivist years at the end of the nineteenth century.

A further interesting and original contribution to the reconstruction of this relatively unknown period for Italian psychiatry comes from an article by Maria Antonietta Coccanari De' Fornari, Andrea Piazzi and Gioia Piazzi.[42] It concentrates on the *Enciclopedia Italiana*, a project that started in 1925 and took over a decade to be completed and published.[43] It involved the most authoritative psychiatrists at a national level. By looking at how some key psychiatry headwords were formulated, the authors shed light on the co-existence of the 'organicist' anatomo-histological tradition and more modern concepts and approaches. The *Enciclopedia Italiana* thus becomes a perfect point of view to demonstrate that the debate among psychiatrists at the time was lively, there was a considerable open-mindedness in giving voice to dissenting or contrasting opinions, and both theoreticians and practitioners were discussing and elaborating outcomes of new and old trends, foreign theories and practical approaches.

Finally, the history of psychiatry during the fascist dictatorship years is complemented by recent publications on the ways in which the regime used the mental health system as a tool for the repression of political dissent. These books refer to Lombrosian theories on the connection between mental and moral deviancy, the pathologization of certain categories of individuals, atavism and concepts of inherited or inborn tendencies to immoral, criminal or degenerate behaviour. All of these subjects are relevant to the pathologization of homosexuality during Fascism. Matteo Petracci concentrates on the Santa Maria della Pietà asylum in Rome and documents the internment there of several anti-fascists.[44] His interest focuses primarily on how the regime extended the role of social control that psychiatry had inherited from theories of the previous century, to include Anti-Fascism among the 'socially dangerous' categories of citizens. His analysis of the legal aspects of internment is very detailed and explains how the law could be bent to accommodate the repressive needs of the regime. Equally, Mimmo Franzinelli and Nicola Graziano reconstruct cases of anti-fascists and Resistance fighters interned in Aversa, the criminal asylum near Naples, as an alternative to prison.[45] Franzinelli and Graziano also mention that, in the context of increasingly severe racial policies, some detainees for common crimes were sent to the criminal asylum once their homosexuality was detected. The authors shed light on the case of G. B. P., who was sentenced for theft and criminal association but was transferred from the Genoa prison to the Aversa criminal asylum in 1933 because he was homosexual.[46] The aim of Franzinelli and Graziano's book, however, is to highlight the continuity between psychiatric practice during the fascist regime and Lombroso's theories, and to prove that many anti-fascists were incapacitated through internment.

In the field of the history of specific mental health institutions, a wealth of titles are being published every year, but only a few recent publications take the fascist period into consideration. Annacarla Valeriano's first book analyses the period between 1880 and 1931, thus including the first few years of Fascism.[47] She concentrates on female patients interned in the mental health institution in Teramo, in the southern region of Abruzzi, and highlights social order, morality and eugenics as reasons for their internment. Her findings are rooted in nineteenth-century theory and her research does not emphasize any peculiarity for the period of Fascism, its theoretical and internment practices, or any specific aspects that might characterize the *Ventennio*. Her second publication centres on women interned in the fascist years in the same institution.[48] Again, and here this is even clearer, there is no intention to identify distinctive traits of psychiatric thought and practice in those years. Valeriano emphasizes the repressive role played by psychiatry to control women's non-normative behaviour, but her analysis focuses on elements of continuity between the years of the fascist regime and the previous decades.

Vinzia Fiorino, in her reconstruction of the activities in the Volterra asylum between 1888 and 1978, covers the entire period of the dictatorship.[49] She brings to the fore interesting specificities for the fascist regime, such as the increased bureaucracy needed to obtain a patient's release, whether definitive or for a trial period. She interprets this increase in bureaucracy as a way to discourage relatives from applying for release and to further isolate the institution from the outside world. She also observes that political loyalty now played an important role within the asylum routine. Membership of the PNF, *Partito Nazionale Fascista*, and its accompanying membership card determined who could work or even provide services, in line with all other workplaces, where beliefs in fascist convictions became an essential criterion for employment. She identifies an intensification of control not only in the political orientation of professionals involved in the psychiatric system but also over patients' sexual behaviour. She observes that during Fascism,

> it is … evident that notes on sexuality and political behaviour will become more and more present in the reconstruction of the ill subject who is liable to being interned.[50]

In addition, Fiorino describes the case of a patient interned during the dictatorship whose medical notes included a mention of his 'tendencies to sexual inversion that manifest themselves in a tenacious push towards intimate relationships with patient G.'. Hers is one of the few mentions of how homosexuality was approached and described in an asylum during the *Ventennio*.[51]

Finally, in the already mentioned Massimo Tornabene's book, *La Guerra dei Matti. Il Manicomio di Racconigi tra fascismo e Liberazione*,[52] part of the history of the Racconigi asylum, in the north-west region of Piedmont, is reconstructed as he focuses exclusively on the period of the fascist regime. He observes that in this institution too 'the organicist direction of Italian psychiatry was predominant: psychology was marginalised and so was psychiatry itself, whose teaching was absorbed by neurology during Fascism'.[53] Within this theoretical and practical framework, he confirms that electro-shock treatment was widely in use in Racconigi and that psychosurgery was pioneered on patients affected by a wide range of mental illnesses. His detailed analysis gives a precise reconstruction of the organization and daily routine of this institution during the dictatorship and constitutes a valid point of reference with which to compare other asylums examined in the course of this research.

The history of homosexuality in Italy: The interwar period

In order to complete a literature overview, to contextualize and ground the research on the topic of this book, I take the historiography on homosexuality in Italy into consideration, privileging studies on the *Ventennio*. The fascist period in Italy, as an overall subject, is still not completely investigated: too many 'secrets' are yet to surface, and many never will. A considerable amount has been written around the memory of Fascism and of the Holocaust in Italy from 1945 onwards, and on the problematic process of reconstructing Italy's uncomfortable past.[54] The relatively recent books by Robert Gordon and John Foot document how memory of the dictatorship was collected and how official and unofficial politics shaped the way in which Fascism was reconstructed, narrated and made public.[55] Issues of collective responsibility were set aside from the post-war period onwards, together with war crimes committed in Libya, Somalia and Ethiopia, to give a few examples of where the silence has been almost impenetrable until very recent times.

In Italy, anything that touches the subject of Fascism is extremely controversial and open to political manipulation. Fascism and the memory of it are at the centre of the Italian daily political debate. Public opinion is divided between those who downplay the regime's repression, crimes or abuses and those who stress the need to concentrate on them.

Within this context, it comes as no surprise that the history of homosexuality, and of homosexuality during Fascism in particular, is a markedly small field of research and that investigation of it started relatively late. From the end of the Second World War, the uninterrupted series of Christian Democrat–led coalition governments did not help foster interest in this field, while the homophobic positions of the Communist Party in the 1950s and 1960s are well known and aptly exemplified by Pier Paolo Pasolini's expulsion from the party.

There are several other reasons for this delay in research on homosexuality during the interwar period. In the years following the war, the biggest effort on the part of Italy's mostly left-wing historians was reconstruction of the history of the *Resistenza*, the fight against the regime. The priority, in the aftermath of the dictatorship and the two years of civil war (1943–5) that followed, was to build a past that could reunite the country around a 'Grand Narrative' of the heroic struggle against the dictator. Thus, the history of political dissent and resistance to the regime was meticulously written from the years immediately after the war. At the same time, the Italian Jewish community's oral testimonies of the Shoah were printed as primary sources, starting with Primo Levi's *Se Questo è un uomo*, published in 1947.[56] Smaller groups that had suffered persecution during the dictatorship, such as Romas, Jehovah Witnesses, Protestants, gays and lesbians, were almost completely forgotten by scholars for several decades.

Only when the official files of the 1920s became available for consultation to the general public, seventy years after their origin, did the subject start to be studied, and Giovanni Dall'Orto managed to gain unprecedented access to archival material as soon as it was made available.[57] His work, together with Gianni Rossi Barilli's and Paolo Hutter's radio interviews,[58] led to identification of LGBT survivors and inspired others to collect oral history testimonies in the early 1990s.[59] However, oral history was gathered too late, when survivors were few and with fading memories. Consequently, the account of the persecution endured by LGBT people remained fragmented and partial.

Moreover, when initial efforts were made to start piecing together the mosaic, it became apparent that the expected counterbalance to the 'Grand Narrative of the *Resistenza*' could not be found. The older generation of homosexuals had lived in the closet and were extremely critical of the gay liberation movement, its visibility, its slogans and campaigns. The experience of living in fear, combined with the need for silence and discretion, dominated. Many older gay men even referred to themselves using derogatory and insulting terms such as *frocio, ricchione, femminella, arruso,* not easily translatable terms, such as *maricon* in Spanish or 'fairy' in English. The generations of Italian LGBT people born after the war were ashamed of these 'grandparents', who came across as helpless victims tormented by guilt complexes, shame and hypocrisy. These were precisely the attributes that younger LGBT people were fighting against. They were uneasy with people they regarded as closeted, who openly disliked Pride Parades and, in expressing nostalgic feelings about their youths, could make politically embarrassing remarks about the 'good old days'. In turn, older LGBT people felt judged negatively and were even more reluctant to speak out. The generational gap widened further and made oral history projects increasingly difficult to accomplish.[60]

Recent years have seen the publication of a number of essays and books that addressed the issue and tried to fill the evident scholarly gap in this area.[61] Among them, Lorenzo Benadusi's book, inspired by George Mosse, gives an interesting interpretation of the cultural stereotypes from which the persecution of homosexuality took its origins and consolidated during the regime.[62] Michael Ebner's publications investigate further and offer tangible proof of the daily routine of violence that Italian homosexuals lived through.[63] Giovanni Dall'Orto dedicates a relevant part of his latest book on the history of homosexuality in Italy to the interwar period in Italy.[64] A recent collection of essays on various aspects of the history of homosexuality in Italy, edited by Umberto Grassi, Vincenzo Lagioia and Gian Paolo Romagnani, comprises an entire section on the nineteenth and twentieth centuries.[65] Studies in the field are increasing in number every year, as many universities in Italy now offer gender studies programmes and history faculties in the last twenty years have witnessed a tangible interest in the history of homosexuality.

Methodology

This book consists of two distinct parts: the first focuses on psychiatric theories on homosexuality, concentrating on some of the most authoritative Italian psychiatrists for the period between the 1920s and the early 1940s. The second part is based on archival research.

I have carried out archival research in the archives of three psychiatric hospitals. Located in three different areas of the country, these were of a different size and relevance in fascist Italy. Santa Maria della Pietà, in Rome, was one of the largest and most well-known institutions during the *Ventennio* and beyond. Its archives are among the best kept and catalogued in Italy. However, they have suffered from frequent changes of location and previous lack of conservation care. As a result, a few Admissions Registers and patient files are missing. The situation is confusing when it comes to the numbers of patient files. Each patient's file contains several numbers referring to each internment, but on occasion different numbers refer to a person interned only once but transferred from one pavilion to another. In addition, files also note administrative numbering, which is sometimes mixed with patient file numbers but refer to a completely different classification. Consequently, I decided not to include the patient file number. The Santa Maria della Pietà archivists do not rely on the numbers; consultation of a specific file depends on having the patient's surname, first name or initials and, if known, the date when s/he left the asylum because s/he was discharged, or transferred to another institution, or deceased while interned. Therefore, in my notes, I report the date when the patient left the institution, together with the patient's initials, surname first. In this way I do not reveal the patient's identity, as required by law (as explained later in this chapter), but I give notes that prove the accuracy of my research as much as possible and allowed by current legislation.

The psychiatric hospital in Florence, named after Vincenzo Chiarugi, but known as San Salvi Hospital after the area in which it is located, was a much smaller institution at the time, serving a provincial city that was a fraction of the size it is today. Its documentation is much more difficult to access and consult. Split into two, its records are held partly at the State Archives in Florence and partly in a locked room next to the University of Florence Faculty of Psychology library, located in the old hospital premises. This locked room contains records of patients discharged after 1940. Access to this second part of the archives is limited and difficult to obtain. When I managed to consult it, I could find only one of the eight patient files I was looking for. This makes it plausible to assume that some documents have been lost or misfiled. Alternatively, they could be kept elsewhere, in a location inside San Salvi and inaccessible to the public. However, the ASL (Italian equivalent of the NHS) employee in charge of the San Salvi part of the archives never mentioned the existence of another collection of documentation. Prof Donatella Lippi, of the University of Florence, confirmed that, to her knowledge, there is no documentation in locations other than the two I mentioned earlier.[66] The chapter on San Salvi is therefore based on the available and consultable documents, keeping in mind that its results are partial. In this case too, patient file numbers are deliberately not mentioned, as they are irrelevant. What counts is the date when the patient left the institution, because of being discharged or transferred, or deceased, which appears in my footnotes, together with the patient's initials.

The third mental health institution archives consulted for this research were the Girifalco asylum archives. This institution was chosen to represent a small and provincial psychiatric institution, far away from major cities and from the capital. Its collection consists of patient files and Admissions Registers only, as all the administrative documentation has been lost.

The criteria used to identify which patient files to consult were identical in the first two institutions I analysed. In the Rome and Florence mental health hospital archives, I examined the files of patients diagnosed as presenting abnormality/ties of character, constitutional immorality, moral madness, erotic delirium, psycho-degeneration, degeneration, state of excitement, dysthymias, depressive states with a degenerative basis, ethic deficiency and amorality. In the Rome asylum's archives, I also took into consideration, randomly, files of patients with diagnoses different from the ones mentioned above, such as hysteria, schizophrenia, paranoid delirium, senile dementia, demented states, emotional excitement based on senility, encephalitis and so forth. My aim was to see whether homosexuality was also indicated under differing diagnostic categories and descriptions. In the Girifalco asylum archives, as diagnoses were not specified in the Admissions Registers, I sample-searched and looked at all patient files for three years chosen randomly within the fascist period: 1924, 1933 and 1939. Files here are catalogued by date of admission.

Research into mental health hospitals' archival records is sometimes difficult from a bureaucratic and logistical point of view, but it is also a painful experience. It brings the researcher in contact with the lives of the thousands of individuals who were intercepted by the psychiatric system and were subsequently isolated from society, separated from their world of affections, given experimental cures, forced to work, often looked after by ignorant and aggressive nurses. The majority of the individuals were not ill, as the crowd of interned people included stutterers, deaf and mute children, rebellious adolescents, anarchists and political dissidents. Those who were mentally ill had very little chances to be cured. To read their letters and the psychiatrists' notes on them, to see their drawings, to be able to look at their picture, day after day, is a moving and at the same time upsetting experience. Often the dust on the folders reveals that these files have not been touched or opened by anyone for decades; in Florence some files are still covered by dried mud from the 1966 flood. Prior to this research, I worked as an archive researcher for television and I thought I could carry out the task keeping a professional distance. However, as I went deeper into it, as I spent more than four years digging out mouldy and dusty documents that shouted stories of trauma, hunger, poverty, abandonment, loneliness, desperation and pain, I grew increasingly involved and felt the duty to make their lives known, to break the silence that surrounded these biographies for so long. I am indebted to those who facilitated my research and to the Wellcome Trust, whose generous grant allowed me to focus on the task with the necessary time and concentration. This research has certainly been an unforeseeable professional and personal journey.

Legal issues and ethics

Legal issues are complex when tackling archival research in Italy, given the existing legislation protecting the privacy of individuals. This is even more the case when dealing with mental health and sexuality at the same time. Research carried out in a public archive in Italy must by law be conducted following the directives contained in Italian decree n. 281 of 1999, with its 5.4.2001 amendments, and decree n. 196 of 2003. These state that, when communicating research results, historians must make sure that no identification of any individual is possible when mentioning issues connected with sexuality, even though these facts took place more than seventy years earlier. Files can be consulted only seventy years after the file's date. In accordance with these laws, I do not disclose any detail that might reveal patients' identities, such as the entire patient file number, name and surname in full, precise place of birth, home and work address. It is however true that, by giving the patient's initials and the date of release or death, I provide a clue to retrace the patient in question. Nevertheless, the accuracy of my research would be questionable if I mentioned no single detail.

Current Italian legislation is seriously restrictive. Historians dealing with archival data collected in Italy face the additional difficulty of finding a way to prove their professionalism while not breaching privacy. Several different approaches have been adopted over the years, according to different interpretations of the law. When dealing with the history of homosexuality, some scholars have chosen to indicate a few dates, or full first names followed by the surname's initial, while in certain cases police file numbers have been quoted in full and in one recent instance all details were disclosed, together with police photographs of gay men sent to the *confino* during the regime.[67] I opted for the method that protected data privacy the most.

However, while I understand that privacy issues are important and must be handled sensitively, I also agree with Wendy Mitchinson and Franca Iacovetta when they maintain that protecting the privacy of individuals of the past leads the historian to marginalize them even further.[68] To keep total patient anonymity cancels identities and deprives these men and women of any individuality. It could also be argued that anonymity is complicit with the idea that homosexuality is something to be ashamed of, as if it were a crime. More than seventy years after the events, it should be possible to reveal the identity of those who were incarcerated because of their sexual orientation. Naming victims of the psychiatric system would partially restore the dignity that was taken from them. Initials make their existence almost abstract, whereas historians should aim to give flesh to events and concepts.

There is also another important issue at the basis of this debate: would the person in question, now deceased, have wanted his or her identity disclosed? Bearing in mind that respect for the dead is a moral obligation for historians and researchers, in some cases we can deduce that those interned because of their homosexuality might indeed have wanted to condemn the blatant injustice of which they were a victim. The case of G., in Collegno, is an apt example of this.[69] G. was a middle-class lawyer who had the tools and assertiveness to make himself heard. He wrote a thirty-one-page-long document explaining why he thought he should not be interned. He demonstrated that he wanted to be heard. Many other homosexual victims of the psychiatric system did not do the same, but most of them wrote letters to relatives, friends and the asylum director, asking to be released and contesting the reasons for their internment. This could imply that the patient wanted his/her case to be heard and known.

To conclude, sometimes patient files stretch over a long period of time, as many patients remained in a psychiatric hospital for years, decades or even for their entire lives. However, because the current law does not allow researchers to consult files that are less than seventy years old, parts of files were removed before I could read them.[70] In one case, the entire file was inadvertently disclosed to me. I could see that the patient was described as homosexual from the late 1940s onwards. When interned during the fascist period, she was defined only as rebellious and morally non-conforming. It is very relevant to note that her lesbianism appeared on the medical notes only after Liberation. It would also have been interesting to highlight the medical and linguistic discrepancies between professionals who operated under Mussolini and afterwards, when dealing with the same patient. This is an apt example to illustrate how current legislation effectively curtails historical research.

Primary sources

This book draws from a wealth of different documents. My main primary sources are, first, the psychiatry manuals, essays and articles of the fascist period on sexuality and sexual inversion. These include texts written by psychiatrists based elsewhere, namely in Germany, Spain and France; as mentioned earlier, these are particularly significant because they inspired many Italian psychiatrists and theoreticians of the *Ventennio*. Some of these publications are in the form of short essays published by psychiatric journals.

Secondly, I use the mental health hospitals' patient files and the administrative documentation of the asylums. Oscar Greco, who dedicates an entire sub-chapter of his latest book to asylum files as a source, highlights that mental health hospitals' notes have been ignored by historians for many years because they were generally thought to be a partial account of psychological problems.[71] They are, however, an extremely valuable container of information that stretches from medical thought to cultural layers and codes inside and outside the institution. Lucia Sandri shows they often include not only medical notes but also a variety of legal documents, poetry and drawings by patients, photographs, intimate correspondence and various certificates issued by different authorities.[72] Therefore, they allow for many approaches to study, from the reconstruction of the procedures of the security forces, to social mechanisms, from the history of the perception of illness and madness to the history of medicine, from the history of emotions to the history of sexuality. Their potential is fully explored in this study as the medical notes are used to reconstruct the social aspect of homosexuality, medical thinking and practice, and hierarchical relationships within the institution.

Terminology

It is essential to explain how I approach the original terminology as the subject harbours several problematic aspects and is highly sensitive. Definitions such as 'moral imbecile', 'perverted', 'deficient', 'sexual invert', 'pederast' and 'sodomite' appear in inverted commas only in this introduction or the first time I use them, to indicate that they are dated expressions, belonging to the era at the centre of this research. Thereafter, the inverted commas are omitted to facilitate reading. These words, which depict prejudice and moral judgement so well, are used deliberately, as they signify attitudes among psychiatrists, relatives and the security forces towards certain categories of patients. In addition, the use of terminology from the time ensures that my analysis is not obscured by anachronistic definitions that belong to the present. Original terms are therefore used not only when quoting psychiatrists' notes but also when summarizing them. It should always be clear from the context that the terms are those chosen by professionals at the time and not by the author.

Finally, I use the capital letter for nouns such as Fascism, Anti-Fascism and Resistance or *Resistenza*, while I use lowercase letters for adjectives, absolute adjectives or adnouns such as fascists and anti-fascists. All foreign terms are in italics, apart from the names of institutions, universities, associations and the like. When quoting book titles, I use capitals for all nouns for titles in English, while I follow the different Italian titles' styles as printed, following the two different traditions. Quotations have been translated into English by the author. I put in bracket the dates of birth and death of people I mention and quote only the first time their name appears in the text. If dates, old journals' issue and volume numbers are not provided, it means that these could not be found.

Book structure

The introduction reviews the existing literature on the history of psychiatry in Italy during Fascism, starting from the few texts that focus on psychiatry and homosexuality. It then reviews publications on the repression of homosexuality under Mussolini's dictatorship, a field that has become of increased interest over the past two decades. It goes on to explain that the research is archive based and that it compares three different mental health institutions located in three different Italian regions. Finally, it analyses the most crucial methodological, legal and moral aspects regarding archive research on sexuality issues.

Chapter 1 reviews Italian psychiatric writing on sexual inversion for the period before 1922–43. It demonstrates how psychiatrists of the *Ventennio* were strongly influenced by their internationally acclaimed immediate Italian predecessors. It also introduces authors from other European countries who directly influenced Italian psychiatric theories at the time. The chapter ends by highlighting other influences on Italian psychiatry of the *Ventennio*, such as the regime's propaganda, Roman Catholicism and pseudo-scientific literature that touched the subject of homosexuality.

Chapter 2 illustrates psychiatric treatises written and published under the fascist regime, which addressed issues of 'sexual inversion', sexuality and 'hermaphroditism'. It brings to light both the novelty and the traditionalism within the psychiatric thinking of the interwar period in Italy.

Chapter 3 illustrates the results of archival research carried out on Santa Maria della Pietà, the Roman mental health hospital. This institution was chosen as it was one of the largest and most important at the time. It attracted several illustrious specialists and hosted a large number of patients. It was also in geographical proximity to the central power and the main institutions of fascist Italy.

Chapter 4 is centred on archival research carried out on the San Salvi asylum archives in Florence. This institution was chosen because it presented several characteristics that differed from the other two asylums analysed. First, and foremost, it comprised a university clinic that functioned as an observation unit. This aspect was investigated to see if it indicated a strong link with psychiatric theories of the time. Secondly, San Salvi had a very strong tradition in terms of famous and influential psychiatrists who worked or were even involved in its original planning. This translated into a tendency to assert complete independence from external interference. Finally, the Florence asylum constituted an element of modernity within the national psychiatric situation. It was known at the time for being one of the most open to 'no-restraint', home psychiatric care, prevention and voluntary treatment.

Chapter 5 focuses on archival research carried out on the Girifalco mental health hospital, near Catanzaro. Located in Calabria, a southern region that was fairly isolated at the time, with a difficult economic situation and underdeveloped infrastructure, this asylum represents a significant group of Italy's medium- and small-sized mental health hospitals. The aim is to compare this remote asylum with the two more prestigious ones, and at the same time to observe whether there were considerable differences in terms of therapeutic approaches or internment and treatment of homosexual patients.

This book presents several aspects of novelty. First, it sheds light on an area, that of psychiatry and homosexuality in Italy during the fascist regime, which at present is understudied. Secondly, it brings together the practical and theoretical aspects of the topic, by comparing archival evidence with psychiatric theory. It highlights where discrepancies are present between psychiatry and its daily routine application, underlining where the work of theoreticians was disregarded and where it was adopted and followed. Finally, it compares psychiatric therapeutic approaches in three different mental health institutions located in different areas of Italy, whereas most scholars have tended to focus on the historical reconstruction of one asylum. This methodological approach allows me to emphasize elements of similarity and difference in psychiatric practice between various parts of Italy and to demonstrate how psychiatry was multifaceted even at a time of extreme conformity such as the *Ventennio*.

Part I

Psychiatric Theory

This part of the book focuses on psychiatric theory, to frame asylum practice in its context of reference and to evaluate whether, and to what extent, theory had an impact on daily routine mental health care in fascist Italy.

The first chapter illustrates the main influences on Italian psychiatry at the time, in its connections with the study of sexuality. First, it concentrates on the most important foreign influences, which came from Germany, Austria, Spain and France. It then considers the imprint left by Italian predecessors in the same field. Finally, it outlines in brief other powerful influences on the Italian psychiatry of the *Ventennio*, such as Roman Catholicism, fascist propaganda and the stereotypes it created around homosexuality, and pseudoscientific publications that spread knowledge of homosexuality among the general public but also had an impact on professionals' attitudes towards their patients.

The second chapter offers a sample of psychiatric theory on homosexuality written by Italian scholars, who were often also practising psychiatrists at the same time and published during the *Ventennio*. The aim is to demonstrate how much of the thought of predecessors and illustrious foreign colleagues was present in their elaborations on sexual inversion and how much was original thinking. Not one of the treatises examined in this chapter was written by academics who also worked as psychiatrists in the three institutions analysed in the second part of the book I. However, the ambiguity of approach shown by the authors considered here is mirrored by daily routine practice in many ways, as Chapters 3–5 demonstrate.

Main influences on Italian psychiatric theories on homosexuality during the fascist regime

The aim of this chapter is to highlight the ways in which, during the fascist regime, Italian psychiatric theories on homosexuality were still greatly indebted to earlier ideas and stemmed primarily from the German school of thought. The chapter is in three parts. Focusing on sexology, the first part outlines the broader European influences on Italian psychiatry in the fascist period: Austrian, German, French and Spanish. The second part examines some of the most influential Italian psychiatrists, at the end of the nineteenth and beginning of the twentieth century, who addressed issues of homosexuality and were a point of reference for theoreticians and practitioners who operated in the Mussolini years. The third part analyses other influences on Italian psychiatrists of the *Ventennio* in their theories and approach to homosexuality and sexuality.

Italian psychiatry of the fascist regime tried to distance itself from the past, in an attempt to become more scientific and less open to interpretation. In doing so, it embraced endocrinological and neurological approaches to sexuality and homosexuality and deployed consistent efforts to discredit psychology and psychoanalysis, which put the patient and his or her memories at the centre of the investigation. It looked to foreign experiences, aiming to revitalize the discipline by grounding it in prestigious theories. Yet it never managed to shake off the burden of its own past, embodied primarily by the Lombrosian approach. The study of sexuality was the battlefield of this war and in fact sexology constituted an important part of most psychiatric literature of the time.

Other influences created an obstacle to new theories and real innovative approaches. Among them, there was Roman Catholicism and its dogma, which in terms of sexuality was impossible to bypass. To add to this, Italian psychiatric thinking and Italian society were also heavily pressurized by fascist propaganda and its moralization and demographic campaigns, at the core of which was the campaign against homosexuality.

Main foreign influences: Austria, Germany, France and Spain

Italian psychiatry has traditionally been greatly indebted to the past. The Lombrosian school of thought, which so deeply influenced psychiatry at an international level in the nineteenth century, was a burden that could not easily be dismissed, or overlooked, and younger generations of psychiatrists were generally cautious when taking a distance from it. However, the trend to look back and take inspiration from the glorious past of the discipline was present even earlier and stretched beyond Italian borders.

Fabio Stok gives a comprehensive account of the main influences on Italian psychiatry, starting from the beginning of the nineteenth century.[1] Like in most European countries, he argues, in Italy, the discipline was inspired initially by the two French fathers of psychiatry, Philippe Pinel (1745–1826) and Jean-Etienne Dominique Esquirol (1772–1840), with their reading of madness as a moral and spiritual disorder. In the mid-nineteenth century, in Italy, however, long before the advent of the fascist regime, there was a rethinking and re-evaluation of Vincenzo Chiarugi's (1759–1820) theories and approach, centred upon the medical aspects of psychiatry. For Chiarugi, a moral cure of the mentally ill was only necessary in some cases, such as melancholy. According to Stok, going back to Chiarugi represented therefore a fundamental shift in Italy, to be read not only in patriotic terms but also within an emerging trend to transform psychiatry into a scientific discipline. This tendency was a constant element in Italian medical culture until well after the Second World War.

Stok also underlines that works by Pinel and Esquirol arrived in Italy, in translation, with a considerable delay. For instance, Pinel's main treatise, published in 1801 in France, had to wait almost thirty years to be printed in Italian.[2] This, for Stok, indicates a lack of interest on the part of specialists to expand the debate to include those who did not read French. In his opinion this can also be observed in subsequent years in Italian psychiatry. As the professional category tried to improve its scientific profile, there were consistent attempts to limit intrusions from outside and to keep the debate among its members only. As observed in the following chapter, in the fascist years, the translation of psychiatric texts seems to have mostly taken place only if there was a seal of approval, in the shape of an illustrative long preface to the work in question by a famous Italian psychiatrist, who explained why he endorsed the publication.

Stok underlines another important aspect of the development of psychiatry in Italy – the continual discussion of the undefined border between legal responsibility and *folie raisonnante* or moral madness. The difficulty in defining this border between the irrational criminal impulse and the deliberate decision to act immorally generated a debate around penal punishment and repression. Italian psychiatry concentrated its efforts on investigating degeneration issues and their connection with criminality. At the same time, Italian psychiatrists wanted to be the figures who decided whether a person was to be charged by the legal system or not. In Italy, the psychiatric legal report, *perizia psichiatrica*, became the tool to assert psychiatry's importance in terms of social order, and therefore its primacy among medical disciplines.[3] Psychiatrists claimed they had priority over judges in assessing who should be punished, who was to be isolated from a social context, who was dangerous and who was not. The original strong link between criminology and psychiatry remained the distinctive trait in the Italian psychiatry of the nineteenth century, and Fascism expanded this already-existing role to suit its repressive needs.

The second half of the nineteenth century brought many scientific advances in terms of medicine and psychiatry, which further encouraged a medicalized approach to the discipline as faith in science was at its maximum during the era of Positivism. And since German psychiatry was at the forefront of medical and scientific approaches to mental health care, all Europe, and Italy in particular, followed German developments with great interest, despite some isolated resistance. Stok identifies Wilhelm Griesiger (1817–1868) and Emil Kraepelin (1856–1926) as the two most important points of reference in this period. Griesiger, who perceived psychiatric disorders as illnesses of the brain, influenced Italian psychiatry well into the twentieth century and inspired a generation of specialists who strongly believed in the predominance of pathological anatomy in psychiatric diagnosis.

Italian psychiatry drifted away from French influences, and in the second half of the nineteenth century, directed its attention towards neighbouring Germany. From then on, Stok rightly observes, it remained subordinate to German psychiatric theory for several decades, and only with the invention of electro-shock treatment did it regain a prominent position at an international level – but only with regard to medical technology, not at a theoretical level. For Stok, even the merging of neurology and psychiatry university teaching originated in the influence of Griesiger.[4] Already in the second half of the nineteenth century most Italian psychiatrists were regularly quoting German and Austrian theoreticians as their main point of reference, and the names of psychiatrists such as Theodor Meynert (1833–1892), who studied the connection between depression and blood circulation in the brain, and Hans Walter Gruhle (1880–1958), who related mental disorders to brain lesions or somatic dysfunction, appeared frequently in the Italian psychiatric literature. As the political situation consolidated the alliance with Germany during Fascism, this translated into a closer bond in scientific, medical and psychiatric terms.

However, in terms of sexology, one of the most influential theoreticians during the fascist regime was, as Alberto Cavaglion points out, Otto Weininger (1880–1903).[5] His famous treatise, *Sex and Character*, published in 1903, was printed twenty-eight times in Italian translation between 1903 and 1947.[6] Weininger's theory, according to Cavaglion, was successful and appealing because it was sufficiently ambiguous and could be interpreted in ways that conformed with the regime's guidelines. The Austrian psychiatrist asserted that all individuals had both male and female attributes and that they sought each other to find completion. This he believed could be proved in a biological, incontrovertible way, as opposed to Sigmund Freud's (1856–1944) debatable theory of the unconscious that so worried positivists. As a consequence of identifying male and female elements in every living creature, instead of arriving at a statement that saw the harmony and integration of two different worlds, Weininger and his followers offered a scientific basis to theories that considered the feminine as the negative and inferior element in nature and the masculine, active, virile element as the positive. Cavaglion highlights how these theories laid the basis for the sexualization of political beliefs – where Fascism was perceived as male, for instance – and for the 'genderization' of nations, people and races. Weininger's thought was used to set a scale from bottom to top, from worst to best, opening the path to pseudoscientific racist and discriminatory theories. Cavaglion gives a very precise account of how Weininger almost became a national hero in Italy. He was quoted and followed by intellectuals, journalists and politicians, including Mussolini, becoming a natural ally in the battle against Freud's theories. He was idealized by the futurists as a symbol of the new era that was about to come. Weininger was used to discredit any feminist battle; women who were demanding more rights were considered to have an unnaturally prevailing masculine side. His theory of the irreversibility of time became the banner against psychoanalysis, whose attempt to go back and interpret the past was now judged as an immoral and feminine type of endeavour. Virility meant action, embracing the future, with no dwelling on the immutable past.

Weininger's words permeated not only scientific language, Cavaglion stresses, but also everyday culture in fascist times.

Another psychiatrist who was often quoted and referred to in specialist literature is Oswald Bumke (1877–1950). His main treatise was translated into Italian in 1927, eight years after its first edition.[7] The German psychiatrist questioned hereditary aspects of mental illness, an idea that in Italy clearly broke with the still strong Lombrosian tradition. He placed great importance on endocrinology as a determining factor in mental conditions and behaviours. Glands were able, according to Bumke, to influence and direct the human psyche, although he admitted that environmental and situational elements could have a direct effect on mental health and that trauma too could have an impact on the mind, even when there was no evident or retraceable hereditary predisposition.

His ideas were new in other ways too. Bumke stated clearly that moral madness had nothing to do with an absence of moral values, but it was, rather, an emotional deficiency. In this way, he effectively cancelled a century-long tradition of moral judgement of psychiatric patients. On masturbation too, he challenged previous theories that saw it as a cause of mental disorder and asserted that it constituted maybe a symptom of a psychiatric problem, and only in certain cases. Neither of these last two positions received great attention from the following generations of Italian psychiatrists.

In his classification of mental conditions, he dedicated a chapter – chapter VII – to will, action and speech disorders. In it, there is a section on morbid instincts, divided into manias, sexual instinct, masturbation and masochism/sadism/fetishism/homosexuality/exhibitionism. Sexual perversions, Bumke stated, were found mainly in individuals who also presented other characteristics of an abnormal constitution. This argumentation had enormous relevance in Italy, as homosexuality was often thought to be a part, maybe not even the most relevant one, of a pathological situation where other 'symptoms' were present. He also questioned the hereditary theory on homosexuality, or at least felt it ought to be downsized in its relevance. Essentially, he framed homosexuality in a wider psychopathological context but considered it to be a disease that stemmed from an endocrinological dysfunction and, as such, curable.

Since sexual inversion was an eminently medical problem, the patient's statement had little relevance to his approach, in clear contrast with Sigmund Freud and Richard von Krafft-Ebing (1840–1902), who put patients' descriptions and recollections at the centre of their investigations. Bumke, as Florian Mildenberger points out, was against psychoanalysis and completely denied the existence of the subconscious.[8] He stressed that a homosexual patient's confessions to the specialist were not to be trusted. This too reverberated strongly in Italian psychiatric practice, where the voice of homosexual interned patients was almost always filtered through the specialist's interpretation and comments. Besides, homosexuals were often described as being liars inherently and were considered untrustworthy in theoretical writing.

Despite his firm belief in an endocrinological approach, in the chapter he dedicated to therapies, Bumke expressed serious doubts on the effectiveness of castration as a cure for homosexuality; experimentation on human beings by Eugen Steinach (1861–1944) had begun, and his results were being discussed at the time. Bumke thought hypnosis might help only if a latent residual heterosexual tendency could be ascertained or if the patient showed shame or repentance.

Together with Weininger and Bumke, Emil Kraepelin (1856–1926) was a third constant point of reference for Italian psychiatrists from the beginning of the twentieth century and throughout the fascist years. Kraepelin considered mental illnesses to arise from alterations of the structures and functions of the brain and nervous system, yet focused on symptoms and on observation of the patient, rather than on the causes of a psychiatric disorder. The psychological aspect was therefore completely overlooked.[9] According to Kraepelin, the main task of a psychiatrist was clinical analysis of the patient, something that Augusto Tamburini (1848–1919), the prestigious author of the preface of the Italian translation of his main treatise, especially appreciated.[10] The director of the Reggio Emilia asylum and of the authoritative *Rivista Sperimentale di Freniatria* praised Kraepelin for opening the path to those who wanted to investigate the anatomical aspect of psychiatry and to those who were interested in studying its endocrinological aspects.

Kraepelin divided the causes of mental disease between internal and external. Among the internal causes he listed sexual excesses but, like Bumke, stated that masturbation was not a cause but a symptom of mental illness and only in few cases. Among the internal causes, together with hereditary factors, he asserted that there were predispositions to mental disease linked with age, gender and race, thus preparing the ground for the scientific justification of racial discrimination. He then listed the manifestations of madness, and in the last category, characterized by excess, alongside impulsive actions, incoercible acts, nudity and the predisposition to be influenced by others, we also find deviation of sexual needs and sexual inversion. In other words, he aligned his position to the predominant view that saw homosexuality as congenital, not acquired. It was a condition that required an inborn predisposition.

However, it is in the second volume of this treatise, published in Italy separately in 1907, that Kraepelin enunciated more clearly his theory on sexual deviance and homosexuality, which, as Mildenberger underlines, was in constant evolution throughout his career and became more conservative and radicalized as the years progressed.[11] In categorizing mental disorders, he dedicated an entire chapter, chapter XII, to the so-called 'originary psychopathic states', which included nervousness, constitutional depression, constitutional excitement, impulsive madness, and sexual aberrations. He stated, partially contradicting himself, that the starting point of all sexual aberrations was masturbation but clarified that it was a normal activity in youth, and only in an adult did it constitute an abnormality because it substituted the natural tendency towards procreation. A sexual aberration such as exhibitionism, for instance, would clearly derive from it. Talking about sexual instinct inversion, he believed it affected mainly men, and most importantly, it implied a psychopathic predisposition, often of a hereditary nature. This concept seems to have received considerable attention during the fascist regime. Psychiatrists of the *Ventennio* often looked for hereditary factors of degeneration when dealing with homosexual patients that proved that sexual inversion was inborn. Furthermore, Kraepelin established a clear connection with sexual precocity, which in his opinion always led to masturbation and which he thought was often a starting point for homosexuality. This is also a concept that greatly influenced fascist Italy's psychiatrists. However, in certain cases, homosexuality could also be induced by external factors, Kraepelin added, for instance by certain types of morbid friendships that could degenerate, if an inborn predisposition was present.

Kraepelin tried to classify the characteristics that would allow a medical professional to identify predisposition to male homosexuality. Among them, he listed intelligence, augmented emotional excitability, often accompanied by artistic and musical talent, and a sweet, docile and dependent character. In some individuals, both heterosexuality and homosexuality coexisted, he realized, and in these cases, he believed that the term 'psychic hermaphroditism' was more appropriate, clearly borrowing this terminology from Karl Heinrich Ulrichs (1825–1895) and Magnus Hirschfeld (1868–1935).[12] Sexual inversion also had an impact on the conduct of life, as it affected movement and posture, often combined with vanity, transvestitism and love for feminine types of work, he observed, while homosexual women engaged in men's activity – they drank, smoked and loved sport and male occupations. The first traces of these behaviours, Kraepelin warned, were already visible in childhood and could therefore be identified very early on by a trained and vigilant eye.

Finally, he admitted the existence of a small group of homosexual individuals who also bore somatic evidence demonstrating their sexual deviancy. Men with high-pitched voices and without beards, with breasts or wide hips and women with big bones, beards, raucous voices and narrow hips were, however, a small minority, he observed. The attention of specialists was therefore to be rather concentrated on behaviour, posture, gestures and choices. The development of homosexuality in the individual was supposed to be very slow, and it was sometimes associated with other conditions. Kraepelin observed that some homosexuals 'feared to be discovered, to be spied upon, they overheard comments about themselves, and were extremely anxious'.[13] This comment shows how mental suffering caused by homophobia was interpreted as persecution complex and anxiety.

The German psychiatrist realized that sexual inversion was not a rare occurrence, although he disagreed with Ulrich's calculation, according to which 1 out of 200 was homosexual. Kraepelin was convinced that it was more frequent in certain professions, such as among tailors, waiters and actors. He believed the diagnosis to be relatively easy when there was a transformation of the personality, both from a somatic and from a psychic point of view, while in certain cases, he admitted there might be no way to detect it, and in these circumstances, as a last resort, it was necessary to believe the patient's statement.

Kraepelin, most importantly, thought that homosexuality grew 'on a terrain of a *morbidly degenerate personality*', but that the environment had a responsibility only in awakening an inborn tendency.[14] Homosexuality, he observed, often started manifesting itself in places where only one sex was present and a first successful encounter pushed an individual to repeat the initial positive experience again and again, to obtain the same pleasurable feelings again. He believed that recent therapeutic experiences showed an improvement or even recovery and indicated hypnosis as a possible cure, together with bromide, a healthy diet and regular physical exercise. At the end of this therapy, the result would always be a degenerate personality, he concluded in coherence with his views, but the homosexual tendencies might disappear.

A drastic change in Kraepelin's beliefs came in the aftermath of the First World War. As Mildenberger observes, he came to accuse homosexuality of being responsible for the decay of society and argued it should be punished, while initially he had thought it should not because, being an inborn condition, it did not imply vice or choice.[15] Kraepelin's students and assistants remained faithful to his teaching, but gradually also absorbed the ideas of Ernst Kretschmer (1888–1964), who connected homosexuality to schizophrenia, as the two conditions were believed to have some aspects in common such as an asthenic body, gonadic malfunctions and infantile emotional attitudes. Kretschmer also tried to establish strong links between physical appearance and mental disease. As this was in line with the Lombrosian school, he was quoted by a proportion of Italian psychiatry theoreticians. Mildenberger underlines how the debate in Germany consolidated around homosexuality as an acquired condition versus homosexuality as a congenital condition – in other words, on two fronts – although positions sometimes shifted, and even Kraepelin's position, as previously shown, changed several times.

Another influential German psychiatrist who was sometimes referred to in Italian medical literature on sexual inversion is Wilhelm Weygandt (1870–1939).[16] Weygandt conceded that not all sexual inversion cases were the product of a special morbid predisposition, because, he added, in some countries and in certain specific historical periods, such as ancient Greece, homosexuality was in fashion and it was therefore a widespread condition.[17] Together with pressure from society in the form of trends and fashions, Weygandt added that pederasty could be observed mostly not only among those who were forced to spend their time with individuals of the same sex, such as prison inmates or boys in public schools but also among those who had too many 'normal' sexual intercourses and looked for new *stimuli*. In his view, it could also be a symptom of certain psychopathologies, such as imbecility, and finally it could be detected among psychic degenerates. His theory therefore combined several approaches and did not exclude external factors, such as environment, education and psychic contagion. However, the theory also included an element of free choice, when Weygandt admitted homosexuality could be determined by the decision of an individual to follow a trend or even to look for different ways to obtain sexual pleasure.

Weygandt too observed that, although there were men with external feminine characteristics and their female counterparts, that is, women with a male appearance, often a homosexual physical constitution did not present any specific morphological sign. These homosexual men took the appearance of the opposite sex through artifices such as shaving, wearing jewels, being fussy about what they wore and using corsets, while their female counterparts put all efforts into behaving like men – they smoked, drank, swore, rode horses and so on. Often sexual inversion manifested itself at an early age, as boys played with dolls and girls with tin soldiers, or through sexual precocity, another statement that resonated in Italy, where sex at an early age was often pathologized. Pietro Benassi and Salvatore Luberto note that Weygandt also gave a strong indication that psychiatrists should intern those who committed 'crimes of outrage, slander, crimes against public order, against morality, against propriety', thus confirming his very conservative attitude.[18]

Among the internal causes of mental illnesses, Weygandt identified marital status as a predisposing factor. This was often quoted in Italian patient files as a concurrent cause for mental disorder, as unmarried people were increasingly described as inherently unstable, incapable of taking responsibility, immature and unfit for adult social life in the regime's demographic campaign climate. This observation gave scientific proof to fascist stereotypes that understood single men and women to be unmarried because of their innate difference, hinting at their degeneration, moral and social inability, selfishness and anti-patriotic feelings.

Among the Austrian and German influences on Italian psychiatry, Eugen Steinach (1861–1944) and his assistants certainly have a place of honour.[19] Their experiments with the transplanting of testicles and ovaries to cure several conditions, homosexuality among them, were followed with great interest in Italy and were often quoted in psychiatric journals and treatises. During the fascist years, they generated optimism that homosexuality could be surgically cured. Together with the experiments carried out in the new field of brain surgery, as illustrated by Zbigniew Kotowicsz, they raised a considerable amount of criticism too, or sometimes judgement was suspended, as results started coming through but could not be considered conclusive.[20] Among those who showed enthusiasm for Steinach's and Lichternstern's experiments, we can cite Augusto Mario Coen, who referred to them in an article on moral madness, where he specifically addressed issues regarding homosexuality.[21] He was clearly convinced that more positive results would come from this type of surgical intervention and described a successful case where a young man had been operated upon and soon afterwards had lost any interest in men. With regard to brain surgery, as proof of the existence of a strong and convinced interest in the subject in fascist Italy, we can point to the presence of Egas Moniz, a Portuguese surgeon who was a pioneer in the field, in the Racconigi asylum in 1937. Moniz was invited by the mental health hospital's director, the neuro-psychiatrist Emilio Rizzatti, who fervently promoted psychosurgery in Italy. Moniz believed that 'a homosexual is an ill person, and generally useless, because sterile and we should fight for his well-being and for society', something that points to his commitment to apply brain surgery techniques to cure sexual inversion.[22] One case that could prove this has been brought to light recently, that of a lobotomy carried out on a homosexual man by Moniz in Racconigi in 1937.[23]

The 'elephant in the room' was Sigmund Freud. His theories were well known in Italy at the time, his name often surfaced in articles in the psychiatric journals of the *Ventennio* and could not be ignored, but Italian psychiatry remained suspicious of a method that placed the patient at the centre of the investigation, that listened and deciphered his or her words, feelings, fears, obsessions and dreams. This methodological approach was dismissed as not sufficiently grounded in science and too open to subjective interpretations. However, this was not the only reason why most psychiatrists in Italy dissented with the Freudian approach. An article by Luigi Scremin, published in 1932, clarified why Freud's ideas could not be adopted in a Catholic country such as Italy.[24] The Padua university professor explained that it was unethical for a doctor to dig so deeply into a person's secrets and intimate thoughts, as the psychoanalytical session could not substitute the sacrament of confession. He warned against the traps of a scrutiny of dreams that were interpreted from the point of view of sexuality alone. In Scremin's opinion, this type of approach was permissible only when a recognizable trauma had taken place. Besides, he added that to reduce every psychological phenomenon or behaviour to sexuality, an attitude that in Italy was termed *pansessualismo*, was 'incompatible with the Catholic doctrine'.[25] Most importantly, conflicts could not be resolved by freeing instinctive tendencies and behaviours, getting rid of ethical considerations and boundaries. Scremin's position was shared by many psychiatrists in Italy. *Pansessualismo* in Italy became a synonym for mechanical and scientifically unprovable associations of phenomena, an excessive focus on sexuality as the originator of most conditions of the human psyche and an ethically dubious medical approach. The same journal, two years later, reported the speech given by Leonardo Bianchi (1848–1927) at the National Congress of the *Società Italiana per lo Studio delle Questioni Sessuali*, held in Naples in April–May 1924.[26] On that occasion, Bianchi voiced his indignation at Freudian methodology, stating that the idea that the sexual identity of a person was forged by his mother's caresses and hugs was not just unscientific but also deeply offensive. 'Italians would never have been able to conceive such a monstrosity that defaces the most noble and sacred among human feelings', he added.[27]

Together with Sigmund Freud, Richard von Krafft-Ebing and Karl Heinrich Ulrichs were discredited, both because of their personal involvement with the 'homosexual cause', which was thought to make their assessments not completely impartial, and because of the attention they dedicated to their patients' accounts, recollections and life experiences. Italian psychiatry saw their work as being essentially in line with Freudian methodology. Sometimes they were accused of naively believing what their patients told them, without being able to understand that the aim of certain statements was to obtain a more lenient judgement from the health professional; at other times, they were suspected of lending in part the ear of an accomplice and not maintaining the correct professional distance from those they were there to cure.

Despite the prevailing trend to observe, quote and discuss mainly German and Austrian psychiatrists, in terms of theories on sexual inversion some inspiration continued to come from France. A point of reference was Marc André Raffalovich (1864–1934), author of a book dedicated entirely to homosexuality.[28] His positions on the subject were extreme, and they influenced the most conservative group of Italian psychiatrists. Raffalovich believed that homosexuality could not be cured and that the only way to solve the problem was chastity. He too showed how physical traits of the opposite sex appeared sometimes, but not always; there were effeminate men who were heterosexual and perfectly virile men who were homosexual. Like Bumke, he asserted that the statements of homosexual patients were not trustworthy as sexually inverted individuals were inherently liars, a common belief in the fascist years in Italy. He also shared the view, which he attributed to unnamed scientists, that 'pederasts are the garbage of the earth, its most beastly entity. They are physically punished, and I think that is the right thing', thus corroborating the stereotype of the equation between lack of virility and ugliness, absence of strength and health.[29] Puberty constituted the most dangerous period of a person's life, he asserted, because innate homosexuality could develop in those years and because young individuals could easily fall prey to seducers in search of new sexual experiences. Seduction could awaken inborn tendencies that had to be repressed. Homosexuals, in his view, did not deserve any of the compassion and empathy that Krafft-Ebing manifested towards them. They were simply individuals who were overwhelmed by passions they were unable to control, and therefore, they deserved harsh judgement like any heterosexual who did not put a limit to lustful desires, such as unfaithful wives. Raffalovich concluded his main treatise with a long comment on the court trial against Oscar Wilde, where he saw Alfred Douglas as a brave hero who went against social conventions, while Wilde was encouraged in his *debaucherie* by a decadent society.

C. Bruni, author of the preface to the Italian translation of Raffalovich's treatise, also wrote the concluding chapter, where he argued that punishment for homosexuality would be counterproductive.[30] As Wilde's case showed, he explained, it would only publicize and promote homosexuality. Bruni thought that it would be sufficient to apply Article 46 of the Italian penal code on mental infirmity and that, ultimately, the confinement, reduction or repression of homosexuality was a matter of ethics. Clearly, he believed that sexual inversion should be repressed without drawing too much attention, a concept that Fascism embraced thoroughly. The regime's Rocco legal code, introduced in 1930 and operational from 1931, never mentioned homosexuality as a crime, leaving its repression to more subtle methods. This is a clear indication for the historian of how isolation in an asylum was considered a valid and less scandalous way of getting rid of homosexuals during Fascism. Society, through its moral code, Bruni continued, had a duty to deal with the problem. In the preface, he introduced the concept, developed by Raffalovich, that homosexual desires were destined to remain unsatisfied, and therefore, he agreed that the only viable option, for society and the patient's sake, was to contain them through chastity.

Another French author known to psychiatrists in fascist Italy and who was deeply rooted in Lombrosian ideas was Jean Baptiste Félix Descuret (1795–1871),[31] who strongly believed in the hereditary element of passions, which even included envy, jealousy, gluttony and drunkenness. Descuret underlined, however, that contagion had a relevant part to play too, because several chronic conditions could be passed on, such as a tendency to suicide, hysteria and hypochondria. In addition, gender, age, climate and diet could, in his view, determine mental disorders, and professions had an influence too. To prove this, Descuret analysed more than 23,000 cases of criminals accused of murder, classifying them by profession in order to calculate what impact this could have on criminal acts; he attempted a similar approach with statistics on suicides. A strong believer that physical traits could be revelatory aspects of criminal tendencies, he listed a series of connections between a particular somatic element and its deviant counterpart.[32]

It was another obvious tribute to Cesare Lombroso, whose teaching in Italy was still firmly rooted in the training and practices of most psychiatrists. In the second volume of his treatise, he talked more specifically about sexual perversions, among which we see onanism, pederasty and bestiality. Their causes, he thought, were mainly hereditary, sometimes combined with other determining factors such as a warm climate, aphrodisiac or excessive food and absence of religious faith. However, in partial contradiction, contagion by bad example, such as idleness, polygamy, going to theatrical performances and attending promiscuous balls, was also possible in his opinion. He offered a moral cure for onanism, which he thought could prevent homosexuality too. This consisted in scaring those young boys and girls who practiced it with terrifying scenarios such as painful operations, death or bad accidents if they persisted.

The author did not mention any cure for homosexuality, which probably implies he did not think there could be one.

Finally, a decisive mark on Italian psychiatry was made by Gregorio Marañon's (1887–1960) treatise, published in Italy in 1934.[33] The Spanish doctor set out to prove that all individuals showed elements of both sexes. The foetus was initially undifferentiated, and after birth all human beings still carried both male and female traits, to different degrees. Marañon quoted Eugen Steinach, who sustained that his histological analysis had revealed that the testicles of some homosexual men contained a certain number of epithelioid cells that resembled ovarian cells. It was the scientific proof of the validity of his theories.

Having stated that all human beings bore the signs of intersexuality and that libido too was initially undifferentiated and only later developed naturally into heterosexuality, Marañon then proceeded with a physical description of hermaphrodites. Hermaphroditism was divided into two broad categories. The first comprised cases where it depended on conformation or malformation of reproductive glands and genitalia, while the second consisted of all those cases where the adult body presented only some physical traits of the opposite sex. Equally, the author continued, homosexuality was often visible and detectable because of the presence of a certain number of physical elements that were typical of the opposite sex. An accurate description of these traits even included the shape of the larynx and the disposition of teeth. However, the author admitted that these elements were not always present. The problem was more complex, he conceded. According to the Spanish doctor, homosexuality's causes were endocrinal and chromosomal, and libido itself came from a chemical, hormonal phenomenon, despite what some psychologists and psychiatrists kept asserting. However, homosexuality was a state of intersexuality 'with the peculiarity that the functional disturbance is much more intense than the anatomical', and with concurring psychological factors.[34] The author emphasized that it was not to be treated as a crime, like in the past. A homosexual's instinct was simply deformed, and therefore, the invert was not responsible for his condition in the same way in which the diabetic was not guilty for the sugar levels in his blood. Progress would mean that 'society should on no account punish the "invert," so long as he does not create a scandal', words that would resonate strongly during the fascist regime.[35]

The normal and natural specification of the sexual object developed, in evolutionary terms, in three phases. In the first phase, from a state of generic and undifferentiated attraction, the sexual impulse became differentiated, the desire for individuals of the same sex lost its appeal, while the impulse concentrated on the other sex. In the second phase, the impulse focused on a certain type of individual of the opposite sex, such as blond women or bearded men. Finally, in the third phase, it concentrated on a particular person. This final phase represented the highest degree of evolution, while the first and second phases were thought to be transitory states, primitive signs of immaturity and underdevelopment that a 'normal' individual would grow out of. The starting point of the first phase, same-sex attraction, was defined as the most hormonal and typical of animals. In some men or races, Marañon explained, sex remained trapped in this phase and homosexual men's frequent attraction for younger men confirmed their being blocked at the stage of infantile sex. The relevance of these statements cannot be downplayed. Considering homosexuality as an inferior degree of human evolution had huge implications and affected the judgement of many psychiatrists of their homosexual patients, both in Italy and in Germany.

Homosexuality, according to Marañon, was an inborn flaw, a mark of inferiority. His theories made homosexuality even more threatening to society; since it was latent in all individuals, it was a dormant genetic condition that could be triggered by external factors. The situation called for extreme vigilance to reduce the possibilities of these sleeping factors being awoken, he warned. It was therefore essential to adequately supervise school children, especially boarders, because external influences contributed to determining homosexuality, Marañon stated, and so did seduction in childhood, when the human organism is more predisposed to 'intermediateness'. Another triggering factor could be excessive, prolonged and intense maternal care of adolescents. Many homosexuals were only sons, he observed, and others the last offspring of a long series of children, while the fixation of libido on the mother, in Freudian terms, led to 'narcissism in which homosexuality takes root'.[36] Narcissism, associated with masturbation, transformed itself sometimes into 'an inveterate cult of self, thank to which the erotic reflex becomes conditioned by a homosexual influence'.[37] Other triggering elements included sexual fear following a first negative experience and 'epidemic outbreaks through the influence of depraved examples'.[38] Homosexuality was sometimes simply a vogue in contemporary society, a fashion 'clearly linked with the decay of existing civilization'.[39] Alcoholic intoxication, cocaine intake and male menopause could also contribute to its occurrence. Yet he did stress, with a sense of urgency, that some factors had an inhibitory influence on the development of homosexuality, such as a strictly virile environment, absence of homosexual seduction and success of the first heterosexual relationship. Religious, ethical and social influences could be a decisive deterrent too.

According to Richard Cleminson and Francisco Vasquez Garcia, who reconstruct the history of male homosexuality in Spain between 1850 and

1940, Marañon's most innovative idea was that homosexuality was potentially embedded in every individual and was not a pathological deviance of sexual desire.[40] This implied that it could be 'cured' or helped to develop into heterosexuality. Another fundamental element of novelty, as the two historians stress, was that he broke free of the traditional division into congenital and acquired homosexuality. He considered homosexuality to be both a congenital and acquired condition at the same time, subverting all previous theories. As sexual inversion was present in every individual, the normal evolutionary process would automatically inhibit it. In the small group of people where this did not happen, it would manifest itself as a sign of lack of evolution. From this, he inferred that it was necessary to intervene to inhibit it, when nature had not managed to do so.

Essentially, Marañon's theory was based on endocrinology, but it considered other elements too. It led to the belief that, if the hormonal context was drastically changed, homosexual desire would be altered, or it would disappear. The Spanish doctor put the sexual question at the centre of scientific and medical investigation. His position seemed to reinstate the old concept that femaleness in general, and therefore being effeminate, was a 'lesser' stage, an inferior and more primitive condition. In fact, although he considered every individual as the sum of maleness and femaleness, to different degrees, he still thought that the male body was to be considered the point of arrival in evolutionary terms, while the female body represented a less evolved state of development. Besides, he was clear that the presence of a uterus, the abundance of fat and the inferior sexual drive defined women's role in society – that of reproduction. In evolutionary terms, women remained in a position between the adult man and the adolescent, something that explained their immaturity and their tendency to be emotional and irrational. As observed with Kraepelin's and Weininger's theories, instead of reading this coexistence of masculine and feminine factors as a sign of a potential harmony, the theory led to a further assertion of male supremacy. Cleminson and Vasquez Garcia interpret Marañon's theories as a response to the national crisis of masculinity and a way to contrast the emerging Spanish homoerotic subcultures and literature that focused on homosexuality. However, he highlighted the determining importance of external factors too, which led him to theorize ways in which triggering factors could be avoided or neutralized. The idea that the human body and psyche were formed by male and female characteristics and that one prevailing over the other could determine sexual preference was absorbed by Italian psychiatrists, at least at a theoretical level, as the following chapter illustrates.

The Italian edition of Marañon's treatise was preceded by a short preface by Nicola Pende (1880–1970), one of the most influential endocrinologists in the country (see later in the chapter). Unfortunately, he did not waste too many words endorsing the translation of his work. The note by the translator is far more interesting for the contemporary historian. In it, Mario Canella (1898–1982) explained that the motivation to translate and publish this work came to him from an article he read stating that from a strong differentiation between sexes, mankind was now tending towards bisexuality.[41] These 'metaphysical digressions' pushed Canella to suggest the translation of Marañon's book, which proved exactly the opposite.[42] He demonstrated the evident points of contact between Marañon's and Weininger's theories, although Marañon had never quoted the Austrian colleague directly. Weininger too talked about a bisexual predisposition common to all human beings, wrote Canella, as conclusive proof that the Spanish doctor's theories were unquestionably right. The fact that every human being presented both male and female characters was incontrovertible in Canella's opinion, but it should not lead us to believe that mankind was bisexual. On the contrary, it simply meant that it was normal and natural to have one preponderant aspect over the other. However, he concluded with slight disappointment, some signs of this original bisexuality had to remain and were detectable, to varying degrees, as it would be impossible to reach a society consisting of only truly male and truly female elements.

Mario Canella's name is connected to the infamous 'racial psychology'. He taught anatomy and anthropology at Bologna and Ferrara universities, where, after the introduction of the racial laws in 1938, he ran courses on the biology of human races. His book, *Razze Umane estinte e viventi* (*Extinct and Living Human Races*) started from the assumption that races were unequal, and therefore, the distinction between superior and inferior ones was scientifically justified.[43] This led to a study of the different psychologies of human races, aimed at setting a hierarchical scale among them. From this, according to these theories, it followed that Jews, being a mixture of races, represented the lowest level of the spectrum. In other words, Canella is a perfect example of how the theories of Weininger and Marañon could degenerate into stereotyping, racism, anti-Semitism and white supremacism.[44]

Marañon's work was often quoted in Italian psychiatric journals of the time. The subject of hermaphroditism attracted special, almost obsessive attention, and psychiatrists shared descriptions and comments on individual cases encountered in the course of their medical activity. Their evident aim was to add elements to the still limited knowledge of the phenomenon.[45] The existence of individuals who remained at an inferior and undefined development phase, where bisexuality was still present and physically evident, seemed to prove the validity of the Spanish doctor's theories. Yet cases differed a great deal, and each psychiatrist offered many physical, psychological and behavioural details to his observations, hinting at the difficulty in reconciling the theory with daily medical practice. Moreover, the idea that homosexuality was latent in every person created fears together with a sense of urgency that measures were needed to force the 'natural' path to adult sexuality whenever nature had not managed to do so on its own. Marañon's words sanctioned, on a scientific basis, the repression of any behaviour that could trigger homosexuality.

Influences of Italian theory of the previous decades

Dagmar Herzog underlines how, at the beginning of the twentieth century, interest in sexuality and homosexuality intensified as venereal diseases and prostitution were perceived as problems of social order and hygiene.[46] However, the interest in the topic had started much earlier in Europe and in Italy too. As Chiara Beccalossi shows, Arrigo Tamassia (1848–1917) translated the German term *Contraere Sexualempfindung*, coined by Carl Westphal, into *inversione sessuale* in 1878, confirming that interest in sexual inversion was present in Italian psychiatry and sexology from the second half of the nineteenth century onwards.[47] In Italy, there was a specific and constant focus on female sexual deviation as well, she points out, and most psychiatric treatises of the period addressed both male and female sexual inversion. Homosexuality became a category of psychopathy from the nineteenth century in most European countries, Italy included, where doctors began compiling case-studies of sexual inverts, trying to distinguish and divide them into groups that had some elements in common. This trend continued in the following decades. Interest in the subject was related to Lombrosian theories that saw a connection between degeneration, hereditary factors and immorality, where sexual inversion was placed.

At the same time, psychiatry in Italy was still firmly anchored to concepts of moral madness, introduced by James Cowles Pritchard (1786–1848) in the first half of the nineteenth century, which was the terrain from which Lombroso's theories had stemmed.[48] In this sense, manuals such as *Manuale di Psichiatria*, by Cesare Agostini (1864–1942), a pupil of Kraepelin in Heidelberg, exemplify the tendency to consider *follia morale* as a deviation of moral feelings engraved on a hereditary pathological condition.[49] In his theory, moral madness included not only tendencies to idleness, dislike of work, rebelliousness, cruelty from a young age but also delinquency, alcoholism, vagrancy, scrounging and a lack of maternal feelings in women. He thought that a cure was impossible and considered isolation as the only effective prophylactic method to contain the phenomenon and avoid contagion. Agostini provided a list of physical anomalies present in individuals affected by moral madness, in perfect alignment with the Lombrosian approach, and among the causes of their condition, he included nationality, age, gender, marital status, profession and race. Sexual perversions, homosexuality among them, he identified as one of four precocious forms of the category named 'arrests and alterations of psychic functionalities in degenerate individuals'.

Beccalossi explains how the debate in Italy also oriented itself initially in two main directions – on whether homosexuality was inborn or acquired – which would also determine whether it was curable or not. Clearly, this debate mirrored what was happening in Germany, but in Italy, the influence of Lombroso was particularly evident. The Turin-based criminal anthropologist had started by considering homosexuality as a delay in development, in Darwinian terms, but later shifted to interpret it as a product of atavism, which meant that an inborn hereditary characteristic deriving from degeneration was not just passed on to the next generation, but it also deteriorated in the process. However, despite the influence of Lombroso's theories and his search for the common physical traits of delinquents, perverts and prostitutes, Beccalossi argues that in Italy, anatomical explanations, and connected anthropometric considerations, of sexual inversion were not as prominent. Italian psychiatrists, she adds, observed that sexual inverts often had normal genitals and searched for the origin of same-sex desire in the whole individual's degenerate constitution, although in some cases they resorted to clitoridectomies to contain the spread of female same-sex practices in asylums, a practice that contradicted the theory. The debate, originally anchored in a clash between two sides, the Lombrosian degeneration/inherited versus the endocrinological/curable, gradually shifted to favour the Lombrosian theory, which was enriched by the findings of other disciplines.

Beccalossi points to another interesting aspect of nineteenth-century Italian sexology and psychiatry:

> Italian sexology grew out of criminal anthropology, political debates and a strong anticlerical sentiment that ensued after the unification of Italy. ... This movement towards the study of criminal anthropology also reflects one of the most salient features of Italian psychiatry: the manifest link between professional

practice and public engagement ... This political dimension of psychiatry was a specifically Italian characteristic.[50]

One of the best examples in this sense is Leonardo Bianchi (1848–1927), a psychiatrist who enjoyed exceptional fame and success and was always involved in government health politics. He was a member of the Italian Parliament, then secretary of education for a year, in 1905, and a senator. Bianchi's work aptly represents the effort to combine Lombrosian hereditary and degeneration theories with a neurological approach. He was in fact primarily a neuropsychiatrist; in 1882, he founded the journal *Annali di Neurologia* and in 1883 *La psichiatria, la neuropatologia e le scienze affini*. At the same time, he remained strongly rooted in a Lombrosian and generally nineteenth-century framework, as testified by the subjects of his publications, such as hysteria and eugenics.[51]

This attempt to reconcile the neurological and the Lombrosian approach is very evident in his *Trattato di Psichiatria*, aimed at doctors and students, where Leonardo Bianchi gave an accurate description of how he thought a typical patient's analysis should proceed.[52] In his view, several steps had to take place, starting from questions aimed at reconstructing the individual's family history. This step had to be followed by a functional exam of the nervous system. He specified that particular attention had to be given to

> the degenerative anthropological aspects. Everything that, in its shape, constitutes a deviation of the individual in question from the average representative of [his or her] race, or that reproduces characters typical of inferior races or also of superior mammals, or that constitutes irregularity or asymmetry, can be considered as a distinctive characteristic of degeneration.[53]

Already at this stage it is possible to note the presence of three elements that are essential to Leonardo Bianchi's method. Family history, and therefore hereditary factors, together with anthropometric considerations on deviation from normality, derived from the Lombrosian approach, followed by neurological diagnostics. In this way, Bianchi's work was a path opener to those who continued the strong Italian Lombrosian tradition in subsequent decades, rooted in degeneration theories, while attempting to link it with a more medical and scientific approach. As we will see later, this is key to understanding the major trends of Italian psychiatry of the *Ventennio*.

Only after these first steps did the neuropsychiatrist indicate that a medical examination should take place. Here, and again in Lombrosian terms, he underlined the need to investigate the presence of hereditary diseases within the patient's family. This phase would be followed by an examination of the family and the environment of the patient. Specifically, Bianchi thought it was crucial to ascertain the presence of eccentricity, alcoholism or delinquency in any of the patient's relatives, as he saw these factors as hereditary. Lastly, the history of the individual had to be reconstructed. This method, which was taught to students during the fascist regime and was often referred to, demonstrates that Lombrosian ideas were still thought to be the pillar of psychiatric investigation. The insistence on inborn factors, delinquency considered as one of them, the importance given to physical measurements to assess degenerative aspects linked to mental and moral disorders, the research into the patient's past primarily to reveal hereditary traits and the considerable lack of importance given to the patient's history, which occupied the last position in the series of steps proposed as paradigmatic, are all clear links with psychiatry's past that survived in the following decades.

Bianchi dedicated a whole chapter of his treatise, chapter XX, to sexual inversions and perversions. In it, he quoted Weininger and stated that anomalies of the sexual instinct took place when the natural balance of maleness and femaleness present in every individual was broken. These anomalies could be quantitative or qualitative. Among the qualitative anomalies, he placed inversions and perversions. Inversions could derive from underdeveloped genitalia or other indications of a fault in development, or they could simply be the consequence of a degenerative situation that was not physically detectable. When this was the case, Bianchi thought homosexuals should be referred to as '*invertiti d'occasione*' or occasional inverts. He also created other categories of homosexuals: those who, 'given the neuropathic nature of the subjects, and their consequent inferior resistance', would become homosexuals through habit;[54] the indifferent ones, a definition that described bisexuals; and men with a feminine aspect, further distinguished between the platonic and those who were 'humble, cowards, used to doing the most vile and disgusting things one can imagine in a man'.[55]

In a further attempt to categorize the phenomenon, Bianchi saw pederasty as a perversion, rather than simple sexual inversion. It could be found in male-only environments, he observed, but while the non-predisposed individuals went back to normality after they left such places, the predisposed became active or passive perverts. As he explained, in Darwinian and neurological terms, 'the most serious forms of sexual perversion are surely the expression of an anomalous or defective evolution of internal sexual organs or of the nervous system'.[56] Bianchi saw sexual precocity as dangerous and, when writing on therapies to cure homosexuality, expressed the hope that public administrations would ban activities that could awaken sexual feelings in young people. He also thought that one of the causes of homosexuality was impotence and saw in its cure a way to decrease the number of those who sought alternative sexual pleasures as the result of this physical problem.

In terms of the neurological approach, Pasquale Penta (1859–1904) was another strong believer in the connection between homosexuality and the nervous system, but with a much more modern approach to the issue.[57] Penta, in Beccalossi's view, established sexology as an autonomous discipline in Italy. He considered a weak nervous system to be the cause of sexual inversion; therefore, in his view homosexuals had no responsibility for their condition and did not deserve any punishment. On the contrary, he believed they had to be understood. He stressed the importance of environmental factors and psychological elements too. Despite his considerably open-minded approach, however, in one of his lectures of the 1899–1900 academic year, echoing Weygandt, he pathologized unmarried status, stating that 'the unmarried and widows and widowers were more prone to insanity than married people. Spinsters and bachelors were considered to have escaped family responsibilities, which explained their accordingly weak moral sense and underdeveloped personalities'.[58] This reverberated not only in Italian psychiatry over the following decades but also in the propaganda of the fascist regime and in the building of the homosexual stereotype.

Another influential contribution to the study of homosexuality in nineteenth-century Italy, often quoted in psychiatric theory during the *Ventennio*, came from Paolo Mantegazza (1831–1910), whose eclectic interests stretched from anthropology and ethnology to pathology, neurology, hygiene and physiology. A true heir to the positivist faith in science, Darwinism and Lombrosian theories, he too had a neurological approach to homosexuality and thought that in some homosexuals an anatomical anomaly brought more nerves to the rectum, as he explained in *Gli Amori degli Uomini*.[59] He distinguished 'a peripherical anatomical sodomy (deriving from an abnormal distribution of nerves), a lustful sodomy (deriving from a desire for tightness) and a psychic sodomy'.[60] This last would be typical of intelligent, cultured and neurotic men, according to him. The first two categories offered a new definition of passive and active homosexuality.

Mantegazza saw masturbation as a cause of physical, mental and moral disorders. Its consequences would include 'cowardice, hypocrisy, brutishness and character's prostitution'.[61] In his view, it killed the body, the personality and the dignity of an individual. As homosexuality involved mutual masturbation, his judgement on it was in line with these statements. Mantegazza did not think that a cure for sexual inversion was possible also because occasionally the somatic changes brought by homosexuality were irreversible. For instance, he thought that women who had engaged in mutual masturbation for a long period of time had a deformed and oversensitive clitoris, which would make them uninterested in penetrative sex. He believed that repression of these instincts was the only way forward. In fact, he observed that homosexuals who retained self-respect were able to self-censor themselves. In his *Igiene dell'amore*, he reinstated this concept, saying that the only remedy he could see for the problem was either self-imposed chastity or, for men, forced sexual intercourse with women.[62] However, he argued that to inflict legal punishment on homosexuals would have no use; he believed it was positive to let them look for each other in an undisturbed way, so that they would not attempt to seduce heterosexuals.

Charlotte Ross observes that Mantegazza demonized sexual inversion, but at the same time admitted the right to seek pleasure and the legitimacy of male and female passions and desires. Ross adds that he cancelled the boundaries between 'normality' and deviancy when he stated, 'It is impossible to mark the borders that separate love's physiology and pathology.'[63] His firm and undoubted moral condemnation of homosexuality somehow took into account the fact that it existed and it deserved attention and not punishment. According to Ross, he is one of the first to have observed differences between women engaging in same-sex relationships, for instance, showing a will to conduct an in-depth analysis, to observe, describe and understand the phenomenon.

On less extreme but equally conservative positions, we find Eugenio Tanzi (1856–1934), one of the most eminent followers of Kraepelin in Italy and of his belief in the biological basis of mental illness. Tanzi considered sexual inversion as 'erotic infantilism that does not decrease under the strength of sexual attraction, but it prevents its normal orientation.'[64] In his *Trattato delle malattie mentali*, published in 1905 and reprinted in 1914 and 1923, he identified inborn and external causes of homosexuality. He saw the possibility of same sex attraction as a temporary choice, but considered 'complete uranism with no return ... as a mark of degeneration.'[65] In his view, male sexual inversion was either connected to immorality, or to imbecility or paranoia, and he did not question the Lombrosian connection between lesbianism and delinquency. He offered a series of cases to illustrate his views. Tanzi was doubtful of a cure for homosexuality but thought that for men contact with the opposite sex, even prostitutes, could be beneficial. Finally, he believed that, if homosexuality was not displayed in public or imposed through violence, it was useless to repress it or punish it, but he equally thought that it was ridiculous to recognize it legally.

At the same time, homosexuality in Italy continued to be investigated from a criminal anthropological angle, as Alfredo Niceforo's (1876–1960) work aptly shows. He was one of the most celebrated pupils of Cesare Lombroso and is generally remembered as the last true representative of the Lombrosian school.[66] He dedicated a treatise to acquired psychopathy, and among the various manifestations of it, he included sexual inversion and pederasty.[67] He saw masturbation and narcissism as the root of sexual inversion. In his opinion, onanism was also the cause of several other disorders, such as memory loss, difficulty in concentrating or difficulty in doing physical and mental activity. It went hand in hand with neurasthenia, which involved lack of sleep and therefore a pale complexion, thinness, decreased energy and determination, aspects that perfectly fitted the stereotype of the effeminate pederast. He believed that inborn bisexuality could easily turn into homosexuality in adulthood if only one side of the personality was stimulated. This, in his view, applied to women as well, who through masturbation developed what he called *saffismo*. Niceforo also reinstated the Lombrosian concept that connected prostitution with lesbianism, the equivalent of female inborn delinquency. A strong believer that the penal code should mention and punish homosexuality, Niceforo included in his treatise several case studies, which in his view demonstrated the validity of his theories.

A year later, he published a book on criminality in Rome, which he observed from a sociological and anthropological point of view.[68] Under his lens, several homosexuals came under scrutiny. He revealed where they met, what they wore and in what kind of activity they engaged during their free time, in a classic anthropological observation approach. His moral judgement was always present and the fact that he included sexually inverted individuals as prominent in his picture of Rome's low-life is proof of the automatic Lombrosian connection he traced between criminality, immorality and homosexuality. This book was in line with his general anthropological interests and his other publications in the field. In fact, he wrote essays and books on the so-called anthropology of the lower classes, on the inferiority of the southern Italian 'race' and related matters.[69] He theorized the possibility of carrying out 'a biological and scientific analysis of social groups. Anthropometry, physiology, statistics, demography, experimental psychology and ethnographic fieldwork were meant to produce a panopticon for the total observation of society that together could turn every aspect of reality into quantifiable figures.[70]

Alongside Niceforo's criminal anthropological approach, other theories on homosexuality stemmed from the Lombrosian school of thought, which can be detected in several psychiatric texts around the turn of the century. Focusing on lesbianism, Nerina Milletti retraces the Lombrosian approach formulated on the pages of the journal founded by Lombroso in 1880 called *Archivio di psichiatria, antropologia criminale e scienze penali per servire allo studio dell'uomo alienato e delinquente.*[71] Her analysis covers the period between 1880 and 1949, as discussed in the Introduction. She observes that on the pages of this authoritative publication, several Lombrosian concepts found ample space for debate, such as the connection between criminality, in this case prostitution, and lesbianism; hypnosis as a cure for homosexuality; the results of foreign experimental testicular transplants; the negative consequences of onanism; the lack of maternal instinct in homosexual women; and pseudo-hermaphroditism.[72] Psychiatrists and anthropologists illustrated, compared and discussed their findings and theories on the causes of lesbianism, the therapies available and even the presence of tattoos on homosexual bodies, and they compared these with foreign studies and the results of experiments. The journal constituted one of the many platforms available to specialists at the time, and the plurality of positions it attracted testifies to the fervid exchange of opinions on sexuality that took place in Italian psychiatry before and during the dictatorship.

Alarming reflections on male homosexuality came in the aftermath of the First World War. The conflict, as explained by most historians who analysed the period, showed the limits of eugenics and Darwinian beliefs: as the strongest and bravest men died, the weakest, those unable to fight, had a better chance of survival and would give birth to an even weaker generation of Italians. As Paolo Giovannini observes, the traumatic consequences of the conflict also determined a considerable development in neurological studies on post-trauma conditions.[73] But, more importantly, for the focus of this research, promiscuity at the front brought to the fore issues connected with immoral behaviour, homosexuality and moral contagion among soldiers. Giacomo Pighini (1876–1969), a psychiatrist who served as a medical officer during the First World War, advocated the elimination of psychic degenerates from the army.[74] He thought it necessary to exclude from military service not only delinquents but also those affected by mental illness, which in his description included immorality, simulation of epilepsy in order to be sent home, rebelliousness, deafness and perversion. Although he never mentioned the word homosexuality, but resorted to expressions such as 'ethical poverty' or 'perversion of the ethical-affective sphere', he had no doubt that it was necessary 'to consider the amoral, the habitually undisciplined, the habitual criminal and the criminaloid individual as a variety of the frenasthenics' big family, that is to say mentally diminished people, and treat them as such'.[75] He saw these individuals as polluting not just the army, but society at large. As they constituted anti-social and degenerate elements of the 'stock', he thought they should be sent off to the colonies. With this last statement, Pighini, a strong believer in endocrinology in the following years and a politically involved fascist, anticipated the punishment that the regime later reserved for visible and 'scandalous' homosexuals, *confino*, which consisted of a period in isolation in a remote location.

Other influences

During the *Ventennio*, psychiatrists in Italy were influenced by several other factors that were not strictly connected to their medical discipline. One of these was the Catholic Church. Fascism had a complex relationship with Catholicism. It wanted to present itself as a non-religious movement, able to replace old beliefs and rites, but it was aware that a total substitution of Catholic traditions in Italy would be impossible. The Church reached Italian society in a capillary fashion that Fascism could not compete with. Besides, Mussolini understood that on some issues, the Vatican had the potential to constitute a powerful ally, because certain interests converged. For instance, the regime's demographic campaign aligned itself in opposition to abortion and contraception, a position traditionally promoted by Catholicism. Prolific mothers were praised by Fascism and the Church alike. In their opposition to feminism, State and Church also agreed. For both institutions, the natural role of women was to be a wife and mother, obedient to the *pater familias*. Women had to stay at home and dedicate their lives to the family, avoiding ambition or requests for equality, which were dismissed as against the feminine nature. Pius XI had sealed the Vatican's positions on the issue with his official pronouncement of 1930, *Casti Connubii*, where he reinstated the primacy of man, husband and father in the family.[76] Another important aspect on which State and Church agreed was the contestation of sexual intercourse that did not have procreation as its aim. A pillar of both fascist propaganda and the preaching of priests was to consider any sexual activity not finalized in having children as selfish, anti-patriotic, sinful, lustful and immoral. The Catholic condemnation of homosexuality as against nature and against God's plans for humanity was shared by the regime, within the ideals of its demographic campaigns, and seen by both institutions as a negative characteristic of modern life in big cities, opposed to rural life and its values, at the centre of the regime's rhetoric. The common enemy was individualism, as emphasized by Paul Ginsborg.[77]

Many of these concepts reflected upon Italian psychiatry too. A high proportion of internees were women who rebelled against the traditional role imposed on them. Women who showed sexual desire were thought to be not just immoral but 'different' and 'unnatural' or 'against nature', rebellious, and therefore to have some personality dysfunction. 'Normal' women were supposed to 'naturally' have less sexual desire than men, as stated by Marañon and others. Also, a lack of shame, the absence of maternal instinct and a display of nudity were particularly pathologized in young unmarried women, but even mature women who had erotic fantasies or were victims of seduction were considered pathological.

Masturbation, a sin in the Catholic faith, as specifically indicated by the New Testament, and a sign of selfishness and tendency to lust, as observed earlier, was pathologized by psychiatry. Most Italian psychiatrists kept insisting on masturbation being unhealthy or even damaging to health. As Alessandro Scurti notes, Italian psychiatry persevered in an authentic crusade against masturbation that had already started in the late eighteenth century and that essentially pathologized early adolescence.[78] Homosexuality, seen as the search for pleasure through mutual masturbation, was seen as its pathological consequence. Onanism often became the cause and effect of sexual inversion at the same time. In alignment with Catholic teachings, pederasty, involving sodomy, was judged more negatively than active homosexuality; many theoreticians specifically distinguished between the two and always placed the first among the worst perversions.

Singledom was also considered a suspicious choice, indicating immaturity, lack of a sense of responsibility or deviancy, and this too fitted with what the Church had traditionally taught, where marriage and procreation were the 'natural' and adult choice of any individual.

Beyond sexuality, many other Catholic concepts were inherited by Italian psychiatry. The religious concept that repentance was the main sign of the recovery of a patient was widely accepted. An interned person was considered to have entered the recovery phase if he or she admitted his or her condition of being a mentally ill person, showed shame for his or her previous actions and changed behaviour. It was considered of vital importance to observe that the patient had learnt how to repress certain habits, even when the root of the problem had not been solved. In other words, the patient was considered recovered only when he or she demonstrated that his or her behavioural problems could be bent to suit social life. Control of instincts was an essential element of Catholic belief and of psychiatric practice alike.

In addition, ergotherapy remained at the basis of psychiatric treatment, although new angles of it were explored and implemented. The intention was that it had to become more inclusive and less similar to forced labour, but in practice it remained coercive and exploitative. Redemption through suffering, pain and labour is a central concept of Roman Catholic faith. The idea that the mental health institution's discipline was a valid psychiatric therapy, for instance, and that recovery depended upon acceptance of figures of authority and the asylum rules came from Roman Catholic values such as humility, acceptance of hierarchy and obedience.

Even the way in which patients were distributed and kept within mental health institutions, as observed in the chapter on the Florence asylum, can be reconstructed in the light of a Roman Catholic mindset.[79] The most agitated and less 'well behaved' patients were the most distant from the central buildings where doctors and the director operated, while the less dangerous were closer. This arrangement, in clear contradiction with therapeutic concerns, can only be read as a way to interpret the institution as the projection of an itinerary that, from perdition and distance from perfection, must be taken in order to improve and achieve freedom. In other words, it reflects the Roman Catholic concept of purgatory, where souls move from the most distant position from God towards heaven.

Despite the evident effort to transform psychiatry into a scientific and objective branch of medicine, taking a distance from the past, the fascist years did not manage to shake off the heavy heritage of Catholicism. In other words, while the psychiatry of the *Ventennio* deployed considerable effort to demonstrate that it had evolved into a scientific discipline, old concepts linked with moral madness persisted. The implication that madness was caused by a spiritual derangement persisted, alongside the idea of it being rooted in inherited degenerative elements. Old diagnostic categories, such as constitutional moral madness, immorality and amorality, remained in use during the *Ventennio*, and patient files seldom questioned this old-fashioned and inherently Catholic type of approach to mental illness. Besides, patient files were full of comments that implied moral judgement on the behaviour, choices and attitudes of internees, often written by nurses, GPs and the security forces, but not radically questioned by asylum psychiatrists.[80]

While in many ways the agendas of the Church and the State coincided, constant tension persisted between the two institutions. Many historians have focused on the ambiguous relationship between Mussolini and the Vatican and on the difficult path that led to the signing of the *Concordato* in 1929.[81]

As Paul Ginsborg explains, within the still predominant Catholic Italian ways of life, the family remained an area that Fascism found difficult to penetrate.[82] The Church imposed on the family the duty to educate sons and daughters, passing Catholic values to younger generations. The priorities of the Catholic Church held, despite attempts by the fascist regime to enter its sphere, creating socialization groups, sports clubs and other options as alternatives to staying at home, under parental and marital vigilance, according to Ginsborg. Fascism introduced mistrust and broke some of the solidarity that existed, for instance, among working-class families on the outskirts of industrial towns, such as Turin, but on the whole, the family structure remained a strong nucleus.[83] Catholicism was always looked upon with a certain degree of suspicion by the regime, and Catholic associations, for instance, remained a thorn in the side of Fascism, as they constituted a sphere beyond the State's control.

This ambiguity of the family, in part supporting some of the values that coincided with Catholicism and fascist propaganda and in part opposing them, can be seen when analysing homosexual patients in asylums. Most interned homosexual patients were referred to the psychiatric system by their families, who even contested the doctors' decisions to release them. In a minority of cases, patients were supported by their families, who showed they were aware of the homosexuality of their interned relatives but did not seem to judge them negatively because of it; they asked the asylum director to release their loved ones and accepted them at home. Psychiatry, in this sense, also played an ambiguous role. It offered its knowledge and services to the State, the Church and the security forces, who wanted to isolate, punish or cure homosexuality; yet it also showed a certain reluctance in having to carry out this role. It did not completely refuse it, so that it could also continue to assert its power, but at the same time, it often tried to disentangle itself from the role of a mere gaoler.

Fascism's position towards the family and its values is emblematically explained in an article published by Egilberto Martire, a member of parliament, in 1929 in the pages of *Politica Sociale*.[84] The author clearly tried to reconcile Catholic and fascist ideals and values, underlining the combined efforts to reach similar targets. He also stressed the common adversity towards feminism and towards those men

> who can do without women. These anti-women tendencies (this euphemism spares us from having to quote Krafft-Ebing) are nowadays fairly common among male youths; among those too, and unfortunately, they are the majority, who have read neither Plato nor Oscar Wilde.[85]

Interestingly, Krafft-Ebing and his theories are quoted as if known even by the readers of a generic current-affairs magazine, not just by sexologists, psychiatrists or other medical specialists. It indicates that, despite the silence surrounding homosexuality at a formal level – that is, legislative and institutional level, the terms of the discussion were familiar to most. It equally confirms that the repression of homosexuality was seen as functional to the implementation of the demographic campaign, something that went hand in hand with the celebration of traditional Catholic and family values.

Psychiatry also absorbed the culture of the period and at the same time produced concepts that were developed by popular culture. We have already seen this circulation of ideas in regard to Weininger's theories earlier in the chapter. Another apt example is the vast pseudoscientific literature on sexuality that circulated from the end of the nineteenth century onwards. Charlotte Ross examines two texts published at the beginning of the twentieth century.[86] She highlights how, among titillating, voyeuristic and satirical descriptions, in this type of literature, there was also space for some empathic understanding of homosexuality. This genre of publications intensified in the following decades, and Ross lists some of the titles, such as *Lussuria e Castità* (Lust and Chastity) by Alberto Orsi, *La masturbazione nella donna: cause e forme, casistica e rimedi (con illustrazioni)* (Women's Masturbation: Causes and Types, Statistics and Remedies – with Illustrations) by Nice Fowell and several books published by the Florence-based publishers Il Pensiero in a series called *Perversioni Sessuali* (Sexual Perversions).[87] The Rome-based publisher Capaccini too, active at the end of the nineteenth century, printed a series called *Biblioteca dei Pervertimenti Sessuali* (Library of Sexual Perversions), whose titles were surely aimed at attracting mostly the general public in search of titillation. However, it is plausible that such publications were among the few available to homosexuals and lesbians who wanted to know more about their condition. Finally, it is not impossible that some of these books informed psychiatric doctors and nurses in search of clarification. The ideas contained in them were elaborations of more serious scientific theories, translated, often made banal, not only for the public, but probably also for those medical staff who did not read high sexological theory. Some of the comments that appear in patient files of the fascist period, written by nurses or by asylum doctors, are in line with this satirical and prudish literature. Capaccini did publish not only scientific texts but also other French texts whose titles do not suggest a scientific approach, such as *L'Amore, la Lussuria e il Libertinaggio* (Love, Lust and Licentiousness) by Martin Laurent, *Le Deformazioni vulvari e anali (anche prodotte dal saffismo)* (Anal and Vulvar

Deformities, Also Caused by Sapphism) by Louis Martineau, *I Delitti di Libidine* (Crimes of Lust) by Auguste Ambroise Tardieu, *L'onanismo nella donna* (Women's Onanism) by Thésée Pouillet and similar works.[88] Giulio Cesare Ferrari (1867–1932), one of the most eminent child psychiatrists of his time in Italy, must have been aware of these texts and their effective influence when he warned,

> It seems to me that someone should make his voice heard against these publications on the topic of sexual psychopathies, that have no use other than to propagate the plagues they claim they aim to cure. Vulgarisations are almost always useless, and those of this kind doubtlessly damaging.[89]

In other words, psychiatry absorbed the general climate too, with its concepts and beliefs from popular culture, which influenced the common understanding of sexuality. Besides, this pseudoscientific literature gave flesh to the theories. It offered readers characters with whom it was possible to have a certain degree of empathy and understanding, and this contributed to a wider acceptance of homosexuality, also among psychiatric professionals.

Equally, psychiatry was influenced by fascist propaganda, or had to show it was, and it rarely took a distance from the stereotype of homosexuality the regime reinforced, at least on the official documents such as asylum patient files and journal articles. The picture of the homosexual as a degenerate individual, idle, selfish, cowardly, without patriotic feelings, pale and devoured by vice was often reflected in the comments and patient descriptions of psychiatrists and nurses. However, when dealing with patients who were interned because, or also because, they were homosexual or bisexual, psychiatric professionals demonstrated that they were able to go beyond the stereotypical descriptions and often even sided with the patient, as demonstrated in the second part of the book.

This contradiction between theory and implementation, a key issue of Fascism, was well exemplified by Mussolini's behaviour. He portrayed himself as the model family man, an example of rectitude for the country, but he never denied or hid the fact that he had many love affairs, some of which lasted a considerable time and were very visible. In the same way, theoreticians pronounced hard condemnations of homosexuality, but practitioners were far more lenient and understanding. Italians were used to such contradictions and the gap between the rhetoric of the regime and daily life, as much as they were used to the difference between official Italian language and their dialect. So, while the regime stereotyped, condemned, persecuted and repressed homosexuality, a theatre character such as Gastone, embodied by his creator

Ettore Petrolini (1884–1936), was immensely popular. Petrolini performed the part of a snobbish bachelor with many unmistakable characteristics of the stereotypical homosexual, such as pale skin, cynicism, affectation, mellowness, thinness and a nasal and feminine voice and gestures. Italian audiences adored his dry humour and his anti-establishment behaviour. Within this scenario, it is also possible to understand how the regime tolerated poets, painters and writers who were clearly homosexual and whose work did not conceal it. Intellectuals and artists such as Giovanni Comisso (1895–1969), Filippo De Pisis (1896–1956), Ottone Rosai (1895–1957) and Sandro Penna (1906–1977), to name a few, offered homoerotically charged iconographic and literary images in their novels, poems and paintings, and their work was known and circulated, within the limits imposed by censorship.[90] Upper-class gay and lesbian circuits existed and were visible – in Florence and Capri – for instance, and the authorities were aware of them but deliberately turned a blind eye.[91]

To conclude, Italian psychiatry remained suffocated by its internationally acclaimed predecessors and some of the most eminent German, Spanish and, to a lesser degree, French theoreticians of the past. The tendencies towards new scientific and medical frontiers were subjected to the influence of the medical practice, sexology and psychiatry of previous decades. The pull towards modernization was dampened by this burden and by the heavy weight of the Catholic tradition. While the profession tried to portray itself as a scientific and objective branch of medicine, cultural and religious heritage was ingrained in its theory and practice, together with the stereotypes that Fascism strengthened. New disciplines such as endocrinology and neurology were explored, but in the end, they were merely added to old beliefs that homosexuality was an inherited degeneration or inborn psychopathic trait.

Italian psychiatric theories on homosexuality published during the fascist regime

This chapter analyses psychiatric theoretical work on sexuality and homo-sexuality, written during the *Ventennio* by Italian psychiatrists, and identifies how previous theories were elaborated, rejected or absorbed by them. The wealth of treatises that discuss the topic, also written by relatively unknown professionals, leaves the impression of a lively debate. Although the results, in terms of new theoretical approaches to homosexuality, were not particularly original, most specialists felt the need and responsibility to share their thoughts and findings on the issue, in an attempt to give new interpretations of the causes of sexual inversion, its origins and possible therapies to cure it, or measures to contain it.

The chapter confirms how Italian psychiatric theory was influenced mainly by German, French and Spanish psychiatry of the time or of previous decades, but at the same time remained indebted to Italian psychiatric thinking of the past. Overwhelmed by so many authoritative influences, Italian theoreticians of the *Ventennio* found it hard to produce a strong new theory. They tried to combine different approaches from several sources, keeping in mind contemporary advances in terms of therapies, endocrinology, neurology and surgery, but remaining strongly anchored to Lombrosian theories that saw homosexuality as hereditary and one of the expressions of inborn degeneration, often with visible recurrent somatic signs. The fascist decades produced a wealth of psychiatric literature that touched upon the subjects of sexuality and homosexuality, but no single strand emerged to dominate the others. I have therefore exercised a choice, identifying the main trends, keeping in mind that the discussed texts constitute only samples of a vast production of essays and manuals.

Starting with the most authoritative voices, Enrico Morselli's (1852–1929) career began in the second half of the nineteenth century with his involvement with several scientific, medical and philosophical journals, together with the direction of the Turin mental health hospital, and university teaching in Turin and Genoa.[1] His eclectic and extremely successful professional activity can be framed within a positivist and Lombrosian general approach, although in the last part of his life his interest expanded to include Freud and psychoanalysis, which he tried to introduce in Italy, as one of his last publications testifies.[2] In his *Sessualità Umana*, published posthumously in 1931, he spent a great deal of effort discussing and proving the inferiority of women, in line with Lombrosian theories and with some of the previously illustrated thoughts formulated by Weininger and Marañon.[3] When he focused on the male climacteric, he believed that several problems connected with this phase could be solved through glandular implants, and quoted Serge Voronoff's (1866–1951) recent experiments in the field. Impotence and low sperm production were among the symptoms that could be addressed by this type of surgical intervention. Discussing issues connected with male menopause and its pathologies, having quoted Kraepelin and Hirschfeld, who identified a connection between the male climacteric and some forms of psychosis, Morselli specifically explained that during this period of a man's life, several perversions could resurface.[4] Among them he listed pubertal narcissism and therefore onanism. He added that new tendencies could appear, such as the search for new *stimuli*, which could lead to sexual intercourse with prostitutes, mutual masturbation, fetishism, paedophilia, anal and oral sex. In fact, sadistic crimes such as rape or uxoricide were usually committed by mature men, he observed.

In addition, there were other groups of patients who could benefit from these new therapies too, in Morselli's view:

> A first group, nowadays very much in fashion, is of those who are affected by sexual inversion, whose secondary characteristics of their gender are not very developed, and whose instinct is directed towards sterile homosexual satisfaction. They could see their perversion corrected with a testicle transplant that would awaken or fortify their anomalous or deviant virility. Here we have a question for the attention of sexologists: in fact, a good number of these uranists, passive ones included, show, as Vidoni demonstrated, eunuchoid characteristics, certainly due to the imperfect action of their genital hormones. Together with their somatic eunuchoidism, their intellect is soft, apathic, indolent, often frenasthenic. To implant a virile active gland could maybe bring them out of their state of physical, psychic and social inferiority, and could at the same time diminish in society the disgusting social plague of male prostitution.[5]

This statement is an apt summary of old theories: sexual inversion must have traceable physical characteristics that frequently consist of secondary traits not considered pertinent to their gender, with a 'good number' of individuals who present 'eunuchoid characteristics'. However, and here one can see the new approach to the issue, these are due to a glandular dysfunction that can be surgically treated. The intervention would radically change the hormonal balance of the person with this dysfunction so that s/he could be transformed into a 'healthy' person, that is, no longer sexually inverted. This manipulation is read in eugenics terms, with the belief that society would improve thanks to this approach, as the plague of male prostitution could be solved.

Morselli demonstrated his belief in endocrinology and his appreciation for the work carried out in the field by his former pupil, and then colleague, Giuseppe Vidoni (1884–1951), whose theories, illustrated later in this chapter, were rapidly gaining esteem and support in Italy. He gave an account of the doubts still surrounding these new therapies, but he focused only on the lack of positive results in attempts to rejuvenate patients, thus not excluding positive outcomes in other fields. In the second part of the book, he revealed how anchored he was to old Lombrosian theories, when he explained how prostitution was the result of an inborn hereditary degeneration and how prostitutes bore physical and pathological signs of their degeneration.

When he addressed homosexuality issues, he showed that external determining factors were important, such as male-only environments, which could be fertile terrain for what he termed 'morbid friendships'. In his view, Lombroso had correctly pathologized this type of platonic love as particularly dangerous because, he reiterated, sometimes positive impressions acquired during puberty could push an individual to seek similar satisfaction later in life. All these concepts came from various sources that have been commented on earlier, nothing completely new on the topic emerged from his analysis. Morselli concluded, trying to give a logical system to his thoughts, saying that there were erotic ties

> among the constitutional anomalous individuals and the inferior types who populate the corrective institutions, the prisons, the public baths, the asylums; but in one-gender only communities … the formation of this type of 'friendships' will not expand beyond the duration of the time spent there, the forced disciplined co-housing, the forced separation from people of the opposite sex.[6]

In other words, he believed external factors not to be sufficient, on their own, to determine homosexuality. In order to develop into a homosexual person, one needed to have an inborn predisposition, he stated, echoing several opinions illustrated in the previous chapter. Strict surveillance was to be implemented by pedagogists in the early phases of childhood and adolescence but, at the same time, as homosexuality was mostly congenital, he did not think that it was necessary to punish it if it did not offend morality and 'aesthetics', which was a way to describe scandal. This position is a clear example of how difficult it was to reconcile theories that considered sexual inversion congenital and the old idea that morality had to be safeguarded with adequate measures, as homosexuality could be triggered by external factors. The Italian way, which closely mirrored Marañon's ideas, is well summarized by Morselli and many others who thought it was prudent to include both stances.

One of the previously mentioned, Giuseppe Vidoni's (1884–1951) main treatise focused on the connections between delinquency and endocrinology, which in his view was a valid tool to study and prevent crime.[7] Vidoni asserted that glands played a fundamental role in an individual's life and could determine both his or her behaviour and physical aspect. A thyroid's insufficiency would stop the development of sexual organs, for instance. He studied the effects of the pituitary gland's dysfunctions, observing that they could produce feminine secondary characters, such as delicate and thin hands. He added that eunuchoidism's hormonal configuration could also have secondary physical consequences, such as longer limbs, especially legs, which he found in 88 per cent of homosexuals observed by him, and *valgus* knees. This suggestion travelled far in Italy where several psychiatrists observed the physical appearance of their homosexual patients, in search of proof that they had longer limbs. For instance, Mario De Paoli came to this exact conclusion in an article where he discussed two cases of homosexuals interned in the Como asylum.[8] Although the two men were different in many ways, as their medical and family history showed, alongside the manifestations of their sexual inversion, De Paoli indicated that they both presented some strong physical similarities, such as longer legs, to be interpreted as a consequence of their hormonal imbalance. In his opinion, the sexuality of both men was determined by their endocrinological dysfunction. He still referred to homosexuality as a serious moral degeneration, though, exemplifying well the contradiction between enthusiasm for modern scientific achievements in disciplines such as endocrinology and the persistence of old approaches.

The search for common physical marks of endocrinological problems was clearly inherited from the Lombrosian tradition and Vidoni pushed the endocrinological approach in this direction, demonstrating a connection, due to hormonal dysfunctions, between feminine aspect and male delinquency, mirrored by a masculine aspect in female prostitutes. He also indicated the presence of breasts as a typical trait of male delinquents and observed genital anomalies in several 'degenerates'. In this way the link between degeneracy, delinquency and homosexuality, a key issue in Lombroso's theoretical thought, was reinstated, and the glandular aspect represented the novel element of the approach. Like most of his contemporary colleagues, Vidoni followed Steinach's experiments and Voronoff's testicle implants with great interest, and in his treatise, he quoted the famous case of the implant of a sadist's testicles on a homosexual and a eunuch.[9]

Martina Salvante has focused on Vidoni and his studies on female and male prostitution.[10] She observes that Vidoni started from the traditionally Lombrosian interpretation of female homosexuality as the typical female delinquent and associated female prostitutes with male behavioural and somatic traits to underline the masculine elements in them. Prostitution, in Lombrosian terms, meant an absence of the most exquisite female characteristics, such as shame, maternal instinct and modesty. Vidoni saw in prostitutes 'a sub-species of homosexuals'.[11] After this first analysis, he then concentrated on male prostitution and published an article based on his observation of some boys incarcerated in the Genoa prison.[12] Eight out of nine cases he considered to be real homosexuals and he read their inborn endocrinological configuration as the cause of their homosexuality. He connected their sexual deviancy to an intellectual deficiency in some cases, to delinquency, such as theft, and use of drugs in other cases. Clearly, in Vidoni's view, homosexuality was congenital and the result of an inborn glandular configuration, but its endocrinological component was malleable, opening the scenario for new therapeutic approaches to correct the condition.

Vidoni quoted Nicola Pende (1880–1951), showing great respect for his writings and achievements. Pende was an endocrinologist and a senator who influenced psychiatry and sexology in Italy and elsewhere. His reputation went well beyond Italian borders, and even the internationally acclaimed Gregorio Marañon, for instance, mentioned his achievements with reverence on several occasions. Pende had a clear awareness that his thought could have an impact beyond medicine and in his work connected his scientific views to extremely reactionary social and political ideas. For instance, his treatise *Dalla Medicina alla Sociologia* stated that cells were harmoniously governed by hormones, able to connect all the other morphological cellular elements with morality, character and intellect in an individual; in the same way society should be led by an intellectual aristocracy that would guarantee social harmony among all its members.[13] In 1924, with *La Biotipologia umana*, he pushed his theories to a further stage and proposed a classification of human bio-typology based exclusively on neuroendocrinology.[14] Like in Vidoni, this type of categorization belonged to Lombrosian thought, but was revisited in an endocrinological way and pushed to the limits. He exemplified the importance of endocrinology by drawing a scheme where the basis of every human being's structure was represented by a square, which visualized his or her hereditary situation. On it lay four walls that represented his or her (1) morphological, (2) physiological or humoral–functional, which he considered to be the most important, (3) moral or affective and (4) intellectual aspect. Hormones were situated between the material and the moral sphere of human beings as they were the hinges connecting body and mind. In his system, they determined everything starting from the physical aspect to personal choices and professions, from which Pende inferred that a certain physical aspect was inescapably connected to a particular job, and vice versa, a person's occupation could be deduced from his or her physical description. Therefore, medical cures had to be differentiated on the basis of patients' professions because, in Pende's view, occupation implied different physical characteristics and responses. In a different treatise, he categorized the spectrum of characters and behaviours on the basis of hormones.[15] The tendency to stereotype human beings through this theoretical approach is evident, as the extreme attempt to find a scientifically objective formulation of social and health conditions. Pende even exemplified his theories using geometrical configurations.

Pende believed that sexuality could be manipulated. This could happen in a number of ways, according to him, including gland transplant, radiation and surgical correction of genital abnormalities. His approach is another perfect example of how the old concept of homosexuality as hereditary and therefore congenital could be enriched by new disciplines, such as endocrinology in this case. As Beccalossi points out, endocrinology was connected with eugenics, and its attempt was to improve the Italian 'stock' through hormonal manipulation.[16] In this way, it responded to needs to embrace the so-called 'positive' eugenics approach, which characterized Catholic countries, and did not advocate the elimination of inferiors, but rather their 'improvement'. Furthermore, as Beccalossi notes, 'hormone therapies were used not only to enhance Italians, but also to normalise them'.[17] The individual could not be cured, but this did not generate a pessimistic view. On the contrary, homosexuals now appeared to be transformable, re-programmable, thanks to science. In eugenics terms, this belief added optimism on the possibility to improve society.

Coherently with his theories illustrated above, Pende believed that the state had to put in place some form of prevention against free choices because they contradicted the scientifically proven peculiarity of every person. His system could not include any individual's freedom, as everything was dictated by gland secretion and hereditary factors. In defining femininity, for instance, Pende identified two main female types, the erotic and the maternal, while men's sphere of action extended to more areas and went beyond sexuality, to include muscular work, cerebral occupations, fighting and so forth. According to him it was vain to rebel against the fundamental law of a natural destiny written in the genetic, glandular and neurological part of each person.[18] This meant women should not ask for any emancipation, which in Pende's view was unnatural. He was also in favour of racial psychology, as he believed races had immutable and identifiable characteristics.[19]

From the most famous names of psychiatry and connected areas of study, this research moves to the analysis of some of the treatises written by less known specialists, to illustrate how major theories were dealt with by those who were not among the most established psychiatrists, but still enjoyed fame and the honour of publication during the regime. Among them was Giuseppe Mariani (1885–1963). The *Dizionario Biografico degli Italiani* tells us that he taught in several universities, such as Pavia, Cagliari and Bari, where he became *Rettore* (rector or vice chancellor) and concentrated his research on dermatopathology connected with venereal diseases.[20] He then focused on the socio-sanitary aspects of syphilis and presumably this was how he came to discuss issues connected with sexuality.

Following the steps of several of his Italian and European predecessors, he identified onanism as a starting point for homosexuality. Masturbation, in his view, was the strongest evidence of selfish behaviour, something that fitted with the stereotype of the homosexual as an egocentric and narcissistic person whose lifestyle was in opposition with the demographic campaign launched by the regime. In his main treatise on sexuality, *La Questione Sessuale. Fisiopatologia, Sociologia e Legislazione Sessuale* (The Sexuality Issue. Physiopathology, Sociology and Legislation on Sexuality), he advocated vigilance during puberty to avert any trend in the direction of homosexuality, and warned against excessively strong friendship bonds that could degenerate into same-sex morbid relationships.[21] He drew most of his considerations from existing literature, insisting on the importance of prophylaxis during puberty and of vigilance so that signs of bisexuality could be detected very early on and elements of dormant homosexuality could be repressed even before they emerged, clearly echoing Marañon, among others.

Mariani identified three groups of homosexuals: where the somatic element of inversion was present and visible; where it was not; and a third category where the physical aspect was only slightly altered compared to 'normality'. He opted for a definition of homosexuality that followed Ulrich's idea of a 'sexual soul' of a different gender from the body that harboured it. However, he thought that this was only applicable in some cases, while in other individuals there were evident non-alignments in somatic terms too, so that the body also bore visible signs of the opposite sex. In women, he observed acutely, homosexuality was more difficult to detect because they were brought up to hide their feelings and did not enjoy the same freedom as men. Homosexual women, in his view, were often either frustrated virgins or prostitutes. Interestingly, though, he saw that sexual inversion had an essentially psychic basis: 'The strong predominance of affection and the intellect, often very intense, over sensory feelings, makes us think that homosexual love is mostly an anomaly, in most cases of a psychic nature.'[22] However, to corroborate his thoughts, he added that even psychoanalysis admitted a psychopathic inborn basis to sexual inversion.

To summarize, Mariani's theories tried to combine several strands that came from various theoreticians. Homosexuality was an inborn anomaly (Weininger and Marañon, among others), which he tried to categorize using the presence or absence of physical traits (Lombroso) considered appropriate to the opposite sex, admitting though that there were 'intermediate' states where both female and male characteristics were present but none was prevailing (Marañon and Kraepelin). As latent homosexuality could be awoken especially in puberty, strictest vigilance was necessary (Marañon, among others). The only point of originality lies in his admission of the psychic part of a person's sexual orientation and consequent lifestyle. As he thought that homosexuality was an inborn hereditary condition, he agreed with most of his predecessors that punishment for homosexuality was therefore both 'stupid and useless'.[23]

Mariani was an authoritative voice in the fascist years, as confirmed by the fact that he was the author of several entries, such as 'erotomania' and 'priapism', dated respectively in 1932 and 1935, for the prestigious Treccani Encyclopaedia. His work is representative of the attempt to reconcile several different positions and to offer a coherent path for colleagues to follow.

Another contribution on sexuality and homosexuality in the fascist years came from Giulio Moglie, who taught psychiatry at La Sapienza University in Rome. His treatise, *Manuale di Psichiatria*, aimed at psychiatry students, was published in 1940.[24] Although very little is known of him nowadays, the preface to his manual was written by Sante De Sanctis (1862–1935), considered to be one of the founders of Italian psychology and one of the most authoritative voices in the field of child neuropsychiatry of his time.[25] This implies Moglie's unquestionable reputation at the time of publication. De Sanctis highlighted the areas of continuity between this work and the Italian school of Morselli and Tamburini, together with the author's evident debt towards Kraepelin and Bumke. In this way, he placed Moglie in the firmament of the brightest stars of the contemporary Italian and international psychiatric context.

Moglie's treatise concentrated on defining moral insanity or constitutional immorality, a concept that belonged to the past but that he thought needed renewed attention. He classified human feelings according to the level of their morality, their worthiness of human being's status and their distance from the ideal that men and women should aim towards. Immoral people were 'egocentrics ... unsuitable to social life'.[26]

When coming to sexual perversions, he wrote that he was deliberately brief on the subject, as these were simply part of more generic pathological situations where the inhibitions had completely or partially disappeared. Absence of shame and inhibitions in the sexual sphere were often described by psychiatrists who worked in asylums and by theoreticians as a signal of mental disorder, especially when combined with sexual precocity. The definition of 'normality' included the idea that adults would have inhibitions, were able to control their passions and instincts, knew what was morally acceptable and what was not, self-censored and recognized there were limits to respect.

Moglie catalogued sexual perversions into two main groups, qualitative and quantitative disorders, mirroring Leonardo Bianchi's approach, but sexual inversion did not fall in either of them. He thought inversion could not be considered as a simple aspect of constitutional immorality, but rather as a special pathological predisposition, a hereditary aspect combined with some form of dysfunction or abnormal organic element. He conceded that knowledge on this was still limited. He also briefly mentioned Marañon, noting that he had aptly explained that an element of infantilism was often at the basis of sexual inversion, related to the concept that homosexuality corresponded to a delay in development. However, Moglie added an important consideration to the 'inborn' theories, as he connected homosexuality with other pathologies. Besides, sexual inversions and perversions were mostly noted as one of the manifestations of a pathological situation consisting of more than one symptom. In other words, it was not just a hereditary factor, it was usually one of the many symptoms that should alert the health practitioner to a complex medical condition.

In Moglie's view, some homosexuals were really perverted because they felt they were in the right to satisfy their instincts, while others were morally sane and were therefore full of shame and remorse, and tried to solve their problem through work, medicine or religion. This attitude, often inherited by psychiatric practice, reveals how anchored he was to old moral madness theories and to the Catholic concept of repentance as a sign of redemption, which in medical terms coincided with recovery. In any case, despite their best efforts, he concluded, homosexuals were 'congenitally sick, a true expression of degeneration'.[27] To cure homosexuality, one had to cure the psychopathic condition, whose sexual inversion was one of the many symptoms, he added. In forms of sexual inversion that were not too serious and not too deeply rooted, he believed that physical exercise, abstinence and lack of masturbation might help. A cure was therefore not possible, but imposing certain behaviours, censoring, repressing and forcing homosexuals to chastity might be a remedy to the problem, to be addressed, as observed, in a wider psychopathological context.

Moglie's theories and approach to sexual inversion constitute a good example of the most traditionalist and moralistic attitudes towards homosexuality, which did not even consider the formulation of a cure. The belief that homosexuality could only be treated through abstinence meant that only repression was believed to be a valid answer to the problem. The idea mirrored Raffalovich's beliefs. Most importantly, to consider homosexuality as one of many symptoms of a psychiatric condition was a way to return to the old degeneration concept that new theories were trying to surpass.

Finally, I examine a treatise, *La base organica dei pervertimenti sessuali* (The Organic Basis of Sexual Perversions), by another relatively unknown author, Alfredo la Cara.[28] The book, published in 1902, but updated and reprinted in 1924, is almost a compendium of all the theories that circulated in psychiatric *milieus* in Italy at the time. From what can be deduced from this piece of writing, the author represents well the group of Italian psychiatrists who concentrated on the neurological explanation of mental illness and homosexuality.

La Cara set out clearly the two ends of the spectrum in theoretical terms, when addressing sexual inversion. Between the two theories, congenital and acquired condition, he declared he sided with Raffalovich, who, as we have already seen, considered it to be a congenital condition that could not be cured, but only repressed through chastity. In line with this, the author of *La base organica dei pervertimenti sessuali* added that external influences could have an impact only on a predisposed subject, and cures could only be successful on those who understood that they were ill, which meant they felt ashamed and still had some 'healthy' inhibitions. In this scenario, like Raffalovich and Bumke, La Cara discredited patient statements and confessions, which, in his opinion, were just attempts to justify themselves. In doing so, he automatically discredited the theoreticians who based their observation and method on these narratives, Freud and Krafft-Ebing among others. La Cara thought that Krafft-Ebing in particular should have read between the lines of his patients' confessions, understanding that these men were merely trying to obtain more lenient sentences, as homosexuality was punished by the German code of laws. The Lombrosian assumption of a connection between homosexuality, lying and wrongdoing was clearly firmly rooted in his thoughts.

La Cara's work shows that he was up to date with his reading on the subject. He illustrated the theories of several German sexologists and psychiatrists who shared the opinion that homosexuality was as an acquired condition and he demolished their positions one by one. He believed that homosexuality was congenital and, therefore, that it could be understood only through psychopathology. Consequently, he thought it was necessary to concentrate on the transmission of *stimuli* between the cortex of the brain and the genitals, in a clear neurological approach. For La Cara, what caused homosexuality was a physical anomaly, namely the disposition of certain nerves which determined pleasure in anal penetration. To corroborate his views, among others he quoted Joanny Roux (1866–1909), a French neuropsychiatrist who believed that the sexual instinct did not just generate in the genitals, but in the entire body.[29] Sexual feelings could be transmitted by the sense of smell and by certain nerves placed in different areas of the human body, La Cara agreed. Interestingly, he contested the traditional division between active and passive homosexuals, which in his opinion was a purely theoretical concept. He had in fact observed that homosexuals usually played both roles. He defended Paolo Mantegazza's theories, which had been attacked. In his opinion, discrediting old theories on sexual inversion was equal to an attempt to look on this condition with less severity; modern views opened scenarios that he believed would soften the traditional sound approaches to the issue.

Coming to Weininger, La Cara summarized his theory of inborn bisexuality and added that he approved of the belief that sexual attraction did not just depend on an impulse originating from the genitals but from several other sexual features in the body. This explained why experiments of castration did not show a complete reversion of sexual impulses, he noted. However, he coherently contested Weininger's concession that some external situations might trigger congenital and latent homosexuality.

La Cara gave an account of all the major theoretical works and the different positions taken, including Pende's endocrinological approach, and concluded his treatise, which only addressed male homosexuality, with a chapter dedicated to social prophylaxis. He too believed that homosexuals who sought cures showed that their moral sense had not totally disappeared. Their level of degeneration he judged to be not too serious and therefore, only in these cases was it possible to think of rehabilitation. For the others, he agreed that cures were useless. Social prophylaxis could prevent contagion, which in La Cara's logical theory could only be seduction of the very young. He saw it was imperative to protect possible victims from seducers. However, if homosexuality depended on the inborn structure of the nervous system, how could education have an impact? La Cara offered Raffalovich's solution, according to which, like bees or ants, human society should have a class of chaste eunuchs employed to work for the community. Chastity, in other words, was the only way to prevent and repress homosexuality, an inborn condition that could not be modified in any way. The author imagined redemption for this group of selfish and unproductive individuals through socially useful work, adding that perversions had been observed mainly among the rich and idle, and consequently work would probably be the best antidote to their debauched lifestyle. It is a clear tribute to the old degeneration theories that indicated metropolitan dandies as particularly prone to moral and intellectual corruption.

Following in the steps of several other theoreticians, such as Marañon, La Cara highlighted the importance of applying strict vigilance over youths to prevent them from becoming victims of seduction. It was important, he wrote, to make sure their readings were appropriate, and that they did not engage in conversation with servants who might bring up unsuitable subjects. He believed that parents should never allow their children to have any knowledge of passions and sexual attraction. Young people had to be taught their moral duty and how to dominate their instincts, together with instilling in them a strong sense of responsibility and self-esteem, he continued. Idleness, attending theatres and novel reading should be avoided before adulthood, he added. In puberty, fathers should teach their sons about venereal diseases and, if they suspected that their children engaged in perverse sexual practices, he believed they should immediately take them to see a doctor. At school, he advised keeping desks far apart to avoid any possible physical contact between students, as it might provoke sexual arousal, and recommended that male toilets had separate cubicles to avoid promiscuity. He considered physical exercise on a regular basis to be an appropriate preventative measure and, if a teacher saw moral alterations in a pupil, s/he had a duty to isolate this person and not allow him/her back in class. Only by following these repressive measures could, La Cara believed, some hereditary tendencies be partially contained.

Even though the Italian intellectual psychiatric landscape appears to have been uniformly conservative and confined within rigid and often antiquated parameters, there were some isolated voices of dissent. These were very few and had a limited incidence both in psychiatric theory and routine practice. Nevertheless, it is worth mentioning, as Babini also observes, that a small group of psychiatrists, which included Marco Levi Bianchini (1875–1961) and Edoardo Weiss (1889–1970), tried to introduce psychoanalysis to Italy, despite the general negative responses to it.[30] Among them, there was also Emilio Servadio (1904–1995), who wrote the first part of the entry 'sexology' for the Treccani Encyclopaedia in 1936.[31] In it, Servadio argued that the most profound modern thinkers on the subject of sexual inversion were Havelock Ellis (1859–1939), Sigmund Freud and Gregorio Marañon, demonstrating an opening up to the most innovative international theoreticians. On homosexuality, which he still included in the category of perversions, he warned that the field was vast and still understudied, insisting that the somatic and endocrinological aspects of the conditions had not been conclusively proven. He continued stating that no strict relationship between a feminine aspect or psyche and male homosexuality had been established and that the distinction between 'active' and 'passive' homosexuals had relative validity. Finally, he added that homosexuality could not depend either on hereditary factors or on psychic anomalies. His views had little echo at the time, but are testimony to the fact that, during the dictatorship, they could find a space in the pages of Italy's most prestigious encyclopaedia, even in the section on the medical sciences, which was co-directed by Senator Nicola Pende, who would clearly have been in opposition to some of them, but evidently consented to their publication. It is a small signal of tolerance at the height of the dictatorship.

Another important voice of dissent is represented by the science historian Aldo Mieli (1879–1950) and his journal, the *Rassegna di Studi Sessuali*, which he founded in 1921, and financed and directed until 1928.[32] He then emigrated to France because his socialist views and Jewish religion made his life increasingly difficult in fascist Italy. Psychiatric journals of the *Ventennio* were published by asylums and generally, when they touched on the topic of sexual inversion, they published reports by a specialist on patients examined and treated in the institution. In other words, authors did not offer an elaboration of psychiatric theory, but rather presented cases to colleagues and commented upon them from an empirical point of view. The *Rassegna di Studi Sessuali*, which continued publications until 1932, was totally different. First, it was completely independent and not linked to any psychiatric institution or university faculty. Secondly, it was entirely devoted to topics connected with sexuality, such as sexual education, prostitution, eugenics and homosexuality, which it analysed from a theoretical perspective. At the time, this was an exception in Italy. Most importantly, several authors, including Mieli, regularly commented in its pages on foreign publications on sexuality and homosexuality; one of the journal's merits was introducing and discussing the work and theories of Magnus Hirschfeld (1868–1935), Edward Carpenter (1844–1929), Havelock Ellis, Benedict Friedlaender (1866–1908) and Hans Blüher (1888–1955), at a time when these theoreticians were largely ignored in Italy, or strongly opposed. In particular, Aldo Mieli reviewed many German language publications, sometimes praising them and other times strongly criticizing them, but in both cases informing his readers of a plurality of points of view. He commented positively on Havelock Ellis's essay on eonism (cross-dressing), for instance, while he judged Hermann Schulte-Vaerting equating homosexuals to intermediate 'classes' in the animal world, such as worker bees and ants, as 'far from being convincing or acceptable'.[33]

Mieli also reported on the current debate on homosexuality in the German Parliament and on the speech given by Hirschfeld and Kopp on the necessity to abolish paragraph 175 that criminalized it; his journal regularly commented on legislation on prostitution, morality and topics related to sexuality.[34] He discussed Hirschfeld's theoretical output on several occasions, and declared he was in partial agreement with his positions, believing that 'internal secretions' determined so-called 'intermediate sexual statuses', although he contested the extreme mechanical application of these considerations.[35] Mieli in fact believed that in some cases, homosexuals presented secondary somatic traits of the opposite sex, attributable to endocrinological factors, but this was not always the case, and in his view the glandular apparatus of an individual did not dictate all of his or her psychological manifestations. He also voiced strong criticism of Enrico Morselli's belief that intercourse with female prostitutes could cure homosexual men, which was often thought to be an adequate method to correct sexual inversion. Mieli categorically excluded the idea that homosexuality could derive from a lack of contact with women.[36]

Showing a considerably open-minded attitude, the journal published articles with contrasting positions, for instance giving ample space to those who identified endocrinological factors as the only origin of sexual inversion. Among them, Proteus or Pr., generally believed to be the pseudonyms used by Nicola Pende, had regular and ample space to review essays and books that focused on endocrinology, his field of specialization. He introduced to Italian readers authors such as Kurt Blum (1895–1932), among many others, who looked at homosexuality from a strictly endocrinological angle, while he discredited the work of scholars who viewed homosexuality as acquired, such as Wladimir Bechterew (1857–1927).[37] He reviewed Marañon's latest developments on opotherapy and demonstrated he was up to date on what happened in his field at an international level.[38] Most importantly, despite his conservative ideas, he stated that all sexual acts were neither moral nor immoral, as they had a 'natural' endocrinological explanation, and advocated the inclusion of sexology in Italian university teaching programmes.[39]

Rassegna di Studi Sessuali offered an opportunity to many theoreticians to publish. Most of them were academics who could find limited space in other psychiatric journals. Among them, there was Ferdinando De Napoli, from the University of Bologna, who published an essay where he argued that homosexuality was an anomaly due to endocrinological dysfunctions that could be addressed and therefore cured.[40] It was a position that Mieli did not agree with. A strong believer in the positive advances of endocrinology, De Napoli thought that homosexuality should be considered an imperfection, not an illness. In his view, it was the result of an imbalance between the masculine and the feminine present in each individual. He mentioned two cases, one of an 'occasional homosexual' and one of a 'congenital homosexual', that he treated with Viroglandolo, a hormone-based drug used at the time to cure impotence and precocious senility.[41] The first patient recovered, according to his observations, while the second one showed less repulsion for women.

Among the essays on homosexuality published by the *Rassegna di Studi Sessuali* it is worth mentioning an article by Ernani Mandolini on the contagiousness of sexual psychopathies.[42] In it, the Argentinian scientist excluded the possibility of contagion of sexual orientation, stating that the endocrinological congenital aspect of sexuality made it impossible to pass it on, and therefore to acquire it from others. In accordance with Marañon's theories, he insisted on the fact that an awakening of latent facets was possible, particularly in certain situations and in adolescence, a life period characterized by ambiguity and hormonal imbalance. This should not be confused with contagion, he explained. In a cultural climate that insisted on censorship and erasing 'bad' influences from society, he then reinstated the old negative judgement on passive homosexuals, saying that, while *uranisti*, homosexuals, deserved respect, pederasts did not, as in his view, they resorted to same-sex relationships only because of their impotence. The same author had another article published in Mieli's journal, on the homoerotic present in friendships that drew on Freud's theories, although the author still believed that when homoerotism prevailed and transformed a friendship into a same-sex attraction, the solution lay in opotherapy.[43]

It is also worth underlining that the journal published articles by some women too, something that at the time was extremely rare. Among them were doctor and surgeon Clelia Lollini (1890–1963), suffragette Alice Schiavoni Bosio (1871–1931) and paediatrician Angiola Borrino (1880–1965). It also ventured into the field of the history of homosexuality. The *Rassegna di Studi Sessuali* was a short-lived but brave attempt to open up the scientific discussion on sexuality in Italy and to free the Italian theoretical debate from its provincialism. Most importantly, it informed the public on what was being debated at the time beyond Italy's borders, when the regime's censorship measures limited the circulation of ideas. The courage of its director cannot be underestimated, as he voiced his views against prejudice and stereotypes, for instance, condemning the old idea that it was considered to be sinful to go with a male prostitute, while it was socially acceptable to turn a blind eye to contact with female prostitutes.[44] Mieli did not refrain from harshly criticizing the work of colleagues he disagreed with, such as La Cara, whose writing on sexual perversions (see earlier in the chapter) he defined as 'an old and antiquated book', specifically contesting his theory of homosexuals' different anal neurological formation. For Mieli they were

> theories today considered false, both in their essence and because homosexuality is thought not to have a local connotation, but to be a general characteristic that primarily lies in the human psyche (albeit determined by constitutional aspects such as the famous internal secretions) and that informs the personality of an individual.[45]

He also rejected the idea, propelled by the regime's moralization campaign, that immoral sexual behaviour could be triggered by exposure to erotic scenes in films, as maintained by many scholars at the time, including Piero Pesce Maineri, whose ideas Mieli defined as 'stupid reactionaryism'.[46]

The journal remained an isolated voice within the Italian landscape. It was rarely quoted in articles in other Italian psychiatric journals and most of its authors did not publish elsewhere. It retained an aura of a *maudit* publication. In this sense, it is most relevant to note that an internationally acclaimed and established author such as Pende would cautiously choose to use a pseudonym when he published in *Rassegna di Studi Sessuali*. In psychiatric journals of the time, the use of pseudonyms was obsolete, and in fact articles always specified not just the authors' name but also their job title and the institution they worked for. The autonomy of the journal, rightly emphasized by Lorenzo Masi and other scholars, appears to have translated into a certain degree of isolation.[47] There are no figures to confirm what impact it had or how many copies of each issue were printed and sold, but the fact that it was not quoted in other publications leaves the impression of a limited readership.

To conclude, the fascist years were a period of absorption and elaboration of existing theories. At the same time, many old concepts remained fundamentally unchallenged and Lombroso's ideas were still referred to as the unshakeable basis of psychiatric theory. Specific cases showing the Lombrosian connection between homosexuality, criminality and immorality were regularly brought to the specialists' attention, as they proved that old theories had a reason to retain credibility. Italian psychiatry also remained anchored to the Lombrosian idea that every moral and mental problem had to have a physically evident and identifiable trait, or at least an organ's inborn anomaly. Psychiatrists kept concentrating on a patient's physical aspect and, even when they embraced new theories inspired by endocrinology, for instance, they still believed that inborn glandular dysfunctions determined detectable physical traits that certain categories of patients shared. In this light, they measured homosexuals' bodies, aiming to find physical abnormalities they might have in common, as a consequence of hormonal problems. There were only very few voices of dissent.[48]

The search for physical similarities originating in hormonal imbalance was an attempt to go back to reassuring Lombrosian ideas according to which deviants, and homosexuals among them, were immediately identifiable. However, as observation showed that homosexuality could be physically undetectable, high importance was reserved for those homosexuals whose body did not present any sign of hermaphroditism or physical characteristics of the opposite sex. This idea, combined with Marañon's theories that homosexuality was potentially latent in every individual, generated fear, because it transformed sexual inversion into a faceless, subtle and omnipresent threat. The fact that certain environments and situations could awaken a dormant inborn deviancy intensified anxieties and urged several psychiatrists to propose countermeasures to limit the risk posed by triggering factors. An accent was put on the fact that homosexuals were a threat to society, as they corrupted young people whose sexuality could be led astray. In other words, if homosexuality was the 'inner enemy' inside each person, homosexuals were the 'inner enemies' of the country, and they could awaken the dormant deviancy that was present in every individual.

The obsession with categorization also belonged to the past and the majority of Italian theoreticians in psychiatry could not abandon these old ways. Psychiatrists tried to group homosexuals, like other patients, dividing them on the basis of the 'symptoms' they showed, their behaviour, their appearance or the causes of their condition. This tendency testifies to the effort the specialists deployed to break down this category of patients, in order to better understand it or to contribute to general knowledge of it. However, this resulted in many fine distinctions and new definitions but ultimately failed to produce any genuinely innovative approach.

The effort to categorize, divide and group individuals identified as homosexuals, or affected by other mental or behavioural conditions, also served the purpose of giving scientific status to psychiatry and sexology. It mirrored what was done for other categories of diseases and it offered a chance to frame knowledge by offering an ordered and logical system. During the years of the dictatorship internments rose steadily, following the trend of previous decades, something that shows that psychiatrists in the end had to accept the role of social control guarantors, sanctioned by the 1904 law.[49] Italian psychiatrists were hostile to this law and had contested it ever since it was approved, continuing to criticize it throughout the regime. Their response was to reinstate psychiatry's medical and scientific relevance, bringing it to equal the other branches of medicine. This translated into an accurate analysis of those foreign psychiatrists who had elaborated theories that saw mental illness as a physical condition, the product of a dysfunction of the brain or of glands or of the nervous system. None wanted to be confused with psychologists, whose study was assimilated to non-scientific subjects and was no longer part of medicine's academic curriculum. Most Italian psychiatrists believed that the correct approach to homosexuality was scientific, based on medical observation, on the understanding of causes and an examination of the patient's anatomy and symptoms. Consequently, there was a strong accent on discrediting psychoanalytic approaches, an attitude also supported by Roman Catholic ethical considerations.

At a more general level, Paolo Giovannini confirms that during the *Ventennio* there was an attempt to find a psychiatric language that could convey greater scientific precision and technical accuracy, which accompanied the firm distancing process from psychology.[50] The trend to see psychiatry as strongly linked with neurology, as the two teachings often merged at the university level, was, in Giovannini's view, a consequence of the study of the effects of the First World War and can also be read as a further attempt to transform psychiatry into a scientific discipline. However, the analyses of asylums archived in the second part of the book show that, in this respect, psychiatric practice remained anchored to a vague diagnostic terminology.

In terms of homosexuality, Italian specialists were aware of the two previous currents of thought that saw homosexuality as a congenital or as an acquired condition. In fascist times, the balance gradually shifted towards the congenital theories, or rather remained rooted in them, as they came from a Lombrosian approach, which nobody dared shake off. According to this theory, sexual inversion was an inborn condition, whose origins were retraceable in a family history of degeneration or psychiatric problems. However, for some, advancements in disciplines such as endocrinology and neurology showed that it began in a hormonal congenital imbalance or physical condition and therefore, thanks to scientific progress, it looked now possible to intervene to alter this inborn constitutional configuration. For the most traditionalist theoreticians, the fact that homosexuality was a congenital condition called for repression and abstinence, rather than cure. For a minority, it decriminalized sexual inversion, as it was a genetic flaw that implied no active choice on the part of the homosexual subject. In partial contradiction with 'congenital' theories, external factors continued to play a key role in the development of sexual inversion; for most psychiatrists, in fact, they acquired crucial importance, as Marañon's ideas became more widely known. The fact that homosexuality was a latent aspect of all individuals made psychiatrists even more aware of the subtle yet real risks of the possibility it could be triggered by the surrounding environment. Therefore, despite the fact that most theoreticians of psychiatry asserted that homosexuality was a congenital condition, they spent some effort indicating ways in which homosexuality could be contained by limiting, banning or censoring triggering factors or contexts. Predisposition was necessary even in case one was seduced, the majority of theoreticians agreed, but incisive and timely intervention could be dissuasive. In this way, psychiatry was key and decisive in the social hygiene and moralization campaign that the regime was implementing. As research in the second part of the book demonstrates, these concepts were absorbed by homosexuals. It appears that most of them knew that to show one had been 'seduced', that is, raped or coerced into homosexual intercourse, was considered more leniently, to admit it was proof of shame and therefore repentance, which signified the road to recovery or at least self-censorship had been taken.

Fascism therefore saw limited concrete advances in psychiatric terms. One of the few positive innovations of the period, as Massimo Moraglio shows, was the expansion of the home visits programmes and the implementation of a system of *dispensari*, drop-in psychiatric clinics.[51] These health care centres were motivated by the need of eugenics to identify the hereditary factors of mental illness, allowing intervention before internment was judged necessary, so they were well rooted in past social hygiene theories. However, they constituted evident innovation, as they provided an alternative to internment. In 1937, as Moraglio notes, they were operating in twenty-six Italian provinces. Psychiatrists shared a strong belief that early release was preferable in many cases, especially when the patient seemed not dangerous, quiet, cooperative and, most of all, incurable. In other words, they tried to assess the medical role of asylums whenever there was a chance to do so, and clearly argued that some patients would not benefit from exclusion from family and society. In particular, they rejected the idea of having to be actors of social cleansing or incarcerators. Most asylum directors were in favour of no-restraint approaches, although it appears that their views on the matter were frequently ignored by nurses. They seem to have been informed and updated on what was being said abroad, mainly in Germany and Spain, and the theoretical debate among them, and between them and provincial authorities, was lively. They certainly contributed in putting psychiatry high on the agenda and all fought for a recognition of its scientific role.

One of the most infamous innovations of the fascist period was the introduction of the idea that, since certain psychiatric disorders were connected with gender, race, marital status and age, it would be possible to develop an *ad hoc* psychiatric investigation for groups of people. Starting from this assumption, several specialists elaborated on a hypothesis of a psychology of 'races', which laid further foundations to stereotyping and discrimination, as observed earlier, and led to the most horrific consequences.

Through the words of theoreticians and practitioners we can see that the tendency towards a scientific and medical approach towards homosexuality could not completely disentangle itself from moral judgement. This contradiction exemplifies well the difficulty of reconciliating modernity and faith in science and progress, with Roman Catholic values, a crucial aspect of the fascist regime. So, while German psychiatrists were moving away from moral madness as a category and tried to free onanism from moral condemnation, their Italian colleagues often did not. The insistence on the need for the patient to feel ashamed, to repent, the pathologization of sexual precocity and masturbation, the belief in the positive value of chastity, control of passions and self-censorship clearly belonged to Roman Catholicism. The idea, widely accepted by psychiatric practice, of considering homosexuality as one of the many 'symptoms' indicating a more generalized psychiatric condition kept alive the old concept of degeneration and pathologized homosexuality even further. Homosexuality, and sexuality in general, remained at the centre of psychiatric investigation, and the debate that surrounded these issues was intense during the *Ventennio*, yet the elaboration of a wealth of not too dissimilar theories did not reach a conclusive new theoretical or therapeutic approach and did not abandon traditional moral judgements. In the march towards scientific progress, eugenics considerations prevailed. The patient was consistently de-humanized, as s/he became only a medical case, a conglomerate of symptoms and physical traits to be deciphered and medically treated.

Part II

Psychiatric Practice

In the first part of the book, I analysed the development of psychiatric theories on homosexuality, hermaphroditism and related topics in Italy and the main influences on the elaboration of these theories. I now move to psychiatric practice in an attempt to ascertain whether theory had an effective impact on the daily routine of Italian asylums during Fascism.

In the second part of the book, I analyse the results of archival research carried out in the archives of three different psychiatric hospitals: Rome, Florence and Girifalco, near Catanzaro, in Calabria. Different in terms of location, size, scientific relevance, tradition and structural characteristics, they represent examples that are as distant as possible within the Italian situation. I aimed to find cases of patients interned because of their homosexuality or out-of-the-norm sexuality during the fascist regime and I focused on these cases.

Before examining individual patient files in detail, each of the three chapters summarizes the history of the psychiatric hospital and illustrates its structure, staff and hierarchy, the role of its directors and the configuration of its premises during the *Ventennio*. There is a special focus on the figure of the director, because, given the relative autonomy every asylum enjoyed, he was crucial in deciding policies, therapies and all aspects of the functioning of the mental health hospital. At the same time, an asylum director had to follow the law and national guidelines, so this figure is also emblematic of the tension between autonomy and coercion, pressure and opposition to impositions that took place in most institutions during Fascism in Italy. The power relations, structure, functioning, therapies and all the aspects of each asylum's activity listed above are significant because they contextualize the data of the patient files and are relevant to our understanding of the procedures and attitudes towards internees.

Patient files at Santa Maria della Pietà in Rome and San Salvi in Florence were consulted following selective criteria based on the type of diagnosis given to patients at the moment of their internment, as explained in the introduction, to ascertain if homosexuals, lesbians or intersex individuals were interned during the *Ventennio*. This meant that, from following the diagnosis written in the Admissions Registers, the relevant patient files were requested and consulted. Methodology had to adapt to the different situation presented by the Girifalco asylum's archives, where Admissions Registers did not list patient diagnoses. Therefore, I decided to sample-search, choosing three years, 1924, 1933 and 1939, and looking at all the patient files of each year. File consultation in Rome and Florence ran from 28 October 1922, the day of the March on Rome and generally considered the official starting date of the fascist regime, to 8 September 1943, the day of the Armistice when Fascism officially ended.

There is a further important point to be made. Apart from Florence, where lists of patients present in the institution during the fascist years, and therefore also of those interned before 1922, were available for consultation, and one case in Rome where the patient was transferred from Rieti to Rome during Fascism, and therefore his admission was marked again in the registers, this research could not take into account homosexual patients already interned prior to 1922 and who were still inside the institution during the *Ventennio*. Most of these patients could not be detected through my chosen methodological approach.

3

The Rome asylum, Santa Maria della Pietà: Quiet disobedience

'*Credere, Obbedire, Combattere*', Believe, Obey, Fight, was one of Fascism's propaganda slogans. However, as Paul Corner notes, there was always an evident gap between the regime's coercion and the Italian people's consent.[1] This gap is key to understanding how Fascism operated; the Rome psychiatric hospital offers a valid example of how *Obbedire* was set aside, or at least interpreted freely.

This chapter focuses on the Rome, Santa Maria della Pietà, asylum archives, and the analysis led to some unexpectedly interesting results. A series of nineteen *Libretti*, booklets of instructions to the staff printed and circulated between 1934 and 1939, makes it possible to compare what was instructed from above, in this case by the asylum directors, with how it was implemented, in the daily routine of one of the largest Italian psychiatric hospitals. These *Libretti* are decidedly relevant to this research as they referred specifically to homosexual patients. Issued by the asylum's director, who had to follow national guidelines and yet was allowed increased autonomy by the 1904 law, these instructions were printed by the Santa Maria della Pietà printshop and were circulated internally.[2] The *Libretti*, compared with what can be deduced from medical notes, reveal a discrepancy between psychiatric theory, translated into instructions to staff, and psychiatric practice.

A question remains unanswered, whether the director of Santa Maria della Pietà knew what went on inside the institution he was in charge of, and therefore tacitly agreed with this form of disobedience, or whether he was unaware of his medical staff's lack of compliance. As the latter seems unlikely, his non-intervention policy equalled acceptance, confirmed by the absence of reprimands to staff for not having observed the directives. It is therefore an apt example of the passive resistance enacted by the psychiatric profession towards the regime, as already observed in another Italian asylum.[3] Psychiatrists had opposed the state's intrusion into their professional field ever since Law n. 36 had been introduced in 1904 and their feelings of resentment did not subside during the regime. As noted in the introduction, they never stopped discussing possible amendments to the law to reduce the social control role it imposed on their profession. The behaviour of Santa Maria della Pietà's directors indicates that a quiet form of rebellion was taking place, under the impeccable appearance this and other institutions were keen to demonstrate. It could be read as an anticipation of what Peloso recently described as a significant presence of psychiatrists within the *Resistenza* in Italy.[4]

To contextualize my research, I here outline the history of the institution, focusing on the *Ventennio*, before illustrating how Santa Maria della Pietà operated during Fascism, the methodological issues that are specific to the research carried out in this archive and analysing the relevant patient files.

Brief history of the institution

In order to understand how the Rome asylum operated during the fascist regime, I first provide a short account of its history and evolution prior to 1922. The first recorded institutional assistance to mentally ill patients in Rome goes back to the mid-sixteenth century, when the indigent people and pilgrims' hospice remit was extended to make it the first asylum in the city. Originally located in the central piazza Colonna, in 1725 it was transferred to premises annexed to the Santo Spirito Hospital, in via della Lungara, in the Trastevere quarter. Owing to the exponential increase in internments, these premises were soon judged inadequate. It became clear that another, more suitable location was required, but it was only in 1908 that building work began on a new asylum in the countryside north of the centre of Rome, in an area called Monte Mario, which is now a quarter of Rome. The new asylum, Santa Maria della Pietà, was already functioning by 1913, but it was officially inaugurated in 1914. Initially, it operated alongside the Trastevere premises and consisted of thirty-seven buildings, plus administrative offices, hospital laboratories and space for patient manual work. In addition, there was also a vast area for agricultural work, meant to occupy and cure patients, and at the same time provide food for the population of interned men, women and children. Some of the via della Lungara patients were transferred there, while others continued to occupy the old premises and were relocated to Monte Mario only in 1924. Despite the size of the new asylum, overcrowding soon became a problem again, and two hospitals in the Lazio region were annexed. One was situated in Ceccano, in the province of Frosinone, and the other in Rieti. These were inaugurated as asylums in 1927 and were primarily used for the Santa Maria della Pietà's elderly and long-term internment patient overspill.[5]

Fascist times: The asylum structure, its directors and staff

The following section examines aspects of the asylum during the fascist regime. It is organized thematically, rather than strictly chronologically, not only because the archival documentation is very fragmented but also because I decided to focus only on themes that are relevant to the analysis of the hospital's files and that are related to the main topic of this research. It would be impossible to understand how homosexuality was dealt with by the institution without framing it in the wider context of the asylum routine, internal laws, hierarchy and architectural structure.

In 1936 Santa Maria della Pietà consisted of seventy-four buildings, out of which twenty-nine hosted patients. It had reached this size in a gradual way, as it started expanding when it had to accommodate the Trastevere hospital's patients. Ergotherapy included shoe-mending, carpentry, gardening, agricultural work, embroidery, silkworm breeding and cloth weaving. The asylum was not only self-sufficient, patient work also generated an income. In 1935, for instance, the sale of embroidered linen gave an income of 9,000 Lire, although the director, Augusto Giannelli (1865–1938), believed it was important that patients were remunerated for their work, even if a small amount. Santa Maria della Pietà included a church, a staff library with over five thousand books, a patient library, a theatre, several scientific laboratories, an autopsy room and a surgical department, which also offered its services in case of emergency to local residents. Nurses were required to frequent a professional school, which consisted of three modules: anatomy and physiology, assistance to medical-chirurgical pathologies, assistance to patients affected by nervous and mental illnesses. In June 1932, radio loudspeakers were installed in every pavilion, in line with other public spaces, schools and offices across the country, so that the words of the regime's propaganda could be heard by the widest possible audience.

When trying to describe the organization of Santa Maria della Pietà during the *Ventennio*, it is immediately apparent that a full and accurate picture is hard to obtain. Available documentation for the years from 1922 to 1943 is not complete. It allows a partial reconstruction of the size and clinical hierarchy of Santa Maria della Pietà only for the years between 1934 and 1941.[6] At that time, the institution employed one director, six senior and six junior psychiatrists, one surgeon, one pharmacist, several consultants, such as obstetricians, eye specialists and dentists, eighty-three nuns, 320 nurses, one secretary, one treasurer, nine administrative workers, one person in charge of coordinating farming activities and 150 generic workers employed on a permanent basis (including cleaners, doorkeepers, canteen staff and so on). Like in most Italian psychiatric hospitals at the time, the number of interned people was far higher than the one thousand units Santa Maria della Pietà was designed to accommodate. In 1934, there were 2,701 patients, almost three times its capacity. In 1935 the hospital's population rose to 3,396, in 1936 it reached 3,681 and the following year 3,834, almost four times the maximum number of patients that were supposed to be cared for in this institution.[7] Meanwhile, Santa Maria della Pietà had expanded considerably: new pavilions had been built and some of the old ones were expanded to accommodate demand. Two pavilions were exclusively dedicated to underage internees: Pavilion XC, inaugurated in 1933, the so-called 'Principi di Piemonte' building, was for children considered *educabili*, curable, while Pavilion VIII was for underage incurables. Interned children were from six to fourteen years of age. Regardless of the constant increase in the number of internees, in 1937 a new disposition made patient release an even more complicated procedure from a bureaucratic point of view. It also became mandatory to obtain official consent from the *Procura del Re* when a patient was about to leave.[8] While it was easier to enter the institution, it became increasingly difficult to leave. In addition, Giannelli pointed out that early release, with the patient being looked after by his or her family, had not given results that he considered very encouraging.[9]

The mortality rate, however, according to the official hospital report for the years 1934–1937, was between 10 and 12 per cent which was judged low.[10] Overcrowding was recognized as a priority, and in 1940 it forced the director to request official permission to ask workers to do up to forty-five hours overtime per week, more than an average of eight extra hours per day in a five-day week.[11] In addition, a prize linked to productivity was seen as a necessity, given the workload.[12] In 1939, the director had already written to the Mother Superior of the Order of the *Sorelle dei Poveri di Santa Caterina da Siena* asking if she could possibly provide more nuns as nursing staff.[13] He was clearly trying to find solutions for a situation that was one of constant crisis.

From the available documentation, it is hard to get a sense of the structural set-up, such as the state of the buildings or whether the medical equipment was up to date. Asylums were often portrayed as symbols of efficiency and of the regime's commitment to scientific progress. However, the only consultable documentation that gives a picture of the actual state of this asylum during the *Ventennio* refers to 1922 and gives a bleak description of the state of the psychiatric hospital.[14] That year, patients complained about the cold, as heaters were out of order and no hot water was available. As a result, Pavilion XIII was reported to be full of dirty patients because there was no hot water to bathe them. Patients often refused to eat because of the poor diet the hospital provided, consisting mainly of beans and chickpeas. In addition, Pavilion I had no provision for ice, although patients with a high temperature were confined there. There is no archival evidence that there were any substantial improvements to this situation in the following years, while there is a clear indication, from complaints and other records available, together with patient correspondence to their relatives, of a high level of suffering, both physical and mental, among those who were interned at Santa Maria della Pietà during the *Ventennio*. The Registers for Surgical Operations reported only one patient suicide – a woman patient hanged herself on 28 December 1944 – but listed other incidents that looked very similar to attempted suicide, such as ingestion of ink and 'other substances' or swallowing needles, which is a clear sign that internment did not solve problems of depression.[15]

While it is impossible to assess, because of the lack of documentation, to what extent the structural conditions of the asylum improved under Fascism, one can deduce that treatment of patients was often below acceptable standards. In 1927, an anonymous complaint was diligently filed. Signed 'relatives of male and female patients' and addressed to the *Commissione Straordinaria per la Provincia*, Special Commission for the Province, it brought to its attention the fact that interned people were never taken to the hospital's garden. Up to forty of them were forced to remain locked in their shared rooms all day: 'some shout, some cry, some laugh, some sing and some argue: a real inferno. Is this the cure?'[16] The director replied, defending Dr Mendicini, accused of being responsible for the deplorable situation, arguing that no more than a maximum of fifteen patients were kept in rooms to carry out 'female work'. He obviously thought this settled the dispute.[17]

As anticipated earlier, the role of asylum directors was decisive. Psychiatric institutions operated fairly autonomously, and much of the way in which they functioned depended on the directives given to staff by the director. The 1904 law gave greater power and autonomy to the heads of psychiatric hospitals, who were supposed to take full control of all aspects of the running of the institution they were in charge of. It is therefore key to understand the cultural and medical background of each director in order to evaluate the choices made towards certain categories of patients.

Augusto Giannelli was the first director of the newly built Santa Maria della Pietà and remained in charge of the institution until his death. He lived through all the drastic changes the hospital went through, including expansion and relocation. However, it is extremely difficult to reconstruct his personality and work at Santa Maria della Pietà because most of the files of his correspondence and *atti*, formal deeds, are missing. Therefore, his life and professional achievements are surprisingly undocumented, despite his prestigious position.

Giannelli had experienced the 'luminous pause' that preceded Fascism and became the most authoritative historian of the institution he directed.[18] In 1905 he published an historical analysis of Santa Maria della Pietà, which centred on the years 1811–12 and 1829–1900, when Santa Maria della Pietà was still in its old premises.[19] In 1937, he published another volume where he focused on Santa Maria della Pietà's admissions for the period 1901–36, which is more relevant to this study as it covers the first part of the *Ventennio*.[20] To this day, it constitutes a fundamental source of detail based on a meticulous analysis of the data available at the time. In the first part of the book, Giannelli illustrated his directives in terms of building the new mental health hospital from a technical and practical point of view. In the second part, he concentrated on the running of the hospital, giving details on patient movements, admissions and therapies. He explained that at Santa Maria della Pietà, therapeutic approaches that 'might seem audacious' were routinely applied, such as malariotherapy and other shock therapies, including insulin-provoked coma to cure schizophrenia, on which Giannelli reserved judgement. He was in favour of keeping isolation rooms for agitated patients, something that had been abandoned in some asylums, although he agreed they were not suitable for all patients and had to be used only on a temporary basis. Straitjackets were no longer in use at Santa Maria della Pietà; these had been substituted by wrist bands, an immobilizing method that he considered necessary but less intrusive. Interestingly, when commenting on the exponential increase in interned patients in the period analysed, he said that it did not depend on an increase of madness in society, but rather on the fact that 'the social body made itself more responsive to the deficiencies and the disharmonies of its components, eliminating those who are not suitable to family and collective life'.[21] He also stressed another important concept. He thought that the *Primari*, the medical heads of each pavilion, competent in general medicine and in their specialised branch of medicine, must have the maximum authority and autonomy in the pavilions they are in charge of; initiatives in the type of cure, decisions on release and ergotherapy must be left to them, within the limits and guarantees the director established.[22]

As I discuss later in this chapter, this statement had important consequences.

Evidently the political climate had drastically changed and Giannelli was eager to show he had conformed accordingly. His second book on Santa Maria della Pietà in fact opened with three quotes from Mussolini and was dedicated to the chair of the First Fascist Rectorate of the Rome Provincial Authority. All the patient library books were marked with Mussolini's motto, 'May books be the weapon of your intelligence, not the poison that kills,' Giannelli was keen to emphasize.[23]

In 1938, Francesco Bonfiglio (1883–1966) was named director. He had entered the hospital as a medical assistant, subsequently became a doctor in 1915, then was promoted to direct the serology and blood tests lab. He remained in office until 1955 and was therefore in charge of the asylum during the difficult wartime period. Bonfiglio is an important name within Italian psychiatry and his career achievements are better documented than those of his predecessor. He studied with Augusto Tamburini (1848–1919) and Sante De Sanctis (1862–1935), two of the most influential theoreticians and psychiatrists of the previous generation. He then taught at university and kept himself updated on psychiatry's progress at an international level, often travelling abroad, mainly to Germany, where he had the opportunity to meet internationally praised scientists such as Emil Kraepelin.[24] The Santa Maria della Pietà archives hold a copy of his *curriculum vitae*, presumably submitted when he applied for the post of director of the institution.[25] In it, he listed all his publications for several prestigious Italian and German psychiatric journals, such as *Rivista Sperimentale di Freniatria*, *Note e Rivista di Psichiatria*, *Il Policlinico* and *Zeitschrift für die gesamte Neurologie und Psychiatrie*. His books document his interest in psychiatric conditions caused by syphilis, encephalitis and cerebral atrophy. Bonfiglio's *curriculum vitae* also mentioned the congress papers that he gave and were subsequently published. In 1937, for example, he presented a paper at the *Congresso della Società Italiana di Psichiatria* in Naples, while in 1938 he intervened at the Fifth European Meeting for Mental Hygiene in Munich. His candidacy for the position of director of Santa Maria della Pietà was endorsed by the most prestigious figures, such as Augusto Tamburini, August von Wassermann (1866–1925) and the previous asylum director, Augusto Giannelli. In 1929, the latter had certified that 'Prof. Bonfiglio has the necessary maturity for the successful management of a major psychiatric hospital.' Ernesto Lugaro (1870–1940), another celebrated name in Italian psychiatry at the time, described him as 'one among the few that Italian psychiatry can really count on'.[26] He seems to have been very meticulous from the start of his tenure. Files of communications to staff are full of clear and concise reminders about fines for those who contravened hospital regulations, norms to follow and the necessity to keep high standards of professional conduct for all employees, not just the medical and nursing staff.[27] He even listed in detail the disciplinary actions that would be taken when staff did not behave as expected. It appears that Bonfiglio inherited an institution with long ongoing, ingrained irregularities that he was all too familiar with. He had in fact worked his way up the career ladder inside the Rome psychiatric institution. He is remembered as a strong believer in the validity of ergotherapy and entertainment for patients, combined with extra-hospital care whenever possible.[28] The overall picture is that of a meticulous professional, open to new ideas, seriously engaged both in the daily practical side of his job as well as the theoretical aspects of psychiatry.

It is interesting to see to what extent the Santa Maria della Pietà's directors imposed changes to please the authorities, and conformed with the new fascist ways and behaviours, at least at a formal level. Appearances, ceremonies and rites were important in fascist Italy. The regime introduced new rituals and expected the population to show their acceptance of fascist ideals by taking an active part in them. All institutions were constantly reminded of the need to show their adherence to these new rituals and the Rome asylum management made considerable efforts to show that it conformed. All staff had an obligation to adopt the Roman salute and were not allowed to kiss the hands of nuns and the chaplain, following the central power's attempt to disassociate itself from Catholic rituals in favour of fascist ones.[29] On 21 March 1933, Giannelli reminded everybody that 'the nuns must refrain from expressing any judgement on what they report'.[30] This is yet another indication of the ways in which Fascism attempted to distance itself from Catholic moral judgement. That said, several points of contact still existed between Catholicism and Fascism, and fascists relied on tacit alliances with the Church in the discipline of what was regarded as out-of-the-norm behaviour. These inherent contradictions are quite typical of the fascist era. For instance, the director reminded doctors, nurses and administrative employees that by order of the *Prefetto*, the Christmas tree had to be abandoned, as it was a Northern tradition, in favour of the *Presepe*, the miniature reconstruction of the scene of the Nativity that was and still is so typical of strongly Catholic southern Italy.[31] Compromising between old and new, Catholicism and Fascism, the regime did not rule against powerful symbols such as the Nativity, an action that would have alienated the majority of the population and a powerful ally such as the Vatican. However, it introduced its own alternative rites. For instance, it revamped an ancient and forgotten legendary pagan figure, the *Befana*, an old lady who flew on a broomstick and brought presents on 6 January, which became an important additional fascist date of the calendar. In this way, the regime was able to please the most traditionalist part of Italian society and at the same time attract younger generations in search of change. In addition, what was new was often portrayed as a revival of a forgotten tradition, so that Fascism could be perceived as an innovative force within a traditional set of values. Santa Maria della Pietà was clearly expected to conform.

Similarly, the Rome asylum adopted a series of measures that reflected the national demographic campaign promoted by the regime. Prizes for staff were introduced that rewarded having children, in line with the conspicuous effort the regime deployed to increase birth rates. The hospital granted small amounts of money to employees when they got married and at the birth of every child.[32] To participate in the selection exam in order to become a doctor at Santa Maria della Pietà, it was by this time necessary to produce a good moral, civil and political conduct certificate, issued by the *Podestà*, a title that had fallen out of use and was re-introduced by the regime to indicate a town mayor, as well as a certificate proving subscription to the PNF.[33] In this era professional merit alone was no longer sufficient. Faith in the regime's ideals and a verifiable political loyalty were equally important requirements, as many historians have emphasized when discussing mental health institutions during Fascism, or indeed simply employment during the *Ventennio*.[34] An excellent example of this is contained in a letter from the Rome asylum's head engineer to the director, dated 9 April 1940. In it, the head engineer reminded Bonfiglio that employment of a new member of staff had to take into consideration factors such as marital status, his or her number of children, and what war and fascist merits he or she had acquired.[35] The letter also shows how different figures of authority within the same institution felt the need to check on each other's conduct, as if they were responsible for being vigilant over colleagues. This type of behaviour in the workplace is not surprising, given the level of policing that went on among citizens and that the regime actively encouraged. Another proof of how politics had entered the asylum is offered by the fact that the person who represented staff at disciplinary commission meetings had to be designated by the Fascist Association of Public Sector Employment.[36] Nurses' notes included in the patient files reveal an increasingly low level of literacy; the nursing staff were recruited on the basis of political beliefs or on a discretionary basis. In an exchange of correspondence with the director of the Ferrara asylum, the Santa Maria della Pietà director underlined that art. 23 of the 1909 Rules, integrating internment Law n. 36 of 1904, stated that nurses had to be employed 'upon the proposal or favourable consent of the director'. The Ferrara colleague had written, asking for clarification because he intended to announce a transparent and public competition to employ nursing staff and solicited an opinion on this procedure. The reply restated that the law gave merit a secondary role while it confirmed the asylum director's powers.[37]

The national march towards *fascistizzazione* also consisted of a series of smaller but symbolic actions and this is reflected in Santa Maria della Pietà's practices. On 10 June 1939 an *Ordine di Servizio (o.d.s.)*, Order to Staff, quoted a telegram by Mussolini where he deplored the fact that public administration employees still used the third-person feminine singular *Lei* as a courtesy form, which 'demonstrates a low sense of discipline and lack of stamina'.[38] In a culture that exalted virility, the use of a female pronoun to show respect could find no place. The regime favoured the second-person plural *Voi*, old-fashioned and gender neutral. Bonfiglio added that 'in the event of any sporadic case [the use of *Lei*] will be severely punished as a serious disciplinary fault'.[39] Language issues were central to the regime. New expressions were introduced, and their use revealed the level of acceptance of fascist ideals and lifestyle. In the Santa Maria della Pietà archives there is correspondence between the provincial administration and the director on the correct terminology to adopt. For example, the word *Prefetto* was to substitute the old head of province, the term *Regio* or *Regia*, Royal, was to be eliminated and the Fascist calendar adopted.[40] October 1922–October 1923 had become year I, the first year of the Fascist era. However, if there was a need to stress the point in 1943, when Fascism was about to end, these impositions had evidently failed to convince the whole population.

Archival documentation indicates that the process of *fascistizzazione* of the asylum was kept under close observation by security forces. In 1943, the *Prefetto* wrote to the director to complain about the fact that several employees attending a ceremony were not wearing the fascist uniform or a black shirt: 'I strongly deplore this infraction …, not wearing the uniform indicates the lack of a sense of discipline and of understanding one's fascist duty'.[41] Staff were also reminded of the province's instructions in terms of flag display for certain events and recurrences. This was declared compulsory on the Queen of Italy's name day, the official day of commemoration of those who died in the war and 'conferences and fascist events', together with a duty to listen to the radio report aimed at the public employment sector.[42] All the asylum's pavilions had to have a radio loudspeaker, in line with fascist policies to make propaganda widely accessible.[43] The authorities seem to have tried to keep up the pressure to observe these newly imposed rules. However, the fact that nobody felt it compulsory to wear a black shirt in the presence of State officials at a ceremony, for instance, clearly reveals the level of reluctance to conform to fascist rules on the part of the asylum staff.

To turn to the documentation on staff, to reconstruct the picture of how the institution functioned, consultable disciplinary commission arrangements, internal correspondence and directives to staff reveal constant misbehaviour on the part of nursing staff, from the Giannelli years onwards.[44] This was seen in other institutions at the time and Santa Maria della Pietà does not seem to have been an exception.[45] There were frequent reports of violent incidents: fights among nurses over money on 18 January 1923, for instance, and physically violent rows among members of staff on 30 March 1931.[46] Frequently, attention was drawn to physical aggression from the nursing staff towards patients. On 26 November 1923 a nurse pushed a patient so violently that he fell and fractured his femur, on 26 September 1941 a report stated that on 8 June a nurse was caught while he was beating a patient who refused to wear a straitjacket, although in theory the use of this coercion implement had been declared abandoned in this psychiatric hospital several years earlier.[47] On both occasions, punishment consisted of a mere pecuniary fine. In the second instance, the internal commission concluded that, as it was the first incident for the nurse in question, a lenient penalty was justified.

Several cases of less serious misconduct were also reported. Despite their seemingly minor nature compared to the ones mentioned above, they give us a remarkably complete impression of the poor levels of ethical and professional conduct and attitudes among the nursing staff. On 11 December 1923 three nurses confessed they had not realized that a patient had found or stolen a saw with which he cut the window bars, managing to escape. It was only one of the many attempted escapes that staff were unable to prevent.[48] Attempts to escape are in fact a constant presence in the hospital's files.[49] Nurses were frequently absent, leaving patients with no supervision, custody or surveillance.[50] On one occasion nursing staff were reported by a nun to have played cards during their shift and we can find several reports of them falling asleep while on duty.[51]

In addition, nurses sometimes committed minor crimes, such as stealing bread, soup, tomatoes, meat, bacon, sheets, towels and cloth. Theft on the part of the staff is documented from 1927,[52] but the situation worsened with the outbreak of war to the extent that Bonfiglio was forced to issue a formal warning.[53] On one instance, the two nurses who had been in charge of accompanying a patient as he was transferred to another asylum stole money from him, which they used to buy food, wine and cigarettes. They even shared these ill-gotten goods with the patient during the journey.[54] There is also written proof of serious sexual harassment. On 13 September 1932, a male nurse kissed and tried to undress a patient's female visitor. Under interrogation by the hospital's disciplinary commission, he confessed, adding that he felt he had been provoked by the woman. The commission proposed a suspension of his salary for ten days, a penalty that seems very lenient in the context of the moralization campaign launched by the regime.[55]

To complete the picture, Santa Maria della Pietà's nursing staff were also caught exploiting patients' work to the point that the director had to insist that: 'It is forbidden to use patients' work time to clean members of staff's bicycles.'[56] Besides, nurses seem to have routinely performed practices that should have been carried out by doctors only. On 4 September 1934, the director issued a circular where he reminded staff that force-feeding using a nose or mouth pump could not be performed by nurses or by doorkeepers.[57]

In the hospital's surviving documentation, there is an anonymous letter denouncing the deplorable situation.[58] Dated 10 October 1941 it was sent to the sub-secretary of the Ministry of Interior, and from there presumably to the Santa Maria della Pietà director. It drew attention to the death of one patient, the successful escape of two patients from Pavilion XVIII (for criminals) and of two other interned women from other pavilions. It also mentioned an accident that involved a nurse. Finally, it reminded the recipients of the death of a patient that had occurred while she was giving birth. In his reply to the provincial authority, the director tried to minimize the facts, but evidently the daily routine of the hospital was far from impeccable.

However, despite the lack of professionality and discipline, which was also the case in the two other mental health institutions examined in the following chapters, at Santa Maria della Pietà we can see that nurses were given a lot of power. Their notes, detailing what patients did and said, went well beyond what could be reasonably expected. They did much more than document patients' sleeping and eating patterns, incidents, bursts of anger, crises and patients' moods. Nurses' *diari*, daily reports, show that they thought it was their duty to question patients on their life choices so that they could summarize and comment on the content of these conversations. This was commensurate with the culture of spying that was backed by the regime. Their opinions and moral judgements seem to have counted a great deal and their descriptions often re-appear in the medical notes, without an attempt to prove or question them. On occasion, doctors reported patients' statements with the same hostility or sarcasm and using the same terms the nurses had utilized. The assumption was that observation by nurses, often from the same working-class background as the vastest majority of internees, would be less formal and would therefore constitute a part of medical evidence that doctors could not obtain when questioning a patient in their office.

In any case, even in the worst cases of misconduct, the asylum director and the disciplinary commission always appear timid in reprimanding and punishing nurses, probably because staff were very difficult to replace and much in need, in a period characterized by overcrowding of asylums. Furthermore, to dismiss anyone could have created problems with the PNF as all employees were increasingly recruited for their loyalty to Fascism. The result is that nurses took full advantage of the situation, counting on almost complete impunity. They carried out duties that were beyond what their job entailed, they stole, exploited patient labour and generally showed indiscipline and a lack of commitment to their profession.

The private lives of nurses are likely to have been scrutinized. Just before the regime took power, on 17 May 1922, a male nurse had to report to the disciplinary commission on his private situation. He had separated from his wife who had betrayed him by having a sexual affair with his brother. According to his statement, she led 'a dissolute life' and neglected the children. The separation court hearing was still taking place at the time of this disciplinary hearing. The nurse was declared fit for work because 'the fact has not created a scandal that makes [him] untrustworthy on the part of the Institute'.[59] This incident provides an insight into the ways in which scandal was not only one of the main reasons for internment, but it also had to be avoided at all costs as it could jeopardize chances of finding or keeping employment. The case also shows how silence and discretion were conditions for survival for everybody, even before the regime officially came to power. Equally, separation from a spouse could transform an individual into an 'untrustworthy' person, and the consequences of this could be redundancy: it gave a strong message for anyone contemplating the idea. However, no similar cases could be found for the *Ventennio* period, so it is impossible to trace continuity or discontinuity in this respect.

While there is a wealth of documentation on nurses, very little transpires on doctors. It appears that the director's major concern was to instruct and discipline nurses only. No evidence suggests that any disciplinary hearing ever took place on the conduct of psychiatrists during the fascist years. The director's main aim seems to have been to rule over a large nursing task force that was increasingly recruited not on merit, often ignorant and undisciplined, that he perceived as unruly. The lack of official reprimands issued against psychiatrists suggests there was a relative harmony between the director and the asylum doctors.

However, there is some trace of how the director formally addressed psychiatrists when new procedures were introduced. In a large institution such as Santa Maria della Pietà, the way the director communicated with medical specialists was by issuing written reminders or special instructions, often in the form of a one-page circular, that was sent to all the pavilions and offices. Sometimes, staff regulations were longer and took the shape of pamphlets, which touched on several aspects of the daily routine of the asylum, including issues of morality and sexuality. These *Libretti*, literally translatable as booklets, were certainly issued yearly between 1934 and 1939, but there might have been other guidelines for staff, for dates after 1939, that could not be found in the archives.[60] One of these internal publications, *Libretto III*, is particularly relevant to this research as it gave official instructions on how to handle homosexual patients.[61] It impressed upon the staff the need to make the presence of homosexual patients – initially mentioned as *anormali*, 'abnormal individuals', then corrected in pen with *omosessuali* – known to the director of the institute. Doctors were reminded that it was compulsory to communicate to the director the names of 'passive' and 'active' homosexuals, both if they manifested these tendencies during internment or if their homosexuality before internment was known. At point 2, the regulations stated that the doctors had to take all the measures considered suitable for the surveillance of these patients, indicating to which dormitory they were to be allocated and instructing personnel on the need for day and night vigilance. In addition, on the first page of the clinical history files of these patients, the doctor would have to indicate: 'passive or active homosexual, reported to the director on', adding the date. It is interesting to note the importance given to the distinction between passive and active homosexual, which had to be specified by professionals, as if there might be a different approach in terms of cure, containment, vigilance or punishment. It is probably just proof of how the two different categories of homosexuality were considered separate and unassimilable.[62] It is also possible that a difference in approach was in place, at least with regard to disciplinary measures, as the results of this research seem to indicate. Looking at the homosexual patients found at Santa Maria della Pietà, it is only the patient described as active who was punished, the others received far greater understanding from medical staff and punishment or containment were never mentioned in their files. The old distinction was probably still in staff's mind, which identified the active homosexual as dangerous, a potential seducer, affected by a 'vice' and possibly contagious, while passive homosexuals were thought to be inborn degenerates, therefore not rationally responsible for their actions. Besides, they were considered incurable and attracted a more lenient moral judgement, although we must remember that one of them was kept for a period of his internment in Pavilion XVIII, reserved for criminals (P.G.B's case is described in detail later in the chapter).

Libretto III added that doctors had to ensure that adequate vigilance was employed by nurses on any homosexual patient. One can easily see how this could have been a weapon against certain patients on the part of violent, abusive and ignorant nursing staff. Furthermore, the need to increase vigilance towards these patients indicates that the idea of danger associated with homosexuality had been conclusively introduced. However, it could also be argued that if homosexuality required a special mention, it probably meant that staff were not particularly attentive to the issue. The fact that the files of the homosexual patients found in this asylum's archives do not contain any indication on treatment or stricter surveillance instructions seems to confirm it. The following year, regulations insisted:

On the cover of the clinical history file one must write with a coloured pencil when these conditions are present, if the patient 1. is a criminal, 2. has a tendency to escape or to commit suicide, 3. is dangerous to members of staff, nuns ..., 4. if the patient has received special cures (such as malaria therapy) ..., 5. [written in pen] if he is a homosexual or exhibitionist.[63]

The list of cases to report continued with the infectious contagious illnesses the patient might have contracted, accidents s/he might have had and so forth. The inclusion of homosexuality in this list of conditions to be highlighted on the cover of a patient's file, alerting professionals and the director, reinstated the idea that homosexuality was to be considered dangerous and almost contagious, as it had to be marked in the same way as cholera, infectious diseases and suicide attempts. Tendency to suicide was in fact treated as pathological and almost contagious.

The fact that on two occasions reference to homosexuality was inserted at the last minute, in pen, might indicate that it was added by the director of the institute, almost as an afterthought, applying only to Santa Maria della Pietà. In other words, it could correspond to a personal interpretation of current psychiatric thought and trends by the director of Santa Maria della Pietà. Or maybe, to manually transform 'abnormal individuals' into 'homosexuals' simply shows there was a need to spell the issue out to staff, as they seemed not sufficiently aware of it or they intentionally gave little importance to the issue.

The use of the masculine plural *omosessuali* must not be interpreted as indicating that only male homosexuality was the centre of the discourse. Although female homosexuality was often referred to with other words, such as tribadism, it was likely to be included, and the masculine was used only because in Italian the plural has grammatically to be masculine when referring to men and women. Having said this, it must be added that no case of lesbians, tribades or sexually inverted women were found at Santa Maria della Pietà for the 1922–43 period, something that contradicts historical trends in psychiatric theory. From the last decades of the nineteenth century, in fact, Italian psychiatrists analysed and discussed several cases of female sexual inversion and psychiatric journals frequently included an article on the subject.[64] There is no trace of this interest in the Rome asylum archives. Besides, the distinction between active and passive homosexuality the *Libretti* drew attention to seems to implicitly refer to male homosexuality as the main focus of interest.

In later years, instructions to staff reiterated the idea of the danger linked with homosexuality and sexuality in general.[65] *Libretto X* contains a leaflet, dated 14 July 1936, by the director, intended to be circulated among staff, where he specified what he meant by danger. Danger meant harmful intentions towards the self or to others and the tendency to escape or, lastly, 'sexual dangerousness both among people of the same sex and among individuals of two different sexes'. It extended danger to all forms of sexuality, although instructions had previously asked to concentrate only on cases of homosexuality.

These directives to staff insisted on two fundamental concepts, that of danger and of contagion of homosexuality. However, the Santa Maria della Pietà doctors seem to have ignored these instructions. For instance, no indication of the patient's homosexuality appears on the cover of P.G.B.'s and L.A.'s file, who were interned when the guidelines had already been issued. It is possible that homosexuality appeared inside the file of patients with diagnoses different from the ones I considered. It is however indicative that, within the wide range of diagnoses I examined, so few cases of homosexuality were noted, especially considering the number of people interned at Santa Maria della Pietà. As mentioned, in 1937 the asylum hosted almost four thousand patients and it is odd that out of such a high number of patients, nobody was described as homosexual on the cover of their file, nor in the diagnosis, and that no episode of same-sex attraction was reported. There is also a total absence of cases of homosexuals being brought for observation to the nearby hospital, while other patients were routinely sent there to be observed 'for study purposes'. In the available registers that list those who were subjected to this practice, none of them is described as homosexual.[66] Equally, available registers that listed surgical operations and surgeons' reports show no record or mention of testicle transplants or hormone-based therapies whose purpose was to alter the patient's sexual orientation.[67] There is no indication that such practices were in use in Santa Maria della Pietà or that homosexual patients were referred to the nearby hospital to undergo such surgical operations. Documentation proves that patients underwent several surgical operations and received medical treatment, as can be expected in such a large mental health hospital. Staff registered everything, from medication for a viper's bite to procedures in the case of wounds, accidents, suicide attempts by ingestion of needles or ink, induction of child birth, miscarriages and, in one instance, removal of 'foreign objects' from a patient's vagina.[68] The asylum registers also listed minor accidents, falls and similar petty health problems affecting staff, temporary workers and patients that required medical care. No mention is present of anything connected with sexuality and the only testicle removal operation was due to a tumour.[69]

Apart from syphilis, there is rare mention in individual patient files of cures for other venereal diseases, something that is surprising as they were widespread at the time. There is an indication that a venereal disease specialist had to be called, as he appears on the register of outside specialists' remuneration in 1939–40.[70] However, medical files I consulted did not include a detailed description of these conditions. Venereal diseases carried a moral stigma and could have been a corroborating factor in a diagnosis of immorality, moral madness or amorality, and it is surprising that no mention of these could be traced. We know that homosexuals sent to be confined on San Domino delle Tremiti were routinely checked for venereal diseases, the description and therapy of which were always present in their police files.[71] At Santa Maria della Pietà, only P.G.B. was said to have contracted condyloma by his admission to the nurses, and this had clearly been linked to his immoral and promiscuous conduct.[72] There is no record of other close medical examinations to ascertain the presence of venereal diseases or to cure them for any patient whose file was consulted, apart from the routine Wassermann test to diagnose syphilis.

Homosexuality does not appear to have attracted punishments or reprimands when it involved members of staff either. Documentation reveals that on the evening of 19 October 1942, at 11.00 pm, two female nurses were found in the same bed by the nun in charge of Pavilion XVII. Interrogated by the disciplinary commission on 1 April of the following year, their explanations tried to mitigate the seriousness of the circumstances. One of the two nurses declared that she was on the bed, not in bed, probably meaning that she was not under sheets and blanket, trying to hide anything. Besides, she added that she was fast asleep when the nun saw her. The second nurse said she had felt unwell and cold because of a pane of glass being broken, so she had gone to bed to keep warm and had immediately fallen asleep. The members of the disciplinary commission might have been convinced by their version. It seems more likely, however, that in the climate of suspicion and *epurazione* (a term that implies cleansing and purification) that had built up, the commission decided to avoid a scandal that could have brought disrepute on Santa Maria della Pietà. It opted for a safer escape, accepting the story of the two women. The penalty was inflicted only because they were asleep while on duty, not for a suspected lesbian rapport between them, immorality, indecent acts in public or any other description one might have expected. Accordingly, the punishment was lenient: their salary was reduced by a fifth for six days.

Specific methodological issues

General criteria to locate patient files have been explained in the introduction. However, I would like to highlight specific methodological aspects of the archival research carried out in this mental health hospital's archives. The Santa Maria della Pietà archives are held in the central building of the former asylum, where its staff library was, and still is, located. I looked at all the Admissions Registers available for the fascist period.[73] There are some evident discrepancies, overlaps and gaps because several registers were open at the same time in different pavilions. In addition, some archival materials have been lost in the numerous moves of premises for the archives. Furthermore, the archives have suffered in the past from damp and water leaks that severely damaged part of the collection.

In total, in the first phase of my research, strictly following the research parameters I highlighted in the introduction, I ordered 123 patient files for consultation, twenty-six of these were missing, so I consulted ninety-seven patient files. In addition to Admissions Registers and patient files, I discovered in the course of consultation that several patients were sent to the local hospital to be observed or 'for study purposes', thus I consulted registers reporting on surgical operations undergone by interned people and files of cases considered worthy of special study.[74] I also consulted files containing documents on disciplinary counsels, sanitary reports, orders, purchases, sub-contracting, special notes on criminal patients, external correspondence, transfers, and the director's official correspondence and communications to staff.[75] In a second visit, I ordered seventy-two files of patients interned for various diagnoses, and consulted fifty-eight. The diagnoses, this time, varied, but were linked with some aspects of excitement and lack of self-control, to include schizophrenia, encephalitis and epilepsy.

Homosexual patients

Having looked at the institution, its structure, hierarchy, directors and staff regulations, I proceed to analyse the files of patients whose homosexuality was noted by health professionals. The aim is to ascertain if homosexuality was considered worthy of internment, on its own as a separate condition or in conjunction with other pathologies. Out of 155 Santa Maria della Pietà patient files that were consulted for this research, no patient was listed in the Admissions Registers as homosexual, lesbian, tribade or sexually inverted and I could only identify five patients interned during the fascist regime where their homosexuality played a role in their internment and medical notes.[76] This section focuses on these five cases, on a case of 'eunuchoidism', the only one present at Santa Maria della Pietà for the period analysed, and on the case of a patient where lesbianism was mentioned. Few other cases are presented to corroborate the arguments made in this chapter.

The first of these five patients, E.C., was diagnosed as affected by 'moral madness', a diagnosis whose formulation can be retraced back to the mid-nineteenth century.[77] It seems to have been considered outdated by the Santa Maria della Pietà psychiatrists, who in fact deployed it in a total of only five cases during the *Ventennio*, plus in one instance where a patient was described as affected by a similar condition, that of 'constitutional immorality'. In fact, E.C.'s diagnosis of moral madness, linked to chronic mania and dementia, dated back to well before Fascism started. Initially he was interned in the Ceccano hospital, on 14 June 1890, because he was referred by the police who described him as being 'affected by dangerous dementia', but his file mentions three previous internments, one in 1885, a subsequent one, whose date is not marked, and a third one in 1888.

In the outside world E.C. worked as a stonecutter and as a coachman, and lived in the Trastevere area, then a working-class quarter in the centre of Rome. On 3 February 1887, presumably the date of the second internment, the police asked that he be hospitalized because he was 'mentally ill and can be dangerous to himself and others', which was the standard formulation. At the time he was thirty-one. Then again on 27 December 1888, the Trastevere security forces referred him to the asylum and he was interned on the following day because he was 'affected by monomania, ambitious and dangerous'. His father came to his rescue, agreeing to take responsibility for his son's unspecified 'morbid acts' and collected him from the asylum against the medical best advice on 2 December 1889, almost a year later. However, six months later E.C. was convicted for aggression and the police referred him to the asylum again. Following this internment, on 19 May 1891, his family history was taken in detail, to ascertain whether there was a hereditary factor for his condition. It seemed confirmed by the fact that his older brother had been in prison for fraud and had a physical flaw, he was squint-eyed. Furthermore, at the age of thirteen, E.C. already frequented the town's brothels 'spending there whole nights'. Sexual precocity was often identified as a sign of inborn degeneration, as both psychiatric theory and many other patient files testify. In addition, at the age of twenty he was convicted for armed aggression, having threatened somebody with a knife; at twenty-four he spent three months in prison for insubordination and physical violence against a municipal guard; and at thirty he was convicted again for the same crime. According to the psychiatrist's description, he then started begging to make a living and had violent fights with his father. The doctor added: 'what strikes you, when examining this patient, is the total lack of ethical feelings'. When the psychiatrist asked him what his ideal in life was, 'he replied: to carouse, to enjoy himself etc'. He referred to his regular prostitutes as his wives. The psychiatrist noted: 'not infrequently he tries to exercise pederasty, and he recounts with some pleasure that once he could not do so inside the asylum on a patient (imbecile) who had invited him to do so'. It is interesting to note that pederasty was mentioned, but as one of the many signs of moral madness, an additional condition of a person who did not show any moral feeling.

However, a few years later E.C. demonstrated that he had an idea of what the institution would have liked to hear on his sexuality. On 7 August 1899, he stated that he was a virgin. 'Asked what his ideal life would be like, he replies: "to work and to find a bride"', the psychiatrist wrote. Despite his effort to adapt his biography to psychiatrists' expectations, these statements were judged unconvincing and his lack of morality was noted again. A further proof of the patient's absence of moral feelings was that once he had found 4,000 Lire in his coach and admitted that he had kept the sum because 'he would have been an idiot to give it back'.

E.C.'s family continued to be very present, feeling responsible and involved. On 5 June 1909, his brother asked the Magistrates' Court to release him, but his request was refused by the asylum director because E.C. 'is dangerous, he is a moral imbecile'. On 4 March 1910, one of E.C.'s nieces asked the director for news of her uncle. But one of the doctors had just written in his file: 'he is immoral. More than once he has been caught while he tried to exercise pederasty on other patients: today he was punched by patient C. because he wanted to insert his penis in his mouth'. On 8 March 1910, he tried to use violence against the same patient to 'submit him to immoral acts'. The road to recovery faded away, E.C. became aware of it and communicated his consequent frustration. A month later, he wrote to his brother, telling him that he kept asking to be discharged to go back to work in Rome, but 'the director pretends not to understand'. He had already written to his sister-in-law, on 27 July 1909, saying he wanted to get out to resume his work as a stonecutter, asking her to give his regards to a very long list of relatives, neighbours and friends. It shows how attached to his previous life, his social environment and work he still felt and how tightly knit his working-class social context was. It also indicates that E.C. was probably aware that his correspondence was read and censored by hospital staff. He wanted to communicate to the director of the institution that he had connections with the outside world, he had not been forgotten and, on the contrary, there were many people waiting for him to be released. It could have been a way to implicitly demonstrate that, in his social environment, he was not regarded as a danger to society. It could also suggest the man's awareness that active homosexuality was not harshly judged by society. Whether his family and friends knew about it prior to internment, or had heard about its manifestations during internment, as is likely, E.C. seems to have been sure they would not mind too much. His relatives certainly showed undeterred support and understanding, continuing to be in touch throughout his internment and actively trying to have him released.

As Luca Des Dorides discusses, patients' letters are a tangible proof of the fact that they were aware of the importance played by their social and family network, something that he aptly names a 'social capital', that could bring several benefits.[78] E.C. is a clear case of a patient who had what Des Dorides terms a 'career in deviancy' within a mental health institution. He knew its rules well and attempted to use the language that he thought could guarantee certain privileges, that of social connections. Patients with many years of internment experience, in other words, tried to play the game by the system's rules which heavily relied on nepotism and interference by powerful people. E.C. believed he could count on his family as a pressure group in his favour and made sure that the asylum authorities knew he was not an isolated or unprotected individual. The family, friends, the mayor of a small town, the local priest were all figures of authority that patients tried to draw in, if they perceived they were on their side. Medical files are full of letters from chairmen of local fascist groups, lawyers and doctors who tried to interfere in the psychiatric system and were called to help speed up a patient's release. Interned people, Des Dorides adds, demonstrated that they knew the asylum rules from an administrative and bureaucratic point of view as well, and tried to implement strategies to obtain better treatment or to be transferred to a quieter pavilion, or to move from Rome to one of the smaller detached hospitals in the Lazio Region, in Ceccano and in Rieti. He argues that they were also aware of some basic pseudo-medical concepts connected with psychiatry and tried to use them in their favour. For instance, in several cases they enacted violent bursts of anger, to then show sudden repentance and overstated criticism of their past behaviour, something they knew was read by doctors as a sign of recovery and would lead to a less punitive treatment.

In 1915, five years after his last medical assessment, E.C. was still described as 'easily excitable, irritable, he quickly reacts to the smallest provocation with insults, threats and violent, aggressive actions ... [.... He has] delirious megalomaniac ideas', but had become 'apathetic, indolent, indifferent to anything that does not directly affect his needs'. From then on, the patient's situation was reviewed every lustre, which confirms he was considered a chronic and incurable, but not particularly severe or dangerous, case. On 6 May 1920, he was again described as 'an active pederast. He is put *in consegna*, [a term that in Italian has a definite military connotation] and will sleep next to the entrance guard.' The fascist regime was already in power on 16 July 1923, when the doctor's notes reported:

> He is affected by almost total moral blindness. He recounts his pranks (thefts, aggressions, incestuous practices) with cynicism and a sense of satisfaction. Also, recently he has often been caught while attempting to commit libidinous acts, even in the yard. He has a high opinion of his technical abilities and would like to give proof of this, but, after some small jobs, he makes a nuisance of himself because he asks for excessive remuneration.

The fact that a patient asked for remuneration was read as a sign of megalomania and lack of recovery, work in the asylum had to be exploitative by definition. On 27 November 1923, E.C. was transferred to Santa Maria della Pietà for reasons that are not specified.[79] His medical file on 16 November stated:

> In the past, in his talk one could notice a complete absence of ethical feelings and complacency for carousals and convictions he had received .... He boasts

about his merits as a stonecutter and as a coach driver. Diagnosis: secondary dementia.

The notes also reinstated the inherited degeneration factors: his father was an alcoholic, his mother died in an asylum, the patient had frequented prostitutes from a young age. These were all clear stigmata of degeneration that pointed to an inborn, congenital nature of immorality, an idea directly connected with the psychiatric thought of the previous decades. In 1925 he was transferred to the Rieti mental health hospital. In his last psychiatric notes, dated 28 June 1928, he was described again as 'euphoric, proud, amoral, depressed'. He died in hospital on 9 March 1929 of bronco-pneumonia at the age of seventy-three.

It is interesting to note that, in a very working-class context, the patient's family seems to have shown a high degree of solidarity towards its relative. The family asked the asylum director to release him on more than one occasion, showed concern, took him home against medical advice. There is no indication of a moral judgement of his relatives on his conduct. Yet, one could argue that in Italy active homosexuality was generally perceived not as a sexual perversion or inversion, but simply as a normal alternative way for a man to release sexual desire, as highlighted by Robert Aldrich.[80] Other considerations surface through the analysis of this case. As mentioned, homosexuality was treated by professionals as an aspect of an immoral and degenerate personality, but it was not considered as a separate and discrete condition. In this case, we have written evidence that it only attracted punishment once, long before Fascism, but of course other disciplinary measures might have been implemented without appearing in the file. The inborn tendency of the patient towards crime and his liking of excess in all fields fitted within a picture of degeneration in all areas of human activity and interests, including the erotic. None of his manifestations of degeneration was listed as preponderant or was focused upon separately. E.C.'s first diagnosis and internment precede Fascism by many years and there was no real change in psychiatrists' attitudes, vocabulary or therapies towards this patient during the regime. In fact, E.C.'s case shows a clear line of continuity, although the moral aspect of his behaviour was more frequently commented upon in the second half of his internment.

The second case of a homosexual interned at Santa Maria della Pietà belongs to the diagnostic category of 'psycho-degeneration' or 'degeneration', which appears to have been much more in use than moral madness in this asylum during the fascist period. Twenty-five patients were diagnosed in this way and their condition was routinely further explained inside their files, as it was usually associated with other symptoms or behaviours. P.G.B. was an eighteen-year-old student when first interned.[81] On 12 July 1932, the doctor justified his internment on the basis of his 'constitutional immorality', although on the Admissions Register, he was defined as affected by psycho-degeneration. It was his father who referred him and explained the reasons for his decisions to the director as follows: 'he is above all a sexual psychopath', adding that the boy did not follow a regular course of studies, was indifferent to disciplinary rules and had often escaped from boarding school. Besides, 'habitually [he is] a liar, slanderer and mythomaniac. He has a tendency towards vagrancy … lately he declared he wants to dedicate himself to theatrical arts.'

The nature of the sexual psychopathy he was affected with must have been discussed and clarified not in writing, between the psychiatrists and the boy's father, or relevant written notes are now lost. Abruptly the file reported that the patient 'admits everything but tries to downplay all aspects. On pederasty, for instance, he only says that once he was the victim of violence from a *compagno d'arte*, a peer who had made him drunk beforehand'.[82] This comment is particularly relevant as it reveals the boy knew it was important to state his diminished responsibility. According to P.G.B.'s first statement, his homosexuality was not a choice taken in full mental capacity but coercion by rape. The nurses' notes added that he confessed he had to undergo a surgical operation at the Rome San Gallicano Hospital, which specialized in the treatment of venereal diseases, as he had contracted condyloma. Venereal diseases were invariably linked to a moral judgement on the patient's private life, and it is surprising that this detail had not emerged during the medical visit leading to the overall patient medical assessment.

A few months later, on 3 December 1932, P.G.B. was said to be 'a psycho-degenerate with a prevailing sexual taint (inversion), who keeps quiet and is tidy. He can be transferred to another psychiatric hospital or similar clinic'. He was discharged on 4 April 1933 but readmitted in the same year, on 7 November. The nurses' daily report stated in very poor Italian, with many grammar and spelling mistakes, and no punctuation, that he was calm but

> talked in a stupid way, he was discharged eight months beforehand and in this lapse of time he led the life of a [unreadable word], he went to Rome, Naples, Palermo, Genoa, and from one place to the other, he always ended up in a police station, he says he led a terrible life because his father threw him out of home, he says he never worked and had many vices, in Naples he dressed as a woman and went around the town, he says he is more a woman than a man.

This report reveals many interesting issues: first, that the police were stopping transvestites in most towns. It is not specified when and for how long, but P.G.B. travelled from one major town to the other and the security forces arrested him in every city. This important detail, so far not thoroughly investigated by historians, is also confirmed by one of my previous oral history interviews. A gay man I interviewed in 2000 for an oral history project told me that during Fascism, as pederasty was marked on his criminal records, he was stopped by the police and sent back to Naples, where he was from, from several different towns he visited; he was also frequently stopped in Naples and held in custody on an arbitrary basis, especially when he wore female clothing accessories, such as scarves in light colours, or make-up.[83] Secondly, Naples was obviously perceived to be relatively more open towards transvestitism, probably because of its centuries-long community of *femminielli*.[84] Finally, it is interesting to note that, when talking to nurses, P.G.B. admitted that he felt he was a woman, a status that today would be described as transsexualism. Unfortunately, it is impossible to know whether the word 'vices' was an expression he used or whether it was the nurses' choice of words when they summarized his accounts.

In a note dated 6 December 1933 the psychiatrist added that the boy 'had volunteered [it is not specified where, in which forces or army corps], but after a month he grew tired and asked to be discharged. When he came back, his father refused to take him home.' Cowardice had come to signify a lack of moral integrity, selfishness, anti-patriotic behaviour and ultimately it was a sign of anti-fascist ideals, lack of virility and homosexuality, as observed by most studies on masculinity in the fascist years and the creation of stereotypical virility and effeminate images.[85]

As time went by, however, psychiatrists continued to express the opinion that the patient was fit to be discharged. On 19 September 1935, the doctor wrote:

> In his long internment he never engaged in [unreadable word] from a sexual point of view [underlined in the original]. There is no doubt that he was a passive pederast during adolescence, but nothing has been proved. On the contrary, [here] he dedicated himself to work. ... He is certainly aboulic, therefore his intentions are not firm: however, after such a long period of internment, considering his praiseworthy behaviour on the whole, and also keeping in mind his age (21 years), and adding that it would not be humane to give up the idea of a second attempt to readmit him into society, considering also that he does not constitute a danger ..., I therefore propose his release.

This statement is in line with theories current at that time, which regarded homosexuality as a phase of development for adolescents, who would then mature, move into adulthood and become heterosexuals.[86] It also proves that, among the medical professionals, some took the homosexual patient's side. The psychiatrist saw no danger to society in this young man, in disagreement with the clear indications given by staff directives, and underlined the necessity of showing humanity towards him. The doctor clearly relied on nurses' reports when he affirmed that the patient had not manifested sexual desires for other interned men. If this had happened, clearly the nurses would have had to note it.

The boy's father, however, questioned the professionals' decision with some force. On 28 September 1935, shortly after receiving notice of P.G.B.'s imminent release, he wrote to the director:

> I am an honourable civil servant, now retired, and I am an old fascist, I am very ill.... He has not recovered and besides he is incurable, like Prof Bonfiglio said, so why send him out of hospital?[87] Your decision means a sentence of sure perdition, with serious damage caused not just to him, but to his family and society.

He added that the boy pretended to have improved the first time, coinciding with his first release, and when he was free and came home, he nourished the purpose to vindicate himself against his father who had referred him to the asylum in the first place. 'He is a deficient, a kleptomaniac and a sexual degenerate,' he added and said he hoped the director would consider this case 'as a man of science, a father and a fascist', reminding him that he had 'also the duty to preserve the family and society from an individual who can be disgusting, scandalous and dangerous'. This man clearly understood all the key issues. Homosexuality was considered incurable, especially, as in this case, if passive, because it was implied that it was inborn. Sexual degeneration was linked to lack of courage, and P.G.B. came back from the front after just one month, to a lack of intelligence and, in Lombrosian terms, to crime, in this case a compulsive tendency towards theft. It also constituted a danger to society and to the family's reputation. In reminding the director to act as a fascist, the boy's father underlined that the regime's directives in this sense were clear. Importantly, he thought he could exert pressure on the psychiatric institution. At the time of the boy's first internment, the director had already received a letter from the *Fiduciario Rionale*, the chairman of local PNF branch who, addressing him as *camerata,* the term used to indicate fellow fascists, to remind him of where his loyalty was supposed to be, pressurized him to take this case seriously and to listen to the reasons of the boy's father 'who is obsessed about the destiny of his son'.[88]

There is other evidence of pressure being put on Santa Maria della Pietà's psychiatrists from patients' family members. In fact, this recurs so often that it is possible to affirm that psychiatric hospitals had been identified by citizens as an automatic best option to get rid of unwanted relatives. They felt entitled to remind the director of Santa Maria della Pietà of what they saw as a duty towards them and society at large.

D.P.F.P., for instance, was interned in 1927 for a depressive state with a melancholic or degenerative basis.[89] The psychiatrists wrote that he expressed his political and religious ideas animatedly and had previously tried to commit suicide with a gun after a reproach from his mother. His psycho-degenerative abnormality was noted, together with 'hysterical notes and suicidal tendency'. Having heard that he might be discharged, his father hastily sent a telegram to the director of Santa Maria della Pietà, asking to keep him in the asylum. On the same day, 11 May 1927, he also posted a letter to Giannelli saying he doubted his son could have recovered in such a short period of time. The man added a threatening sentence: 'in any case, if you think the time of release has arrived, I inform you that from now, for anything my son might do I, as a father, decline every responsibility'. His words are another good example showing how people thought psychiatry was a malleable, adjustable tool in their hands, almost a service in obedience to patients' relatives and the public security forces. The man even involved the *Comitato Centrale dei Veterani e dei Reduci*, the Central Committee of Veterans and ex-Service Men, who intervened in support of his cause.

In another case a patient's father tried to influence the psychiatrists' choices. His son, D.B.R., a pharmacist, was diagnosed to be affected by a state of excitement on a degenerative basis and was interned several times, starting in 1923.[90] He was referred by his father, who in a letter dated 18 July 1930 described his excesses and explained to the director that,

> he had brisk manners with the family, ate with great voracity, went out to commit bad actions, fraud, etcetera ... It was necessary not to contradict him, to let him do what he wanted, otherwise he would threaten us.

He lamented that, after a small accident which immobilized him for a short while, the young man

> started his debauched life again: he stole family money, sold objects, tried to obtain goods from shopkeepers and did not pay for them, came back home at two or three at night and sometimes in the early hours of the morning, he was drunk, he demanded some food, sometimes wanted money, slept very little ....

> I felt it was my duty, for his sake, to refer him to an asylum again, but my plans failed, and I suffered the consequences. In fact, the following night my son came back at two and kicked me and threw at me everything he could find ... so that in the end, seeing the terrible situation, we shouted 'help'. The police came.

This man, who had clearly lost authority over his son, added bleakly that he had confidence in psychiatry, or at least he wrote so, in order to make his request sound more convincing: 'I beg Your Excellency to try to find every means that science disposes of to improve my son's condition, that at the moment is most disastrous.' In a polite and respectful way, he attempted to push all the right buttons in order to remind the asylum's director of what he perceived to be his duty, even hinting that it was the psychiatrists' fault if he had to suffer his son's aggression after one of his releases.

However, what makes the case of P.G.B. unique is that there is a very interesting twist to his story, as the boy's stepmother intervened in the dispute to defend him. She wrote to the director several times and exerted as much pressure as she could to question the boy's father's decisions and the medical professionals' judgements. On 12 August 1935 she explained: 'he has been the scapegoat, the major victim of the storm that an evil woman started in our home'. In other words, she had been replaced by another woman and insinuated that P.G.B.'s father wanted to get rid of his son as well, to start a new life. The former stepmother sided with the boy as they had both been expelled from the man's new world of affections, and this alliance, based on love and solidarity, went beyond common morality and the traditional nuclear family. According to her letter to the director dated 29 April 1935, the boy had contacted her several times asking for help. Determined to get him out of the psychiatric institution, she demanded to know what psychic degeneration his father had the boy interned for. She added a conclusive 'he is not a criminal', and requested that he be sent from Pavilion XVIII, for criminals, to Pavilion XII, for dangerous patients, maybe to underline that his behaviour was not against the law.[91] It is certainly relevant to note that the boy was kept in the pavilion for criminals, a very harsh choice on the part of medical staff. Despite the woman's resentment at her former husband's betrayal, her letters reveal a genuine concern that challenged authorities and the establishment with a certain degree of courage. Also, the fact that she thought P.G.B. should not be interned because he was not a criminal indicates that in public opinion, prison and asylum were easily mixed up. Most importantly, this woman's voice is proof that people, despite the propaganda they were subjected to, were not unanimous in condemning homosexuality at the time. They were sometimes even prepared to challenge an authoritative figure such as a psychiatric hospital's director in order to defend somebody who had been interned because of it. The woman's attitude also seems to suggest that the Zanardelli Code, which did not penalize homosexuality, and the Rocco Code, which also avoided any mention of sex between people of the same sex, were firmly rooted in people's mentality. This woman's reaction to the authorities is proof that the fascist moral code did not sink in, and that at least a part of the population was not convinced that homosexuality was a crime or that it should be punished.

The psychiatric profession offered its services according to what families – in this case the patient's father – and security forces asked when they referred a homosexual person. However, here there is also a clear indication that psychiatrists were not totally and uniformly convinced that homosexuality could be treated in an asylum. In P.G.B.'s case the specialist insisted that, in view of good behaviour, a young age and absence of homosexual behaviour inside the institution, a second chance should be given to the patient, also in view of the fact that he did not seem dangerous in any way. Whether doctors thought homosexuality could not be cured because it was part of an inherited, inborn degenerative tendency, or whether it was thought not to be dangerous in some cases and therefore not worthy of internment, the conclusive impression is that doctors were uncertain of how to handle it from a medical point of view. No cure or special treatment appears to have been prescribed for P.G.B.

Most importantly, the psychiatrists here give clear proof that they dissented with the belief that incurables, and homosexuals among them, should be interned. While the patient's father believed the place for incurables was the mental health institution, the doctors replied with the opposite. The boy could be discharged, they said, precisely because a mental health hospital was an institution only fit for those who could be cured. In other words, they highlighted the medical role of asylums. At the same time, they also contested the idea that homosexuality constituted a danger and therefore, as the patient was considered cooperative, calm and disciplined, they stated that he could be looked after by his family. Both are strong statements that reveal an attitude far from being condescending and passive. Psychiatrists wanted to convey the message that they were not prepared to act as guards of a detention centre for social misfits, neither did they accept impositions and regulations from above that intruded on the medical aspect of their job. They totally rejected the obligation to match homosexuality with danger. P.G.B. was discharged on 8 October 1935. As nobody agreed to take care of him, he was handed to the head of police, according to standard procedures defined by Article 65 of Law 36/1904. Clearly the boy's father was not convinced by psychiatrists and remained firmly committed to his intransigent position.

The third case of an interned homosexual is the case of a patient diagnosed as affected by clinical depression linked with degeneration. A total of eleven patients were interned for depression at Santa Maria della Pietà during the *Ventennio*, but only five of them were described as having depression 'on a degenerative basis'. This diagnosis too, like that of a state of excitement, psycho-degeneration, amorality, constitutional immorality and moral madness, covered a wide range of conditions, such as tendency to suicide, delinquency, rebelliousness, Anti-Fascism and, in one instance, homosexuality linked with violent reactions and bursts of anger. B.P., a fifteen-year-old boy born in Switzerland, had spent three years prior to internment in a young offenders' prison where at some point he was kept locked in his cell for four months after he had tried to commit suicide by ingesting ink.[92] On 2 May 1923 his admission file reconstructed his health history, stating that he had suffered from an unspecified 'fairly serious' illness that entailed two months of hospital care, and was then brought up in an 'immoral environment'. He was described as affected by a slight depressive state on a psycho-degenerative basis, and was an onanist, the quasi-religious term used to indicate that he masturbated. At the time of internment, he was awaiting trial because he had been charged of causing bodily harm to the director of the prison for minors, whose report was inserted in the patient's file. He had referred the boy to the psychiatric institution because, on his account, he was calculated, obstinate, indifferent and violent. Furthermore:

> He does not have a perfect notion of what is good and what is evil, of what is right and what is wrong, of the duties he has and the rights that belong to him .... He is a moral idiot, in him there is an insufficiency of intellectual faculties that prevents him from an exact knowledge of the idea of morality. ... he manifests instincts of sexual perversion; at present he nourishes a morbid and unruly love for a mate of his, he frequently asks to see him and because he is not allowed to, as it is natural, he has violent and often dangerous reactions.

An official statement, also dated 1 May 1923 and signed by four witnesses, presumably prison workers, reiterated that 'he should be continually kept under surveillance because he threatens anyone who comes close to him and attempts to commit suicide'. On this basis, he was referred to Santa Maria della Pietà. At the end of the first two weeks of observation, his medical file was noted: 'he is a bit depressed, silent, had some crying fits', but, apart from these isolated episodes, he was 'calm, disciplined, respectful'. The medical notes added an important part of the puzzle. While in prison

> he was beaten up by his superiors several times, with fists and with a key [presumably held in the fist, protruding] and was always kept inside his cell. One day, his superior unfairly hit him more than once, he rebelled against him and hit him twice with his fist. This is the reason why he must go to trial.

Evidently, he had been the victim of bullying and physical aggression on the part of prison staff. Interestingly, the doctor did not specify that this was the patient's account, he reported it as a true version of facts, siding with the patient. The boy's observation period was prolonged, as allowed by law, a fact that signals that the asylum staff had some uncertainty about this case. In fact, B.P. remained at Santa Maria della Pietà only a month and a half from the end of the observation period, another sign that indicates a distancing of the psychiatric professionals from the diagnosis of a mental health problem. He was declared 'affected by a slight state of depression on a psycho-degenerative basis' and judged 'recovered during the period of observation' in a note signed by Giannelli dated 18 July 1923, after the boy's official release date. Following routine procedure, B.P. should have gone back to the prison for minors, but the Novara Tribunal had already issued his release, so he could not be readmitted there. The director of the prison asked that he be sent to his father in Switzerland, which is presumably what happened.

Many questions remain unanswered: why was this young boy imprisoned in Italy, while his family lived in Switzerland? His file holds no correspondence to or from his relatives: could this mean a family rejection? On which charges was he imprisoned? Vagrancy? Crime? Why was he sent to Rome and not to a mental health hospital in Piedmont, where he had been detained? What we do see, however, is how the psychiatric institution representatives avoided addressing or even mentioning homosexuality directly. Despite being informed that B.P. nourished a loving passion for another boy, they did not consider it medically relevant and, in any case, they did not think psychiatry could do very much about it. The fact that the patient was discharged shortly after the period of observation, being judged not suitable for internment, hints again at the lack of interest at Santa Maria della Pietà for homosexuality as a psychiatric condition, curable or not. Furthermore, psychiatrists here openly sided with the patient. The way that the violence of the prison staff was reported reveals an understanding of the causes of the patient's 'depression'. In this case, the medical professionals responded to pressure from the director of the prison, the system of the legal and security forces, and did not refuse internment as requested, but they clearly decided to cooperate no further. B.P.'s internment took place before the *Libretti* of directives to staff on homosexuality were issued. Consequently, there was no official obligation to mark it on the file's cover and the patient's homosexuality only appears inside his file, in the prison director's words.

This is not the only case where psychiatrists openly showed support towards an underage patient. There is in fact copious evidence of a connection between the understanding attitude shown to B.P. and to other minors interned at Santa Maria della Pietà. D.P.V., for instance, was diagnosed as having an 'hysterical degeneration of character'.[93] According to the patient's mother the girl had been leading an unruly life for years and had never accepted any discipline, always came back late at night, engaged in fights and lied. The situation worsened after the age of twelve, when her behaviour became 'even more strange and rebellious: she was never at home, did not want to do any type of work, often argued with her mother'. However, the professional noted that her parent used to hit her hard and once wounded her, to the point that in the past the neighbours had denounced her for violence. The psychiatrist observed that the girl carried a visible mark of this, a scar on the right side of her chest. He was also eager to note that her mother had divorced twelve years earlier and co-habited with a man by whom she had three children. His moral judgement hit the mother harder than the daughter, hinting at the woman's 'disordered' lifestyle, outside social conventions, such as co-habiting rather than re-marrying, and having children out of wedlock. The girl was taken care of by the psychiatric institution, despite no clear evidence of a medical conviction or the presence of a mental health problem. She was interned on Christmas Eve 1942 and discharged on 31 March of the following year. A second internment took place shortly afterwards, ending on 7 August 1944. In this case, there seems to have been some consideration on the professional's part of what would be the best solution for a patient who was clearly a victim of domestic violence.

In another case, M.P., eleven when in 1941 he was admitted for the first of five times, there is a clear indication that the boy rejected his mother.[94] Referred by her because of his stubborn rebelliousness and bad behaviour, when at Santa Maria della Pietà he was always described as a well-behaved child who had remarkably good school results. The mother, in turn, was implicitly accused of using the institution to get rid of him as she obviously had a problem keeping him under control. Her views were not supported by the psychiatrists at Santa Maria della Pietà in any way. Their medical notes always referred to M.P. as having 'regular behaviour' and as being 'intelligent', in contrast with what the woman kept saying. On one occasion the doctor even wrote, 'his coming back to the hospital is due to disagreements with his mother', and in general all medical notes on him identified the mother–son relationship as the root of the problem, pointing out that it was the mother who described 'irregularities of conduct'. At some point M.P. must have asked the hospital staff to try to locate his father. His request was seconded. The boy's file contains a letter by the administration to a man with his surname, which was returned, still sealed, to the sender. However, it is important to see that even when the medical professionals appear so unanimously convinced that there was no evidence of a mental illness, they accommodated the family's request for internment. In this case too they probably saw internment as the best available option for a minor whose family situation was so clearly hostile to him.

The fourth case of homosexuality I found is that of L.A., a twenty-nine-year-old ice-cream maker, interned on 7 May 1936 and discharged a month later, which indicates that the patient was kept at Santa Maria della Pietà for an initial period of observation of two weeks, renewed once and therefore extended to four weeks in total.[95] His initial diagnosis is 'state of excitement', but the word 'psycho-degeneration' follows it, in brackets. The psychiatrist's notes on this patient, written on 21 May 1936, tell the story of a person that we would define, nowadays, as transgender:

> Already he was seen [unreadable word] around in the company of an ex-internee of this Asylum, with whom the patient started a friendship that later degenerated into a homosexual relationship. The patient began to say that he was a woman, he displayed himself naked to his mother [unreadable word] and [unreadable word] I am a woman, you see, I have growing breasts, etcetera. He could not be convinced of the opposite. C. [i.e. the former internee mentioned earlier] was always around him, telling him that he would obtain a certificate so that he could marry him, he spoke about moving in together, he described to him the female clothes he could wear, and so forth. The patient was excited by this idea. One day, as the other man had to go away for work from time to time, the patient threatened him with a razor.

This description, which does not leave many doubts on the existence of a homoerotic relationship between the two men, is shortly followed by a sudden confession. L.A. 'states that he took all his false ideas out of his head. He says that now he is convinced he is a man, he wishes to go back home and start a new life'. This act of repentance shows that the patient understood what the psychiatric system expected from him. Repentance, as explained earlier, was considered a decisive step towards recovery. It demonstrated that the patient understood s/he had adopted a 'wrong' behaviour in the past and that s/he was finally managing to dominate his/her instincts. As s/he proved that s/he could exert control over his/her instincts, s/he was considered fit to re-enter society. It is interesting to highlight how patients demonstrated to know the language that the institution used and expected of them. In this case particularly, as the patient's partner had been interned earlier on, information on how to behave is likely to have been passed on. It is important to underline how lenient the psychiatrist's position was, given the 'scandalous' relationship between the patient and his partner which, in the intentions, was to become public and recognized. It is also worth highlighting that the patient is described as being influenced by his partner's views and decisions, thus insinuating that he had diminished responsibility. When the doctor wrote that C. *'gli stava sempre attorno'* (was always around him), the health practitioner seems to imply that C. was somehow not letting go, insisting or interfering with L.A.'s decisions, hinting at the fact that L.A.'s excitement was determined by C's descriptions, for instance. To a certain degree, L.A. would have been excited at the idea of wearing female clothes because of C's description of these clothes. To show that the patient had been talked into doing something, in other words 'seduced' by someone else, allowed the psychiatrist to release the patient after the observation period.

It is also relevant to underline that L.A. was interned on his family's request. Nurses specified in their daily notes on 7 May 1936, the first day he spent inside Santa Maria della Pietà:

> He comes from Policlinico [one of Rome's general hospitals], he appeared to be calm, he says that he was taken to hospital because he changed gender and, as he kept repeating this to his parents, they refused to believe it and he wanted to kill them and so they decided to take him to hospital.

Also in this case, where the patient's sexual inversion was evident and self-declared at first, the psychiatrists judged his repentance a sufficient element for his release. The only comment that suggests an attempt to investigate this case further was the request of a neurological exam, judged negative, and the observation of L.A.'s genitals, that resulted to be normal, as noted on his file on 7 June. Even though by 1936 internal directives imposed a mention on the front page of the patient's file of his/her homosexuality, if it was active or passive and if the patient was to be considered dangerous, none of these elements appears on the cover of the file.

A last element worthy of particular notice is the self-awareness demonstrated by the patient on his condition, his coming-out to his mother and his, and his partner's, firm intention to transform their relationship into an officialized form of marriage, much ahead of times, with the idea of even trying to sort out the situation from a bureaucratic point of view.

The fifth case of homosexuality I found is that of B.E., admitted a first time in 1918 and a second time in 1923 as affected by schizophrenic syndrome, with precocious dementia.[96] The patient's first internment was caused by the trauma experienced when he served at the front, during the First World War. B.E., initially suspected of simulating madness not to go back to the front, was then declared unfit for military service. His file shows that there was a third internment in the 1930s. On 23 March 1939, the psychiatrist noted: 'He shows active homosexual tendencies. He will be transferred to VI,' which meant Pavilion VI, where quiet male patients were kept. The decision is in a way unjustified because the patient had violent anger fits, but is coherent with the Santa Maria della Pietà psychiatrists' shared idea that homosexual patients were not to be considered dangerous.

In 1923, at the time of his second internment, an interesting detail had already emerged. 'When asked if he is married, he remains uncertain, then he shrugs, then first he says yes, then he says no and finally he remains silent.' Maybe, in the light of what we learn from his third internment's notes, this was a way to indicate the existence of a homosexual relationship, not sanctioned but steady, that the patient found difficult to define. B.E. died while interned, at the age of forty-eight, of tuberculosis. His clinical file specifies: 'schizophrenic syndrome with apathy, intermittent states of excitement and impulsivity. Tendency to tear and to break objects. Soon [he showed] symptoms of dementia, with associated noisy manifestations.' Also in this case, homosexuality is not mentioned in the official diagnosis, it does not appear on the cover of the patient's file, there are no detailed comments on the young man's behaviour, genitalia or dangerous behaviour. There is no trace of any special cure, surgical operations, sedation, punishments or isolation.

As explained in the first part of the book, the subject of eunuchoidism attracted great academic interest because it was supposed to explain crucial evolutionary theories. According to these theories, all individuals were born bisexual and developed into 'normal' heterosexuals after puberty. Eunuchoidism and hermaphroditism were thought to be marks of this original bisexuality, retraceable in individuals where this 'natural' mechanism had not worked properly. Cases of hermaphroditism and eunuchoidism were closely analysed in other asylums at the time and considered precious from a scientific point of view, but only one such case can be found at Santa Maria della Pietà for the fascist years.[97] P.D. was interned in April 1929.[98] He was referred by the mayor of a small village near Rome, because he showed religious mania, refused to wear clothes, was violent, broke objects and threatened anyone who came near him. But this fifty-year-old convent cleaner was of some interest to the medical professional who visited him for another reason. Diagnosed with a 'state of excitement in idiot. Eunuchoidism', he was observed in detail. According to the medical notes, 'he has never known women and never felt the desire to do so either'. The so-called *Esame Obbiettivo*, which was another way to refer to the initial medical assessment, added,

> He shows signs of eunuchoidism and of femaleness. He is quite tall, his penis is puerile, the scrotum is small and concave on the front, with very small testicles; his pubic hair has a feminine disposition; sparse moustache; absence of beard and of hair on the chest and limbs; gynecomastia [presence of breasts]; [unreadable word] large with fat accumulated on the hips and thighs.

The rest of his body too was described in fine detail, from the lack of certain teeth to the low forehead, in the presumed attempt to compare his appearance with that of other similar individuals psychiatric professionals were discussing at the time in specialized journals, or simply to ascertain the presence of anomalies. However, in this case, the patient did not present what doctors at the time were specifically looking for, which was hermaphroditism, as they were concentrating their efforts on analysing individuals with sexual organs or a physical appearance that bore traces of male and female, such as beards in women and breasts in men, for instance. The patient was only observed, measured, analysed, commented upon and even spied upon in observance with routine practice. However, after the first assessment notes, there was no consideration of his state of mental and physical health, no mention of a cure, remedy, therapeutic prescription or surgical intervention, and his file does not contain any photographs.

In addition, I found one more case where the mention of 'hermaphroditism', made by the patient, was ignored or not given importance by the health practitioner in charge. L.E., interned in April 1924 and diagnosed with schizophrenic syndrome, was described as having several delirious ideas, such as the conviction of being the son of Queen Margherita, to quote an example.[99] He was also described as threatening to his relatives and prey of hallucinations. Among the various statements made by the patients, the psychiatrist noted that he said he was a hermaphrodite. The disposition of his body hair was described as irregular, as it was abundant on the upper limbs, scarce on the lower limbs and absent on the chest. His genitals were observed and found to be normal.

No further action or reaction seems to have taken place after this confession, no further questions appear to have been asked to the patient on it and no special attention seems to have been drawn to his lifestyle prior to internment.

I also looked for cases of female homosexuality in my research, a topic that had attracted great medical and psychiatric attention from the decades before Fascism onwards. However, I could not find any female patient who was admitted because she was identified as lesbian, tribade or sexually inverted during the fascist regime at Santa Maria della Pietà. Nevertheless, there is an indication that lesbianism was a familiar concept among patients of this asylum. A.B. presented 'reactive dysthymic states' together with psycho-degeneration.[100] She was defined as delirious and was observed to be rancorous towards her violent mother and her very strict father, felt thwarted by everyone, constantly persecuted and criticized. Interned in 1943, a year later she was said to have no sex life: 'Her sexual life is silent.' It is the only time, among the cases analysed for the period in question, where such a statement is presented as a symptom, as usually it was the presence of sexual desire in women that was pathologized. When questioned, she replied that 'she never wanted to get married for fear of becoming her husband's and sisters-in-law's slave. She did not feel the need for sexual intercourse because she only desired a young man who courted her for a long time. Now she would like to become a nun.' A month later, an interesting comment appeared on her medical file. According to the patient 'everybody [at Santa Maria della Pietà] teases her … scares and denigrates her, accuses her of making love with other female internees'. The absence of desire for men would have immediately been interpreted by everybody as lesbianism. Or maybe the patient voiced to the psychiatrist her inner fear of being thought a lesbian because of her lack of desire for men, which is again an indication of how quickly the label of lesbian could be assigned and how fearful women were of it. Or she might have had one or more relationships with women interned at Santa Maria della Pietà and this was the reason she was ridiculed. We will never know, as her conduct was not investigated further, and her comments were just reported to hint at a persecution complex. It is impossible to draw certain conclusions from this case, because so little appears in the patient's file to support any further deduction. However, it is interesting to note that, while the regime's propaganda imposed an almost total silence on lesbianism, the notion was so clear in people's minds as to induce fear of being identified as such. This unmarried woman felt anxious about being judged and perceived as 'different' and 'out-of-the-norm'. While other unmarried women must have been present in the asylum, both among staff and patients, they probably consisted of an increasingly smaller minority, considering that employment was now linked to marital status and number of children, as remarked earlier. Besides, propaganda, marriage incentives and a tax on celibacy were not successful in reversing falling birth rates but had managed to transform single people into dangerous elements of society, perceived as 'others'.[101]

Conclusions

In looking at the available documentation for the fascist period, this research has sketched how Santa Maria della Pietà functioned. Staff regulations, pressure from fascist institutions on the director, problems connected with a lack of professionality, overcrowding and structural deficiencies help us frame the role of this asylum, one of the largest and most significant in the country during the *Ventennio*, particularly given its geographical proximity to central government. This also provides the necessary context to understand attitudes towards patients and homosexual patients in particular.

First, it is highly relevant that I found only five cases of homosexual patients, with one case of eunuchoidism, and a woman whose lack of sexual desire was associated with lesbianism by other patients, according to her statement. Interestingly, the cases of homosexual patients were registered at admission with another diagnosis and their homosexuality only appeared inside their files, where the individual case was discussed more in detail. There is no indication of homosexuality on these patient file covers either, a practice that contravened the director's staff guidelines issued from 1934 onwards, which should have applied at least in relation to the patients who were interned after the staff guidelines had been issued. It is also puzzling to notice that, in a population of almost four thousand patients in 1937 according to Giannelli's calculations, no episode of homosexuality was ever reported to have taken place, other than E.C.'s violent attempts to have sexual intercourse with another patient.[102] It is far more credible that staff did not think it necessary to report it or make it prominent in patients' files. It seems unlikely that the Rome asylum directors were unaware of this disobedience on the part of their staff. It is as if they felt pressurized to pronounce strict directives in this sense and yet they were prepared to turn a blind eye when they were not implemented. This impression is corroborated by the lenient penalties inflicted by the disciplinary commission on the two female nurses who were found in bed together. Again, personnel chiefs and the director of the institution avoided making an issue of it and swiftly swept the incident under the carpet. It is improbable that the only reasons for this approach were fear of political reprisals or safeguarding of the institution's good name, although they certainly played a part.

Secondly, there was a lack of conviction among doctors that homosexuality constituted a real danger and that it was curable through psychiatry. The Santa Maria della Pietà psychiatric staff said loud and clear that a mental health hospital was not supposed to keep incurables, especially if not dangerous. These patients, in their opinion, could be dealt with by families. P.G.B.'s father argued that his son had to remain inside the mental health hospital precisely because he was incurable and therefore could not be readmitted into society. The doctors firmly replied they refused to play the role of social control. It was a strong statement to make, in view of what the regime was trying to implement and it represents an important assertion of the profession's autonomy and dignity, in spite of institutional and family pressures.

On a more general level, it is surprising that, despite the wealth of Italian theoretical publications on sexuality and sexual inversion, illustrated in the first part of the book, the Santa Maria della Pietà medical staff were so unwilling to investigate the cases of homosexuality further. The relative lack of interest in the patients' homosexuality, together with the small number of patients whose sexual inversion was noted, contradicted official trends. Psychiatrists working at the Rome asylum were not only disinterested in cases of homosexuality from a scientific point of view. Also relevant is their relative lack of interest in eunuchoidism. As discussed in Chapters 1 and 2, psychiatrists often presented and discussed cases of hermaphroditism, eunuchoidism and what we would now call inter-sexuality in essays and medical journals articles. However, only one case was diagnosed in this way at Santa Maria della Pietà, and even then, the patient's file does not show a particularly detailed analysis.

The Rome asylum's psychiatrists kept a distance also from the contemporary moral condemnation of sexual inversion. The harshest moral judgement was expressed against E.C., a patient whose lack of humility, commotion, frequent requests for remuneration of his work inside the asylum, interference by relatives who came and obtained his release against the best medical opinion and other aspects of his personality could have irritated and distanced doctors and nurses. His active homosexuality was negatively remarked upon, but as part of a whole situation characterized by a lack of morality. For the other cases of homosexual patients, there was a much more sympathetic approach. A young age was considered a factor that could help 'recovery', as homosexuality was certainly read as a phase one could grow out of in adulthood, which is completely in line with psychiatric theory of the time. Social factors, such as family rejection or violence inflicted on them by their superiors or relatives, were also taken into account by medical staff in a sympathetic way.

There is no indication of a therapy being adopted for any of the homosexual patients, no mention of close physical examination, no particularly intrusive questions posed by doctors on their life prior to internment, while, as we know, intrusive questioning took place in other instances as described in psychiatric journals of the time.[103] Only in the case of P.G.B. did the nurses ask him to talk about his life outside the institution and it is thanks to their inquisitive curiosity that we learn about his trips to Naples and elsewhere, his wearing of women's clothes and his frequent arrests. In the case of E.C. we read he admitted he had frequented brothels from an early age, but not many questions were asked about his private and social life. Some questioning evidently took place in the case of L.A. who described his lifestyle, but the psychiatrist does not seem to have wanted to obtain more details. One is left with the feeling of a general lack of concern or even scientific interest in homosexuality and hypothetical cures for it.

Finally, the use of broad categories to diagnose patients with different conditions and symptoms gives evidence of a general suspension of judgement. Santa Maria della Pietà's psychiatrists seem to have been uncertain of the theoretical tools available to describe and address mental health issues connected with morality. More than one diagnosis was given to a patient during his or her internment and the same term was used to describe conditions with little in common. The fact that most diagnostic categories stretched to include criminality, immorality, cerebral problems, and Anti-Fascism, with evident overlaps and changes of diagnosis during internment, signals that ambiguity offered a chance to escape rigid medical classification. This indicates that psychiatry was undergoing a change, it was questioning traditional terms, approaches and practices. Yet, it hints at the fact that this set of loose definitions was embraced as it constituted a comfortable and safe option. Broad categories were non-committal from a diagnostic point of view, allowed for second thoughts, easy transfer of patients between pavilions and revised diagnoses.

Also to consider is the role that families played in the repression of non-conforming individuals, through psychiatry, during the *Ventennio*. It appears to be central in most cases of people referred to the institution for diagnoses that have to do with morality, discipline and sexuality. Apart from underage orphans, where we find a recurring pattern of their rebellion against the orphanage or convent where they were kept, and referral to the mental health hospital for this reason by the orphanage staff, the vast majority of the patients analysed in the course of this research were interned because they were referred by their immediate relatives, such as siblings, fathers and mothers, or by their husbands. Interestingly, no patient, among the cases analysed, was referred by his wife. Several were referred by the police, mostly for having committed a wide range of crimes, including bursts of anger and prostitution, and were brought from police headquarters to the asylum through a joint decision by security forces and the doctor who signed their medical certificate at the police station. Others ended up in a psychiatric hospital claiming diminished responsibility for the crimes they had committed, because current theory had expanded the connection between criminality and madness, and they were trying to use this to avoid incarceration. We also find a relatively conspicuous group of people sent to the asylum because of their political views.

The majority, though, were referred by their families simply because of unruly or immoral behaviour. Most of them were women. This shows clearly that people considered the asylum an apt measure for the behavioural correction of a rebellious, difficult or scandalous relative. It could be argued that the same happened in earlier decades. However, the way in which relatives addressed the asylum director when they contested release or when they asked for internment to be prolonged shows a hardening of this mentality. Fascism had sanctioned the role of psychiatry as a form of punishment for immorality, rebelliousness and behavioural problems. With few exceptions, in people's minds the asylum was the place the family could look to when all other disciplinary methods had failed, when children rejected their stepmothers and stepfathers, when young women refused to marry the men their brothers chose for them or to behave as they were expected to. It was also perceived as an alternative to divorce, at the time allowed only in extreme cases and difficult to obtain. Often, the family contributed to the creation of deviancy. In fact, relatives' accurate descriptions given to security forces and medical professionals, as observed by Des Dorides, often constituted the basis for psychiatric diagnosis. Relatives' moral judgement, together with that of neighbours, priests and local mayors, was extremely influential and in certain cases determined doctors' responses.[104]

Against the propaganda image of the cohesive and harmonious Italian family, the behind-the-scenes situation was obviously different. Families could harbour resistance to the regime, especially given that they were more rooted in Catholic morality than in fascist ideals, as noted by Paul Ginsborg.[105] At the same time the family could be an environment of coercion, where generational conflict might lead to negative consequences. The willingness to punish young rebels reveals a widening intergenerational gap. Several young women and girls had evidently begun to reject the patriarchal family's impositions and were punished by their relatives through psychiatry. This is a very important aspect of Resistance that should be taken into consideration when analysing opposition to the regime. Several individuals were prepared to pay a high price, and did so, to assert their right to be who they were and to lead their lives the way they chose, despite the family and the regime impositions. Importantly, family attitudes were not uniform and in fact the cases of homosexual patients I found show a contradiction in respect of the role played by families. In two cases, that of E.C. and P.G.B., some relatives showed support and affection throughout, in opposition to the regime's propaganda and beliefs on matters of sexual behaviour.

Furthermore, a shift in mentality can also be observed among psychiatrists. While before Fascism they contested, but generally accepted, the social control role the law assigned them, during the *Ventennio* they not only gave clear signs that they resented this aspect of the law, but they started disregarding it. As psychiatry became central in the moralization campaign launched by Mussolini, several specialists in the discipline indicated that they considered the part of the diagnosis connected with morality as something that belonged to the past. They could not escape obligations to intern those who were referred by families or by the security forces for issues involving morality or sexual behaviour, but in some cases, they took a firm distance and refused to collaborate as much as they could. In this way, it is also possible to interpret the relative absence of diagnosis of moral madness, as it was seen to be a symbol of the role psychiatrists were now rejecting. Their refusal to keep three out of five homosexual patients inside the asylum or to consider them socially dangerous testifies to a stubborn defence of psychiatrists' professional ethics and of their autonomy of thought.

Santa Maria della Pietà's directors were eager to prove that they insisted on conforming to fascist rites and directives, but at a second look, this was a way to avoid closer, more in-depth intrusions. Appearances were spotless, so that the institution seemed perfectly in line with central power's expectations. What went on within the asylum walls, however, was considerably non-aligned. As mentioned earlier, this gap between the regime's coercion and the Italian people's consent is key to understanding how Fascism operated and how its orders were, or were not, implemented.[106] Santa Maria della Pietà is emblematic of the gap between impositions from above and how they were translated into practice. Italians were used to it. At a local level, under the appearance of strict discipline, parades, displays of fascist symbols, administrators enjoyed a considerable degree of freedom in carrying out their duties. It was the price the regime paid to the localities. By guaranteeing space for movement, the regime expected loyalty and political alignment, and conceded non-interference and unquestionable authority. Italians at the time were used to this distance between appearances and the essence of things, as Corner points out.[107] Nationally, people were accustomed to local chiefs not submitting to the central power's directives and taking their own initiatives. The fascist government never completely succeeded in bending provinces, with their old and multilayered structures of power, to its directives. As observed by Guido Melis, when he considered the difficult and contradictory rapport between central government and various local institutions, such as regional chambers of commerce,

> Certainly, the regime kept trying for twenty years to succeed in a gigantic operation, that of modelling society so that it would follow its project of national political mobilization: uniforms, fez, badges, boots, martial hymns, big and small parades, local district groups, sport, cheap rhetoric, the myth of the new man. But at the same time, almost immediately it adapted to compromise, to the perpetuation of the old world.[108]

Something similar happened with regard to psychiatric hospitals, which were asked for obedience at a formal level and were left relatively free in exchange. Non-alignment by the Santa Maria della Pietà director might not have surprised any of the doctors and nurses. In fact, the indication from the Rome asylum is that psychiatrists were aware of government directives, received regular updates on them and continued adopting the procedures and the diagnostic definitions of their choice. Nobody appears to have been reprimanded for not having conformed with the instructions to staff issued in the years of the regime. In other words, Santa Maria della Pietà was perceived, by doctors who worked there, as a relatively safe place for quiet dissent.

4

The Florence asylum, San Salvi:
Precarious balance

Florence has long enjoyed an international reputation in terms of psychiatric theory and practice. Vincenzo Chiarugi (1759–1820), considered to be the founder of the discipline in Italy, was born there. The city was ahead also in introducing the teaching of psychiatry at university in 1802, while the rest of the Italian universities had to wait at least another half a century for these developments.

During the fascist regime, the city population was expanding. From a population of 247,455 residents in 1921, ten years later it had reached 305,447, according to the calculations of the 1931 census.[1] Florence was a small town by Italian standards of the time, compared to Rome, which in 1931 had almost a million residents, but its cultural significance made it more relevant than its many Italian equivalents, during the *Ventennio* and in subsequent decades.[2] It had a lively and large community of artists and intellectuals, many of whom were foreign, and it had been the capital of Italy, although for a very short time.[3] Even in terms of psychiatric care, its asylum was different from most Italian asylums and had some specific peculiarities, as the chapter shows. To underline the continuity with the illustrious Florentine past, it was named after Vincenzo Chiarugi in 1924.

Brief history of the institution

Florence's old asylum, located in the San Bonifazio hospital from 1788, was substituted by a totally new one, inaugurated in 1891.[4] It was built in an area called San Salvi, now part of Florence but at the time just outside the town. In 1895, the provincial administration enriched it with an additional building to host the Institute of Superior Studies of Psychiatry, later simply known as the psychiatric clinic or just the clinic, used for teaching purposes and as the asylum psychiatric hospital observation unit. Patients referred to the asylum were admitted here first, and after a period of observation, they were either interned in the asylum of the province of residence or discharged. The clinic also comprised another building where there was a scientific laboratory. From an administrative point of view, it depended on the university, while the asylum depended on the province.

As mentioned earlier, the Florence asylum differed from most Italian mental health institutions in some ways. The first was that asylums in Italy were usually housed in old convents or general hospitals that would later be transformed and expanded but always retained their main original structure. San Salvi, like Santa Maria della Pietà and a few other asylums in Italy, was built specifically for its purpose and was planned by a group of experts led by psychiatrist Augusto Tamburini. Secondly, the fact that it comprised a university clinic, functioning as a relatively independent observation unit, put it in a small minority of Italian psychiatric institutions. Most asylums in Italy had a dedicated pavilion or section for patient observation that was part of the asylum. Usually, during internment, patients could be sent to a nearby hospital for specific study purposes but only for a very short time, as we have seen at Santa Maria della Pietà. In Florence, the clinic had a primarily didactic role, but it was also in charge of assessing whether a person referred to the psychiatric system was worthy of internment or not. The standard observation period functioned as a learning process for future psychiatrists and in fact some patients could be called back from the San Salvi asylum to the clinic when they were considered 'interesting', so that they could be observed for scientific purposes by students and clinic doctors alike. This constitutes an interesting point of contact between theory and practice. It allowed theoreticians to examine and study patients, sometimes over a prolonged period, something that had obvious advantages for them, as it allowed for a more in-depth analysis of each patient.[5] The parallel existence of these two relatively independent entities in the same premises produced medical notes written by two different teams of professionals. This unusual situation allows historians to analyse similarities and discrepancies between the academic and the medical psychiatric approach.

Fascist times: The asylum structure, its directors and staff

The asylum structure consisted of a central body where the administration offices, the director's office and main services were located, surrounded by buildings where patients were housed. These were grouped according to their behaviour, as has been noted, not necessarily on the basis of their pathology.[6] The calm and well-behaved patients were kept closer to the central building while the most agitated, dirty and dangerous ones were located further afield. In defiance of good sense, which would have called for more difficult patients to be nearer health care workers, the pavilions' disposition seems to reflect the Catholic concept by which correct conduct is prized with proximity to God, the centre of the universe, while those who sin and misbehave are condemned to be the most distant from him. It illustrates well the punitive feature that characterized mental health institutions in the past. The director of the clinic, named *Sopraintendente*, was also in charge of the *pensionario*, where paying patients were hosted, while the hospital in the nearby village of Castel Pulci that functioned as a hospice came under the jurisdiction of the asylum director.

Donatella Lippi indicates that no major structural changes took place between the original plan and the following years, up until the 1930s.[7] During Fascism, she adds, there were some minor changes in line with regime policies. As observed earlier, the name Vincenzo Chiarugi was given to the institution in 1924, in line with the regime's insistence on the need to celebrate national history and illustrious Italian personalities, although people continued to refer to the institution as San Salvi. A cinema for patients was built, although it was frequently used for *adunate*, mass gatherings, and to host nurses' teaching sessions. Due to the constant increase of the interned population, there were some small but necessary expansions. Patients affected by tuberculosis were isolated in a new pavilion from 1936, those affected by post-Parkinson's disease encephalitis from 1937. The C.I.M., *Centro di Igiene e Profilassi Mentale*, Centre for Mental Hygiene and Prophylaxis, aimed at providing home care and carrying out prevention work, was officially inaugurated in 1939, although a health care drop-in centre, called *dispensario*, offering this type of service had been operational since 1866.

It is through Gino Simonelli's words that we have a picture of what San Salvi was like at the end of the fascist years, when he was its director. In 1939 he wrote an article on the institution's history upon the request of Carlo Ferrio, who needed background information for an essay he was writing for the *Annales médico-psychologiques*.[8] In this obviously edulcorated account, Simonelli remarked that the combined clinic and asylum 'allowed the San Salvi Psychiatric Institute, as a whole, to carry out fertile scientific and hospital related activity'.[9] He stressed that the hospital had provided a first career step for a number of psychiatrists who went on to take important roles in asylums nationwide, such as Ernesto

Lugaro.[10] Simonelli added that initially the morphological approach prevailed, while in the late 1930s the biological, that is, immunological and biochemical, studies had significantly increased. The director was eager to emphasize that constant scientific updating was in place and that Lombrosian morphological examination was gradually leaving space for other types of patient observation and psychiatric care.

Beyond the proud and official recognition of San Salvi's merits, Simonelli had to admit that it was originally created for six hundred patients, but in 1939 it held a population of 1,700 with a capacity for 1,900 beds. The Castel Pulci branch, for long-stay chronic and non-dangerous patients, could host up to five hundred people. The total number of patients in 1939 was therefore 2,200, a very high figure considering the initial declared capacity, but not as dramatic as in Santa Maria della Pietà, where the number of interned people reached figures that were almost four times higher than the stated capacity of the institution. Simonelli duly listed all the expansions that had taken place in the previous decades and during his direction, to show that some measures were adopted to solve the problem of overcrowding. In the article, he also announced his intention to expand the structure further, to include a department for so-called *nervosi*, the 'nervous' patients, which referred to those affected by neurological conditions, while other projects were being evaluated. He wrote of the innovative aspects linked with therapeutic approaches in use at San Salvi, adding that no-restraint was the 'absolute norm', together with individually tailored therapeutic approaches and ergotherapy, while modern cures for schizophrenia were being experimented with. Patient turnover, indicating the number of internments and releases, was considered very high. The director indicated that between 1934 and 1938 the percentage of those discharged was between 43 and 48 per cent. He underlined that early release was favoured at San Salvi, and that patients were followed during their first period at home. He portrayed the hygienic conditions of the institution as 'excellent', although, as observed later, he lamented several problems from this point of view in his direct correspondence with the provincial authority.[11] He also described how staff was deployed. By the time Simonelli's article was drafted, the clinic had one director and four doctors. There were two doctors in charge of encephalitic patients. The asylum had one director, ten ordinary doctors plus three extra-staff doctors. In another article he wrote for a local magazine, Simonelli added that the *dispensari*, later called C.I.M., provided home care to two thousand patients, a result he could rightly be proud of.[12]

Analysing some aspects of the procedures of the Florence institution, it is possible to say that both the asylum and the clinic enjoyed an unrivalled reputation and at the same time they were suffocated by it. In some ways, the institution was characterized by conformity with the past and a strong commitment to keep alive its prestigious tradition. For instance, as Lippi points out, Tanzi's nosological categories, a focus of his 1905 book *Trattato delle Malattie Mentali*,[13] were adopted for many years after his direction and remained almost unvaried. Inspired by Kraepelin, Tanzi had a slightly personal approach to Kraepelian theory and thought that its rigid symptomatic categorization criteria left some pathologies out of the picture. He therefore adapted Kraepelin's theories because he believed it was necessary to combine the observation and categorization of the symptoms with an in-depth anatomical examination. This approach would allow for an identification of the organ where the disease was thought to reside and the nature of the illness. Tanzi also insisted on the need to distinguish between external and internal causes of psychiatric conditions, which meant that he thought the social environment, life conditions and similar external factors played a part in the mental well-being of an individual. As meticulously reconstructed by Lippi in her detailed monograph on San Salvi, Tanzi was tied to a traditional therapeutic approach based on medicines and hydrotherapy, such as warm baths to calm agitated patients. Warm baths with mercury and iodine, later substituted by arsenic, were utilized on progressive paralysis as well. Opium and morphine were used in severe cases of agitation, strychnine was administered after fits. For pellagra a rich and varied diet was prescribed, although at a terminal stage it probably had little impact. In terms of shock therapies, prior to electro-shock, diffused pus infections were induced by injections of tuberculin and oil of turpentine, and malariotherapy was widely used. Lippi observes that in the clinic too there was a fundamental continuity with the past, without major changes even in diagnostic terminology.

Despite the weight of tradition, which resulted in conservative attitudes towards therapies and diagnoses, there were some openings to modern ideas and approaches, such as no-restraint, ergotherapy, early release, home care and prevention. These aspects made San Salvi famous throughout the country and ahead of the times in many ways. Together with the deployment of old-school remedies, medicines and approaches, there was systematic research on new pharmaceutical treatments. For instance, fever fits were also induced as a cure for progressive paralysis, for certain psychosis induced by syphilis and for catatonic schizophrenia, something that at the time was regarded as innovative. As mentioned earlier, the C.I.M., *Centro di Igiene e Profilassi Mentale*, provided home care, offered drop-in consultations and carried out prevention work from very early on, compared with the rest of Italy, and constituted a clear sign of openness to modern approaches.

Given its role and reputation, it comes as no surprise that San Salvi had a long history of differences and tension with the provincial authority it depended upon. This aspect became extreme at the turn of the century, when Tanzi was in charge of both asylum and clinic. Being one of the most authoritative names in Italian psychiatry, he made his voice regularly heard, mostly to complain about interference on the part of the province. He had insisted he had the right to nominate his direct assistants in total autonomy and had rejected or harshly criticized the province's requests on several occasions. The Florence provincial authority had often responded with acrimony, contesting or not approving several of his projects, including that of expanding the clinic. Besides, bypassing Tanzi, the province had placed surplus patients in the nearby asylum in Volterra, for instance, disregarding his advice to expand San Salvi's capacity.

In 1931, after Tanzi's decision to remain in office as the director of the asylum alone, Mario Zalla (1883–1960) took over the position of director of the clinic. He is generally considered to be a follower of Tanzi, although he also tried to implement changes. A good part of his activity was dedicated to attempts to institutionalize a separation between psychiatric and neurological patients, in line with the increased importance that neurology was given in the fascist years, combined with the felt necessity to differentiate it from psychiatry, emphasizing its specificities. He anticipated the need to create an independent and isolated neuropathological department, which was officially inaugurated in 1940, but was already functioning in 1938. In addition, he intensified extra-hospital care and prevention services. Zalla remained in office as director of the clinic until 1953.

There is a longer list of directors for the asylum. After Tanzi's resignation in 1903, when he decided to remain in charge of the clinic alone, Giuseppe Bosi remained in office until 1905. After him, Raffaelo Gucci took over for just a year and then Paolo Amaldi (1865–1956) accepted the position of asylum director in 1906 and remained in office until 1937. Amaldi intensified ergotherapy, something Tanzi had strongly believed in, but introduced few changes to it. He ensured that semi-agitated patients were also involved in it, and he expanded it to include several manual jobs, from carpentry to shoe-mending for men, from embroidery to cloth-mending for women. Importantly, he allowed for work to take place inside the pavilions as well, transforming them from places of idleness and boredom into spaces of activity, where female and male patients could work together. Amaldi was also particularly in favour of no-restraint. He deployed part of the money coming from ergotherapy work to buy books for the internal patient library. Under his direction, the nurses' training school was founded. He wanted to separate further the clinic and the asylum, so that one figure only, the asylum director, would emerge as the point of reference for the province.

After him, from 1937 to 1957, Gino Simonelli was the director of the asylum, covering the final years of the *Ventennio*, the war years and the first years of the post-war period. He tried to update the hospital equipment, buying new X-ray and electroencephalogram devices, and employed a teacher trained for special needs children in the patient school for minors on a permanent basis. As the available San Salvi asylum documentation only covers the years 1935 and then from 1937 onwards, Simonelli is the best documented of the two asylum directors of the fascist years, whereas Amaldi is documented only by files for one year of his time in office, 1935. This analysis therefore concentrates on the last part of the fascist regime.

Simonelli was strongly in favour of home care from the very start. In a report to the head of the province dated 1939, he emphasized that, although he agreed in principle with the fact that patients cured at home were costly to the local administration because they received a subsidy, he argued that they made the number of internees decrease, thus saving public funding.[14] He therefore saw an expansion of the *dispensario* services as positive and strategic, both from a medical and economical point of view. However, during Fascism, despite the San Salvi director's opinion, its funding was reduced and home visits were no longer offered to patients.[15] Evidently, the regime did not share the same commitment to early release for psychiatric patients and invested in expanding mental health institutions, so that internments could increase. It is a further tangible proof of the discrepancy of views on the role of psychiatry, between medical professionals and fascist authorities. The latter thought of asylums as isolation and detention centres, where social misfits could be kept distant from society, while doctors kept insisting on the medical and therapeutic function of mental health institutions and those who worked in them, emphasizing the necessity to reinsert psychiatric patients in society.

Simonelli believed there was room for improvement on many fronts. He must have been aware of the low professional standards, not just from an ethical point of view but from the point of view of medical knowledge too, since he asked the head of the province, who accepted his request, to prolong the nurses' training courses. From one year, nurses' training was extended to two years and included anatomy, physiology and pathology. Like at Santa Maria della Pietà, staff malpractice was a constant presence, as can be seen in the director's correspondence files. Many nurses were found asleep while on duty, they did not submit a doctor's certificate when taking sick leave and were often reprimanded because they arrived late for work. They also committed petty crime such as theft. On 11 May 1943, for example, it was reported that some of the staff had systematically removed patients' shoe-soles, presumably to sell them outside.[16]

Aggressive or exploitative behaviour of nurses towards patients was also denounced. In 1935 a nurse was accused of mishandling a patient, mimicking a kick in his backside, while another was caught selling cigar stubs to internees.[17] In 1939, the director signalled more serious misbehaviour and he wrote to the provincial authority to say he was convinced that some nurses took medicines from the pharmacy for their friends' use.[18] Like at Santa Maria della Pietà, malpractice was such an ingrained and frequent problem that in 1943 it was necessary to call for an amnesty for personnel. However, both the nature and quantity of episodes reported and reprimanded is lower compared with what went on at Santa Maria della Pietà, but it is difficult to assess whether this depended upon less surveillance, an overall higher level of staff ethics or lack of documentation.[19]

The most interesting case of San Salvi staff misbehaviour, for the purposes of this research, is an event that generated an internal inquiry in 1942. Two nurses were reported to have bartered cigarettes to two underage patients, in exchange for bread.[20] The fact was later dismissed as the statements were changed after the first official disciplinary hearing. However, the director wrote to the head of personnel saying he was convinced that this was what had really happened. Interestingly, one of the two nurses who acted as informants underlined in his statement that he thought the evident intimacy between the two members of staff and the two patients was problematic, to the extent that he recommended that the two boys be kept in isolation.[21] Evidently, distance from patients was considered an essential part of professional good conduct, but the suggestion that the two underage patients should be punished for excessive intimacy with nurses seems to imply a hidden accusation of them having solicited it and seems motivated by a suspected homosexual attraction on the part of the boys for the nurses in question. Documentation does not reveal if the director ordered a punishment for them or not. However, it is relevant to note that nurses in this instance proposed disciplinary action for supposed intimacy between individuals of the same sex. Unfortunately, the Florence asylum medical files do not contain nurses' daily reports on patients, as I discuss later, so this is one of the very few instances in which we can deduce what the nurses said and did at San Salvi.

Contrary to its illustrious tradition and to what might be expected by a university psychiatric clinic and annexed asylum, the language used to describe patients was often very crude. Especially when talking about women under observation, the San Salvi clinic professors used terms that were heavy and offensive even by the standards of that time. P.C., born in 1923 and admitted on 28 July 1941, was a regular morphine user. She was described as 'stupid'. A.O., born in 1915, admitted for the first time on 29 June 1941, also a morphine user, was defined '*tipaccio slavo*', nasty Slav character and '*robaccia*', trash.[22] The asylum files disclose a similarly abusive language. B.U. was described in the medical notes as a 'moral deficient who would be better taken out of circulation for public peace and safety'.[23] Another interned patient, admitted for moral imbecility, was said to be 'good at doing nothing good'.[24] For G.D., an underage boy admitted for perversion of character, psychiatrists used terms such as '*supermascalzone* [very nasty character], thief, bossy, perfectly amoral. Any pedagogical attempt is useless apart from … kicks in the ass!'.[25] In this respect, San Salvi, both the clinic and the mental health hospital, greatly differs from Santa Maria della Pietà and defies expectations. The doctors' expressions contradict the hospital director's best efforts to give dignity to the institution and to emphasize the importance of its scientific and care role.

The Florence psychiatric institution's particular situation that saw two centres of power, the hospital and the clinic, seems to have enhanced the asylum director's awareness that he needed to continually re-assert his authority, defining his sphere of intervention and that of others. The available archival documentation allows us to frame the underlying constant tensions in this sense, alongside a persistent spirit of collaboration and complicity. In addition, the dialogue between security forces, local government, fascist authorities, families and the director of San Salvi hospital reveals a formal, diplomatic, yet very tense and precarious balance. As all these institutions exerted close vigilance over what the others were doing or intending to do, it is relevant to comment on their exchange of correspondence as it is emblematic of how decisions were taken, how impositions were rejected or discussed, who backed whom in this complex system of strategic alliances.

The intricate maze of messages between the major players involved in psychiatric care and its administration, such as the provincial administration, the *Prefettura*, the PNF and other fascist authorities, together with some of the San Salvi directors' answers to these pressures, is of fundamental importance. In this sense, San Salvi's archival documentation offers a unique portrayal of the tensions and the conflicts of power in place at the time, the asylum director's constant battle to retain autonomy, prestige and authority, contrary to the ways other institutional players increasingly looked upon psychiatry.

It is possible to reconstruct the first level of pressure exerted on the director by fascist organizations, the PNF and various figures of authority embodying the central government. As we have seen, the fascist regime wanted to ensure that every Italian asylum was moving towards a total *fascistizzazione*. The director was constantly reminded that San Salvi had to conform to the party's directives. Solicited also by the provincial authority in this sense, Amaldi asked staff to remember that all employees were required to be present at mass fascist gatherings in Florence.[26] A few months later he provided the federal secretary of the party with a list of those who could not attend one such gathering because they were in service at the asylum, so that those who were absent because of their reluctance to participate would be known to fascist authorities, a gesture of total collaboration with fascist authorities.[27]

The voice of the dictatorship could be heard through the *Prefettura* as well. In 1938 the *Prefetto* reminded the asylum director that the use of the third-person singular *Lei* for the courtesy form was officially banned and that the correct way to address employees was by using the second-person plural *Voi*.[28] The director's reply is not available, but he probably accepted it as the files prove that he transmitted these directives to staff. During the war years, a stamp with Mussolini's intimation '*Vincere!*' (Win!) was even put on most official correspondence from the asylum director and administrative department and Paolo Amaldi expressed in writing his elation when Ethiopia was declared Italian.[29] Therefore, at a formal level, both Amaldi and Simonelli were extremely zealous in following party impositions. Genuinely felt or not, these expressions of fascist faith were probably aimed at keeping the authorities satisfied that San Salvi was 'marching' in the right direction.

However, this was obviously not sufficient to satisfy the authorities. There is correspondence that testifies to pressures from fascist organizations or individuals in order to obtain special treatment, favours and promotions. For instance, on 28 February 1939 the *Fiduciario Provinciale dell'Associazione Pubblico Impiego*, head of the Fascist Province Association of Public Employment, wrote to the head of Personnel, who forwarded the request to the director, asking him to employ a particular person of undoubted fascist belief.[30] On another occasion, the director reassured a Consul that his letter 'about the Black Shirt B.L. of Florence [had] been transmitted' to the competent figure of authority in the asylum Personnel Office.[31] The Fascist Association for Employment in the Public Sector made its voice heard too.[32] In a letter dated 11 July 1934, it reminded the asylum director that fascists should be taken into special consideration with regard to career advancement. In a smaller and provincial context, nepotistic requests were probably not unusual. But here they seem to be a way to test to what extent the director was prepared to accommodate demands as well. In Florence's case, there was a higher level of pressure compared to Santa Maria della Pietà in this sense, something that fits with the picture given by several historians who examined how Fascism functioned at a local and regional level.[33]

Only on a few occasions did the director seem to have resisted external interference of this type. For instance, on 23 June 1938 the Rovigo *Fasci* Federation, coordinating the local branches of the fascist party in the small town, asked to see a copy of the internal regulations and a map of the hospital, to which Simonelli drily replied that he could not as they were under revision.[34] However, on the whole, the impression is that directors took it in their stride that to comply with bossy demands and requests of *fascistizzazione* was inescapable. They seem to have regarded it as part of the daily routine during the *Ventennio*, the normal price to pay in order to enjoy a certain amount of power and freedom of movement.

At a second level we find that the security forces, especially the *Prefettura*, maintained constant vigilance in regard to San Salvi and exerted pressure whenever possible. This comes as no surprise, since the role of psychiatry was increasingly thought to be that of detention of individuals perceived as a social threat. Consequently, the security forces felt entitled to enter the management of asylums as they saw these institutions as tools of their coercive and punitive functions.[35] For example, on 25 February 1939 the Florence *Prefettura* demanded to know what the San Salvi doctor/patient ratio was, commenting that a similar survey had been launched by the British Medical Association.[36] It is a request that should have come from the province, as it pertained to the functions of the asylum, and had little to do with security issues. On 6 March 1939 the director replied that there were eleven doctors plus three extra staff doctors and a capacity of 2,200 patients.[37] It was far higher, he proudly underlined, than at the Banstead asylum, which counted one full-time and six part-time doctors and two assistants for 2,737 patients, or at the Shenley asylum, with one full-time and one part-time doctor and four assistants for 1,555 patients.[38]

With efficiency as a pretext, the *Prefettura* seems to have wanted to interfere with internal medical procedures as well. On 23 February 1935, it asked if there were any lethargic encephalitis patients among the interned patients at San Salvi, presumably to ascertain that the request for a special pavilion for this type of patients was justified.[39] It sounds like a way of putting the director's requests and best judgement on trial, since neither the proposed new pavilion nor the allocation of encephalitic patients had anything to do with public order issues.

The same year it sent a note to the director with a request to justify cases of staff dismissal. In both instances, this should have been handled by the province. On 14 June, the director replied briefly and rather bitterly that he never sacked an employee without previous warning and one or more formal reprimands.[40]

Finally, the *Prefettura* showed concern for issues that were more pertinent to its role. For instance, it asked for information on patients that were considered criminals, such as drug users. On 2 October 1935, the director was asked to provide a list of interned patients with a history of drug use for the previous year.[41] From 1938, with the introduction of racial laws in Italy, Simonelli was also expected to provide an updated list of Jewish patients, needed to issue certificates 'to be exhibited for dispositions of a racial nature'. Italian Jews were asked to prove they had never been interned in order to be allowed to flee from Italy.[42] In these cases, the *Prefettura* signalled that in certain cases the asylum and the police were supposed to collaborate, working hand in hand in guaranteeing public order and implementing the law. Perhaps not surprisingly, no similar request was made in regard to homosexual patients, as homosexuality was not outlawed by the Zanardelli Code or by the Rocco Code.

The provincial authority was another major player in this behind-the-scenes battle for power. In fact, the province was in charge of asylums in its geographical area of competence. It handled aspects linked to funding, management and personnel, and checked that wealthy patients' families paid their internment fees. It also ensured that patients who were registered as resident in another provincial authority area of competence would be transferred. It managed the asylum's budget and it had representatives on the asylum's *Consiglio di Amministrazione*, ensuring all operations were conducted in obedience to the law and internal regulations.

As mentioned earlier, the relationship between the San Salvi asylum director and the province was traditionally problematic. A good example of the tensions generated by the interference of the provincial authority into the hospital's routine is given by the following episode. On 10 February 1939, Simonelli had reminded the province of his proposal to create a department for neurological patients in the asylum structure. He had insisted that the department should be managed by the clinic's director, but that the asylum staff could continue to intern those patients who were considered 'interesting' from a scientific point of view. Diagnostic and therapeutic tools could be shared, but competences had to remain separate, he stressed, and the San Salvi asylum had to retain the right to bypass the clinic's authority in studying certain patient pathologies. He concluded by emphasizing the fact that his reservations 'were aimed at safeguarding our hospital's and doctors' prestige'.[43] He was obviously concerned that his sphere of influence could be diminished by new dispositions and at the same time defended the scientific role of the asylum, which he did not want to see reduced to a mere care, or detention, centre, with less status than the clinic. On 16 February 1939, the head of the province approved the creation of a special department in the clinic, for internment and care of *malati nervosi*, ignoring the director's recommendations. This department, the province specified, should be separate and distant from those where mentally ill people were kept and it would shelter only voluntary patients prepared to pay for their own care expenses.[44] The reply from the asylum director arrived promptly, only a few days after this decision was communicated to him. On 25 February, he underlined once again that there was an agreement between him and the clinic director, by which the hospital's doctors had the right to intern neurological patients that interested them and to cure them in full autonomy. Besides, he added, only if and when the *malati nervosi* reached a number that the province considered high enough for them to be split and interned in two sections would it be the asylum director's responsibility to move these patients to other premises.[45] Clearly, he wanted to assert that these patients had to remain within the asylum's control, and did not let any trespassing into his sphere of action go uncommented.

However, the province tried on several occasions to take some of the chronic patients out of the San Salvi asylum, in order to transfer them to the clinic or elsewhere, and the director resisted these plans asserting it was his decision where to allocate them. Presumably the provincial authority thought that chronic patients would be better looked after in the clinic, a structure that did not host so-called 'dangerous' patients. Generally, the province continued to take decisions without consulting the asylum director, implicitly insisting that it could do so, as it had the necessary and sufficient power to go ahead disregarding his judgement and comments. The mental health hospital director always replied that his opinion counted, implying that he was not prepared to silently accept decisions taken by bureaucrats.

In addition, the province frequently reminded the director of his duty to implement PNF directives, meaning that he was accountable to central government through its local authority representatives too. It is difficult for the historian to assess whether these pressures were generated by suspicion that there was a lack of conviction in implementing these directives or whether reminding the medical authorities about duties to Fascism was considered routine practice. The provincial authority also applied pressure so that fascists would be favoured in terms of employment. For instance, in 1939, the province sent a copy of Law

n. 762, of 29 May 1939, which stated that citizens who had been identified as *squadristi*, which meant they had been fascist supporters from the early days, with at least two years' service seniority, had the right to be employed on a permanent basis.[46]

From the documentation available for consultation that starts from 1935, it is possible to see that the directors generally agreed and accepted most of the directives they were given when these involved the introduction of small and superficial behavioural changes to adapt to the fascist new 'rites'. But they were extremely keen to resist interference and to reassert their power. Authorities and institutions were often reminded of their areas of competence. In the Administrative Commission series of documents, there is a file on discussions relating to a reform of staff rules, which is extremely telling of attitudes in this sense.[47] It contains a series of small amendments to the staff regulations that were then in place. There is no mention of major changes, but the director insisted on reformulating certain clauses so that his authority could be reinforced. For instance, Article 23 previously stated that certain administrative decisions could be taken 'having heard the director's informed opinion'. Simonelli asked for it to be reworded into: 'upon the proposal or favourable opinion of the director'.

Both Amaldi and Simonelli often addressed the provincial authorities with requests, focusing on several problems and inadequacies the institution was suffering from, implying there was an unforgivable lack of interest on the part of those who should have been in charge. To quote a few examples, in 1935, Amaldi signalled that the administrative offices were in a state of 'indecent decay', in 1938, Signorelli lamented that in every asylum he had visited there was X-ray equipment, while in Florence there was none.[48] On the same day, he also insisted on the need to modernize the telephone system.[49] The same year he asked for more nursing staff, while in 1939 he alerted the authorities that the male toilets were without water, the basement of a pavilion had damp infiltrations and the heating system in the *Pensionario* was not working properly.[50] That year, he also reminded the province that it would be appropriate 'to elaborate a concrete organisational plan for a Malariotherapy Centre', thus implicitly criticizing the previous absence of a concrete plan.[51] In 1942, he drew the province's attention to the recurring emergency of the seasonal invasion of flies, and he asked for nets to be installed on windows of most rooms and common spaces.[52] The San Salvi location was not particularly salubrious and typhoid infections were a routine problem.[53] Amaldi's and Simonelli's insistence gives us a picture characterized by exasperation, dissatisfaction and the constant demand of recognition.

Simonelli also contested therapeutic impositions. For instance, in 1938 he received a *Circolare* from the direction of the Ministry of Interior, dated 16 October, where the treatment of precocious dementia via fits induced by Cardiazol or via glycaemic coma was said to have had positive effects.[54] He was prudent, when writing to the provincial authority, and made it clear he had reservations. In 1939, he replied to the head of the province, who had presumably raised cost issues involved in these therapies, repeating that it was too early to express a judgement, as this type of therapeutic intervention had been introduced so recently.[55] Simonelli, as shown earlier in this chapter, was very interested in other therapies and approaches, but here he was stating that judgements in this area were his competence alone.

In fighting a fierce daily battle to reinstate their authority, the San Salvi asylum directors seem to have spent a considerable amount of time following every minute aspect of the institution's daily routine, from purchases to repairs, from insurance policy renewals to staff dismissals. It is as if they insisted in following everything, with the precise aim to demonstrate that they were in charge of everything and therefore could not easily be pushed aside or ignored. They certainly appear much more concerned about losing power and authority than their Roman counterparts.

Specific methodological issues

Research in Florence took longer than expected because San Salvi's archival materials are split in two. Files referring to patients discharged before 1940 are kept at the State Archives, whereas files of those discharged afterwards are held at the old San Salvi premises, in a locked room next to the university library.[56] The State Archives collection is under the jurisdiction of the *Sovrintendenza Archivistica*, the branch of the Ministry of Culture that supervises state-owned public archives and libraries, while the other part of the documentation is administered by USL, equivalent to the NHS. This meant double bureaucratic procedures. Although there are several limitations, mostly due to lack of funding and staff, and almost all the San Salvi materials are out of catalogue and have to be ordered separately by a dedicated archivist, the State Archives have specialized staff and fixed opening hours, a system of ordering files to view is in place and consultation is guaranteed. A different situation operated, at the time of consultation, for the archival collection kept at San Salvi, which was very difficult to access. Bureaucracy was exceedingly time-consuming in this case, but even after having fulfilled all obligations in this sense, the staff simply was not available to open the locked room and supervise my consultation. When an appointment was finally taken, thanks to a volunteer, it was clear that many documents were missing and that patient files in the available folders were not always ordered alphabetically. In addition, time to conduct research in the archives in the old San Salvi premises was extremely limited and, given the lack of cataloguing order, it was impossible to search in detail.

To start with, I consulted all available Admissions Registers held at the State Archives for the *Ventennio*.[57] Through these, I identified patients with diagnoses that were relevant to my study, following the criteria explained in the introduction. A total of forty-one patient files were requested, thirty-four at the State Archives, of which twenty-three were found and consulted, and seven at San Salvi, where only one file could be found. An additional file was requested after consulting the clinic's documentation (see later). Out of the forty-one asylum files requested, the diagnosis that was utilized most was that of moral madness (nineteen cases), in its various guises, such as moral imbecility, deficiency, mental deficiency or weakness, that is, frenasthenia. The second most utilized diagnosis was that of character perversion, used for nine cases in total, followed by immorality, diagnosed for four patients. Other diagnoses analysed are: character anomaly (three cases, one of them described as serious behavioural anomalies), degenerative imbecility (one case), manic excitement (one case), degenerative psychosis (one case), obsessive psychosis (one case), state of excitement (two cases). In the files consulted, mention of homosexuality appears only inside the patient file and not in the diagnosis marked on the Admissions Register or on the file's cover. The diagnosis of the patient identified through the clinic's documentation was initially '*acromegalia*' followed by 'psychic infantilism', which in the subsequent hospital file became dangerous dementia.

I also examined all available files in the series named *Direzione: Affari Diversi*. As mentioned earlier, these refer to the years 1935 and from 1937 onwards. I consulted files up to 1943. They contain official correspondence on the whole, between the director, the provincial authority, the *Prefettura* and various representatives of organizations linked to the fascist regime. They include correspondence from the director to service providers, insurers and so forth.

For a separate series of files, simply called *Commissione Amministrativa*, Administrative Commission, there is a digitalized index, but unfortunately the titles of the files give very little idea of what they contain or refer to. I therefore requested anything that seemed even vaguely relevant. Out of the forty-nine files I asked to consult, forty-five were located. Most of the files refer to personnel issues, such as promotions, early retirement and overtime pay. Others relate to patient movement to home care or to other asylums. Very few document disciplinary procedures against members of staff, while several files contain documents on accidents that took place on the San Salvi premises, purchases, insurance policies and similar issues. A very promising file entitled *Regolamento organico e speciale: riforma, affari relativi 1920–1927*, Special and Ordinary Staff Regulations: Reform and pertinent matters 1920–7, refers only to issues such as promotions, maternity leave provisions, requests for early retirement and similar aspects, but never mentions professional conduct or care directives.[58] However, it contains some interesting material, especially on the ratio of doctors to patients and on the nurses' training programmes. Both are discussed in the paragraph on San Salvi's structure and organization during Fascism. In this archival material series, there is also some evidence of pressure applied on the director from various institutions, and I mention them in the relevant part of this chapter.

Much later, when I thought that my archival research in Florence was concluded, I discovered that the town's State Archives held another area of documentation that sounded very relevant. I learnt that there is a collection of files entitled *Storie Cliniche dei Ricoverati*, Interned Patients' Clinical Histories, on patients who were referred to the clinic for observation. Most of these patients were discharged after the period of observation, while some of them were 'transferred', which meant interned either at San Salvi or elsewhere. As people referred for observation and then discharged exceeded by far those who were interned, this part of the collection is vast. Therefore, I decided to sample-search. I consulted files referring to men and women referred to the San Salvi clinic for the years between 1924 and 1939.[59] There is no register available for admissions to the clinic, so I had to go through each individual file to see what each patient was referred for. Although some folders indicate on the cover that they refer to dead patients, I could not find the date of death in the patients' individual files. I deduced these were pre-printed file binders used by the clinic staff to hold files of patients under observation. As explained earlier, out of all the clinic files that belong to this archival series and that I consulted, only one fell into a diagnostic category that looked relevant to this research, although it did not fit the list of diagnoses I examined.

Interestingly, since the general practitioner requiring internment was asked to fill in a form, the *Modula Informativa*, rather than simply write a short certificate, it is possible to compare diagnoses and terminology deployed by doctors with different specializations when describing the same patient.

Often there were substantial discrepancies between the diagnosis assigned by the general practitioner, by the clinic and by the San Salvi asylum specialists. G.D., for instance, was referred a first time to the psychiatric system because, according to the police, he was 'affected by fixed ideas of kleptomania'.[60] The *Modula Informativa* confirmed the same diagnosis, on 1 May 1935, the day of the police statement, adding he was 'restless, irascible, with fixed ideas. He has a tendency to steal. Diagnosis: fixed ideas. Kleptomania.' However, the San Salvi psychiatrist gave him a diagnosis of 'character perversion', specifying he was a constitutionally immoral individual, revealing an approach that focused on morality. A later *Modula Informativa*, relating to a subsequent internment of the same person, stated: 'He is very agitated [unreadable word], hallucinated; he throws himself against his mother in a threatening way. Diagnosis: mental confusion, serious neurasthenia.' On another previous internment, the *Modula Informativa* dated 23 March 1935 stated that G.D. was affected by 'manic-depressive psychosis'.

Homosexual patients

There are only a few cases of homosexual patients being interned at San Salvi, three in total. Like at Santa Maria della Pietà, their homosexuality appears inside their file for two of them and is not mentioned in their diagnosis. The only case where 'perversion' was mentioned in the diagnosis is that of a man referred to the asylum through the legal system.

The first of the three cases is P.M., a young woman interned three times, the first time in 1920, at the age of 16, for moral and intellectual imbecility.[61] Documentation reveals there was a previous internment in the criminal asylum of Aversa, in 1919, but no detail on this is present in her San Salvi file. Her notes reveal a series of aspects that are familiar, as it has been observed in the Rome and several other Italian asylums.[62] P.M. was a rebellious girl, described as impulsive and 'erotic', who liked drinking alcoholic beverages and had lost her virginity to a man at an early age. She also admitted that she did not feel like working, another worrying sign of degeneration for psychiatrists at the time, as historians have pointed out.[63]

However, in this case, the usual pathologization of a stubborn, undisciplined and sexually precocious girl was accompanied by an important additional comment: P.M. had marked sexual impulses towards women. The girl was said not to deny her past sexual rapport with a man, and at the same time she scandalously admitted liking alcohol and having 'homosexual inclinations', adding they were part of her personality. Prior to internment, her mother had sent her to the countryside, to be looked after by a married woman who regularly informed her on the girl's behaviour. Probably it was both a punitive measure and a decision taken to hide a scandalous relative. The woman, however, repeatedly wrote she was unhappy taking responsibility for the girl and expressed her discontent on more than one occasion. Her correspondence, addressed to P.M.'s mother, is part of the patient's file, presumably because it was handed over by the recipient to the hospital's medical staff as proof of the patient's mental condition. The carer wrote largely to complain that P.M. was stubborn, that she clearly refused to follow any discipline and wanted to do as she pleased. In addition, the woman reported that she was seeing a boy with whom she regularly went out. The girl told him of her previous internment, the woman added, but he did not seem to mind much. The young man, when confronted about the seriousness of his intentions, scandalously replied that for the moment he only intended 'to make love'. According to the woman's reports, P.M.'s unruly and promiscuous behaviour had drawn the attention of the village parish priest, who complained about the indecency of her conduct. As a result, the woman lamented that nobody in the entire village wanted to go near the girl.

The mother's replies to these reports are not in the file. However, she wrote to the director and these letters were attached to the medical documentation. While the woman in the countryside described the current situation, P.M.'s mother offered an account of the girl's background. She gave a very bleak picture of her daughter, saying she had been insubordinate and stubborn from an early age, and she had suffered from frequent hallucinations where she heard voices ordering her to poison her mother. She added that she was expelled from the religious school where she studied because she had fallen in love with one of the nuns. She had already manifested sexual desire for herself and for her female schoolmates from the age of seven or eight – she continued – thus showing sexual precocity, together with sexual inversion, onanism and a tendency to cause scandal. To complete the picture, the mother provided additional information that in her view corroborated her daughter's immorality and degeneration, proving the need for internment. For instance, she wrote that she bit her nails, she was breastfed by an alcoholic woman until she was three or four months old and she ate raw or rotten food. Often, the mother added, P.M. tore her clothes and manifested hatred towards those in charge of looking after her. She had sexual intercourse with both men, even married men, and women. In the past, the reason for her unruly behaviour, her mother reported, was initially ascribed to a malignant spirit and therefore 'she was blessed in church', which might indicate she was subjected to a rite of exorcism as a child.[64] Finally, she had suffered from vaginal infections, the woman added, showing how she connected a diseased womb with a mental condition, in accordance with the nineteenth-century belief that saw the uterus as the organ responsible for the development of hysteria.[65]

The girl's mother concluded by reporting that her family doctor had initially diagnosed her daughter with nervous hysteria. However, the *Modula Informativa* of 19 July 1920 only stated that the girl had an anomalous character, it confirmed she had suffered from hallucinations, had manifested suicidal intentions and was thought to be a liar, ending with a diagnosis of constitutional immorality. Hysteria, homosexuality, sexual precocity and scandal did not appear in the G.P. notes. It is interesting to see how the patient's mother pulled all the known triggers to guarantee that her daughter would be interned, including hysteria, a diagnosis that during Fascism was becoming obsolete, but that clearly survived in popular belief as a women's condition worthy of psychiatric care.

The San Salvi psychiatrist observed that P.M. could be jealous, violent, stubborn, slandering and fickle, naughty and *capricciosissima*, very unruly. He confirmed her tendencies to suicide and added she was thought to be a liar. The patient's statement dated 22 August 1920, where she wrote she had repented and she would behave better once discharged, was dismissed as a lie and proof of cynicism. P.M. was reported to have stated that 'she liked alcoholic drinks very much [underlined in the original text]' and she recognized she did not like working. Coming from a family with some genetic degenerative signs, such as a 'nervous' father and a mother who had nine miscarriages of a total of thirteen pregnancies, the girl had wet her bed until the age of twelve, the doctor added, presumably to reinforce the idea of a delay in the evolutionary process connected with an inherited degenerative overall picture. Thanks to indiscipline, she was said to have been repeatedly dismissed from school and from seven religious convents where she was sent to complete her education. While not challenging the words of the girl's mother and caretaker, the hospital doctor added that she had lost her virginity when she was sent to the countryside, to be looked after by a local family. The psychiatrist transcribed the account according to which P.M. left her door ajar so that a man could enter her bedroom, thus soliciting sexual intercourse.

The patient initially showed a challenging attitude towards psychiatrists, confirming aspects of her behaviour that she must have known were considered immoral in a woman, such as admitting she liked drinking alcohol. She was uncooperative towards San Salvi staff and was described as offering little collaboration when she was subjected to the gynaecological visit. Roughly a year after admission, she was still said to exhibit 'disordered behaviour, eroticism, tendencies to obscenity'. The following year the situation had evidently worsened as she was depicted as 'deeply agitated, aggressive, violent'. She then quietened down, although she continued to have some spells of violence.

In 1926, she was admitted again, and she was reported to have said 'she did not know why this internment had been decided, not having committed, in her judgement, anything strange'. Two months later, her family's refusal to take her back and look after her at home triggered violent rage:

As she understood that her mother does not want to collect her, she started to get angry, to quarrel with other female patients, to annoy everybody a thousand times, including the nun in charge of her department. She then rolled on the floor, threatening to break the window glass and to hit the nurses. She is sent to the pavilion for agitated female patients.

Seven months later she was described as calmer, but she was 'still hoping that her mother would come and take her away from the asylum'. When she understood that, once again, this was not going to happen, she had another crisis and was sent to the pavilion for agitated female patients, where she refused to eat for several days.

In this file, we also have the patient's voice, as there are two letters written by her. In one of them, writing from the same pavilion where she was intermittently kept, on 27 December 1926 the girl addressed her thoughts to the senior psychiatrist who was following her case. Stating that she did not feel understood by the San Salvi nurses and nuns, although she conceded they were generally nice to her, she also candidly admitted she could not recognize herself any longer and that she found it difficult to express her feelings:

I am not mad, and neither am I normal ... I am tired of this life that is so painful, so unhappy, like no other ... I am sad and melancholic, I spent my youth so badly [not legible word] of my terrible family who refused to recognise me as part of it and never showed any affection towards me.

P.M. was initially assertive and bold in her statements, defending her lifestyle and choices, and showing a high level of self-awareness. The psychiatric system, her family and carer managed to instil in her the idea that she was 'different', an isolated, not normal individual, with a problem to solve. The complaints she voiced clearly addressed these issues and identified the family as the cause of her rebelliousness and difficult youth. From simple undisciplined behaviour, with an attempt to live her bisexuality freely, the patient had withdrawn into a guilt complex, feeling not understood, abandoned by her family to the psychiatric system, as the last resort of an alternative home care situation had also failed. Her case is a clear example of the damaging consequences internment could have. Her file does not report any cure undertaken. It is possible that she was sedated only when she had violent fits, but otherwise she was probably just kept inside the institution, in the hope that the orderly, disciplined life of the asylum could work as a therapy.

Undoubtedly this case is a further proof of the type of pressure families thought they could exert on a psychiatric institution, which they expected should have a disciplinary role over rebellious individuals when all other punitive measures had proved unsuccessful. At the basis of this case there was family rejection, but, unlike the Santa Maria della Pietà medical staff, the San Salvi psychiatrists following the case were more willing to play the role of moralizing and social control. They did not question the patient's mother and caretaker, they never focused on the problematic mother–daughter relationship and, implicitly, they morally condemned the girl. The medical professionals in this case seem to have accepted working in conjunction with the patient's family to ensure that a scandalous and immoral individual was removed from society.

As sexual desire was considered to be unnatural in women, there are several other cases of 'erotic' women among the diagnoses analysed in the course of research in the San Salvi archives. The case of C.L. bears surprising similarities with the one described above, although homosexuality is missing.[66] Interned in 1926 at the age of twenty-one for moral madness, and then again in 1927, C.L. showed sexual precocity, rebelliousness, *capricciosità*. She was said to be disrespectful, to reject her family and to be considered scandalous by her entire village, together with being a liar. She was also totally uninterested in work, not even in domestic tasks, a signal usually interpreted as a worrying refusal of a woman's role in society. She accused her father of having sent her to the asylum because she refused to marry the man he had chosen for her, exactly like P.M. had accused her mother of having sent her away and then to the asylum because of her non-conforming behaviour.

The second case is that of D.M., a young woman interned in 1917 at the age of seventeen.[67] She was described as erotic and as a person with a total absence of moral sense. For these reasons, she 'committed dishonest acts, reporting them with no shame. While under observation, she was said to continually create scandal, giving herself to anyone without shame, even in the open air.' Once interned, she was diagnosed as having intellectual and moral deficiency. She was interned a second time in 1918 and died in hospital in 1931. Her diagnosis belonged to the era before Fascism, but later psychiatrists did not question it nor did they update it, showing how much psychiatric practice during the *Ventennio* still relied on previous theories and approaches.

There is a third case of an erotic girl aged fifteen, documented in the correspondence between San Salvi and the psychiatric hospital San Nicolò, in Siena.[68] R.L., interned there on 16 January 1936 for 'biopathic frenasthenia' was said to show 'alterations of character with amoral and erotic tendencies'. She improved and was judged fit to be discharged, but her mother was not thought to have 'the necessary moral requirements to exercise custody'. Therefore, the Siena asylum director enquired if it would be possible to transfer the girl to an asylum in the Florence province, presumably to keep her far away from her mother's influence. Even the morality of female relatives, when deciding a patient release, was a key issue for San Salvi medical professionals.

These cases aptly illustrate how the Florence psychiatric institution acted as a moralizing and disciplining force. In this sense, at San Salvi there was a strong element of continuity with the past compared with Santa Maria della Pietà, combined with a desire to conform to the new fascist directives in terms of a moralization campaign. It is most significant to note that this moralizing action took place mostly in the presence of female patients.

A thoroughly contrasting attitude was shown when dealing with male homosexuality and immorality. The other two San Salvi files where homosexuality was noted refer to two men. The first one, C.D., was interned in 1927, a month after he was arrested for 'homosexual practices'.[69] On the Admissions Register his internment was motivated by 'perversion' and 'moral madness', while homosexuality was mentioned in his file. He was described as

a deaf-mute man who, in the outside world, lately abandons himself to homosexual practices that brought about his arrest on 1st March. Here [in the asylum] he keeps a calm disposition. He is tidy, works hard and behaves correctly. There would be no reason for him to remain in the asylum.

The last sentence of this statement shows that male homosexuality at San Salvi was not thought to be a sufficient reason for internment. Like at Santa Maria della Pietà, if there was no other aggravating factor, a male homosexual patient was simply declared fit for release. In this case, this is even more important, because here we have a man who was convicted for his homosexuality and was subsequently linked to scandal. In fact, this thirty-three-year-old tailor, married with children, with a level of education judged as high, had been convicted for *oltraggio al pudore*, roughly translatable as indecent behaviour. He was then referred to the asylum by the legal system because his crime was thought to be a consequence of a *vizio di mente*, a mental problem.

The Tribunal's file referring to C.D.'s case is also kept at the Florence State Archives.[70] Unfortunately, it contains little documentation. It shows that on 1 June 1927, the Commander of the *Carabinieri* Headquarters in the village where the man was resident stated that, despite the precarious financial situation of the man's family, which included a deaf-mute daughter and an unemployed third son, with a father who was a builder but was unable to work, C.D. could be looked after at home. In fact, he was described as a good tailor with a considerable income. Clearly security forces thought that C.D.'s income was needed by his family. In other words, for them he would need no particular care, on the contrary he was thought to be fit enough to look after his incapacitated relatives. Even the *Carabinieri* seemed to share the psychiatrists' view that in this case there was no reason to intervene with detention or internment. As observed by Des Dorides, considerations on the economic status of patients were an important factor when deciding on his or her release.[71]

The patient's file shows that on 9 June that year he was handed to his father, who evidently had no moral problem in taking responsibility for his son, even though he had been charged because of his homosexual acts. It further demonstrates that, like in E.C.'s and P.G.B.'s case at Santa Maria della Pietà, sometimes, among the Italian population, same-sex relationships between men were not judged negatively, despite the government's propaganda and moralization campaign. In C.D.'s file there is trace of a second internment, which started on 1 August 1927, but insufficient documentation means it is impossible to understand why he was interned again. Neither the cover of the file nor the Admissions Register show any mention of C.D.'s homosexuality, although it was the reason for his arrest and first internment, but only state his perversion.

The second case where male homosexuality is mentioned is that of D.B.E.[72] Born in 1885, this married cobbler was admitted to San Salvi on 21 May 1938 the first time, then again in 1940 and a third time in 1943. He was described in the Admissions Register as an individual 'affected by a state of excitement in a degenerative psychic constitution'. In his second internment notes, he was said to come from the concentration camp of Manfredonia, a camp in southern Italy where civilians, mostly Jews, Slavs and anti-fascists, were kept.[73] As his surname does not bear direct connection with Jewish or Slav surnames, it is plausible that he was interned because of his anti-fascist opinions or activity. This would also be corroborated by the fact that, once in the asylum, he was reported to have insulted the Italian king and Mussolini, and to have offended figures of authority. On his second internment, he was also diagnosed with paranoid psychosis and was said to have been previously interned in the Nocera Inferiore asylum, a large psychiatric institution in the south of Italy, where he had been transferred from the Volterra asylum, in Tuscany. The patient had clearly spent several years of his life in different psychiatric institutions and detention centres.

In 1939, he was described as 'a subject with a psychic degenerative constitution, unstable in his mood and character', but who 'never committed dangerous acts'. However, few months earlier, he was reported to have tried to commit 'obscene acts on patient M.M.' in the men's toilets. This indicates that at San Salvi, like at Santa Maria della Pietà, homosexuality was not thought to constitute a danger. In this case it was punished. The patient was kept in isolation (*cameretta*) after this episode, but it is not specified for how long. D.B.E. was later described as quarrelsome and chatty, showing excitement and a tendency to suicide, together with having pronounced offensive words towards state authorities. In November 1940, he was said to be trying still to carry out 'libidinous acts on his fellow patients' and for this reason he was transferred to another pavilion. He was also believed to instigate other patients to rebel against the psychiatric hospital staff. However, on the cover of his file, together with a diagnosis of degenerative psychic constitution, alcoholism was marked, but not his homosexuality.

D.B.E. was not considered particularly dangerous and his homosexuality was only mentioned as one of the several aspects of degeneration present in his personality. Like in E.C.'s case, interned at Santa Maria della Pietà, he too was punished for having tried to have sexual rapport with another interned patient. However, apart from this action, the medical staff did not seem to have prescribed any specific therapy, to have carried out close observation or to have judged him as particularly dangerous.

As mentioned earlier, one additional relevant case was found in the *Storie Cliniche dei Ricoverati*, Clinical Histories of Referred Patients' files, which consist of documentation of those who were referred to the Florence psychiatric system. Initially admitted to the clinic, the largest percentage of them was discharged after the observation period. If interned, their patient files were usually sent to the asylum where they were assigned, unless the clinic thought that a particular patient was an 'interesting' case for study purposes. Therefore, this series of documents mostly illustrates cases of those who were not thought to be worthy of internment and is a peculiarity of this institution, San Salvi, where, as seen earlier, the clinic and the asylum co-existed but were separate entities. It also includes several files of men and women who asked to be interned on a voluntary basis and also from this point of view it was important to double-check if there was anyone among them who referred themselves to the psychiatric system to be 'cured' of homosexuality.[74] From my sample-search investigation, nobody appears to have referred themselves to the Florence psychiatric institution for this reason. Some files, like the one examined later, referred to patients who were subsequently interned, but presumably their observation file was kept in the clinic archives much longer for study purposes.

It must be noted that the observation period was often longer at San Salvi than legally prescribed. By law it should not exceed fifteen days, and in special situations it could be extended to thirty, while here the rules were frequently bent, and several patients were kept in the clinic much longer. For instance, Z.T. was admitted to the observation clinic a second time on 6 May 1923 and was under observation until 20 June.[75] It could be read as a sign that the clinic pushed towards gaining more authority in certain instances, ignoring legal impositions and claiming the right to indicate a therapeutic path that did not lean on the nearby asylum. It is a further proof of the delicate existing balance between the two branches of the same psychiatric institution.

In the *Storie Cliniche dei Ricoverati* files I consulted, the word 'degeneration' was never used, and the word 'immorality' was rarely mentioned. Plausibly this means that cases of degeneration and immorality were always interned, so these patient files are held in the main hospital patient files collection. In this series of documents, I found only few cases of moral imbecility, but this definition in one case was connected with a tendency to steal. In the other case the patient, a minor whose father was imprisoned for having killed his wife, the patient's mother, was said to have a 'disposition to violence and depravity', together with being 'very poor in the ethical-moral sphere'.[76] There was one case of moral and intellectual deficiency that described a man who indulged in betting, alcohol and incest.[77] Also, the case defined as 'constitutional immorality and epilepsy' had nothing to do with the patient's sexuality or morality, as it was used to describe a person with bursts of violent anger.[78]

When patients were analysed by the clinic staff from the point of view of their sexuality, some were accused of scandalous behaviour because they had sexual intercourse with anyone, also in the open, such as D.M., a woman whose case I examined earlier because she was interned.[79] There are two mentions of sexual perversion, which turns out to be voyeurism in one instance and exhibitionism in the other.[80] Both cases refer to male patients. The first one was discharged after a few months, while for the other there is no date of release available, but it is plausible that he was discharged after observation, since his file is in the clinic's collection. This would confirm a more lenient attitude towards male patients on morality issues.

In any case, if, as observed earlier, the majority of patients with scandalous behaviour or a sexual dysfunction were interned after observation, the fact that the clinic did not consider any of these cases 'interesting' from a scientific point of view (other than D.M., as the presence of her file in the clinic's documentation seems to suggest, and N.N. on whom I comment later) is very telling and, as noted at Santa Maria della Pietà, in total contradiction with theoretical trends of the time. In fact, while, as previously stated, there was a high degree of scientific theoretical interest in cases of sexual inversion, intersexuality, hermaphroditism and sexual abnormalities, this does not seem to have permeated the San Salvi clinic's daily practice.

In my sample search, I could only find one clinic patient whose sexuality seems to have attracted the medical professionals' attention. N.N., originally a farmer who then became a miner, was diagnosed as having '*acromegalia*. Psycho-infantilism'.[81] This diagnosis was not in my original list, but I decided to look inside his file, as his condition was linked to a glandular dysfunction. N.N. was admitted on 4 July 1918, well before the fascist regime started, at the age of twenty-one. His lack of interest in women was noted during the observation period. In addition, his genitals were defined as 'scarce: small testicles and penis', his secondary sexual traits as 'female-like disposition of body hair'. The patient was also said to have a tendency to violent bursts of anger, during which in the past he had threatened a colleague. Besides, according to the doctor, he 'spent his money on silly objects, sweets and alcoholic drinks', which led to him being defined as childish. N.N. left the orphanage at the age of four and was raised by a succession of three couples of farmers. They are never called adoptive parents in the file, but '*tenutari*', an obsolete term which implies they took the boy under their jurisdiction. It is unclear why the boy was passed on from one couple of farmers to another, when still underage. One of these farmers declared he saw N.N. some years later, and stated that he had become 'physically misshapen', subject to a physical decay that in the psychiatrists' mind probably corroborated the suspected degeneration, in Lombrosian terms. Homosexuality in N.N.'s clinic file was therefore not mentioned but simply hinted at, as the patient did not manifest any interest for the opposite sex, had underdeveloped genitalia and a physical attribute that was judged as feminine. N.N.'s clinic file contains two photographs of him, something that proves a deliberate intention to classify, study and observe his physical appearance. It is the only file that contains photographic documentation among those I consulted at San Salvi and at the Florence State

Archives, demonstrating further the scientific interest raised by patients with sexual primary or secondary traits considered 'abnormal' or 'ambiguous'. In the head-and-shoulder profile shot, in two copies, the patient's torso was stripped of clothes, probably with the intention of showing the shape of his chest, the presence of breasts or the disposition of hair. The second picture shows the entire patient's body as he stands frontally, completely naked, with his hands on the front of his thighs so that it is possible to see them clearly. N.N. was interned after observation.[82] His asylum file did not dwell on his hermaphroditic physical appearance, it rather concentrated on his anger fits, his strong headaches, his behaviour inside the asylum where he showed an interest for work, while in the outside world he was said to be uninterested in it. N.N. was assigned to ergotherapy. Initially he took care of the animals used to test medical substances, and then he worked in the laundry. He was kept in the clinic, for observation, for sixteen months, a very long period of time, considering that observation, by law, could not exceed four weeks. He was transferred to the Castel Pulci branch in February 1922 and a note in his asylum file states that a psychiatrist intended to continue to study him there. In any case, the clinic retained his observation file at the time, obviously judging it worthy of further examination, or maybe because of its potential didactic use, but his asylum file shows that in the fascist years there seems to have been a lack of scientific interest in this patient. He died of peritonitis while interned in 1925.

Conclusions

Available documentation does not reveal consistent written official communication between the San Salvi hospital director and the psychiatrists who worked in the mental health institution. There is also no trace of regulations to staff or *ad hoc* directives on practice and conduct. In the absence of this type of document, it is impossible to know what instructions the directors gave San Salvi's doctors or what he appreciated or disliked in their work. It is also impossible to know whether the directors read the psychiatrists' notes, but, despite the considerable workload, it seems that they must have been aware of the general attitudes of medical professionals towards interned people and the language they sometimes used. This would indicate that doctors at San Salvi enjoyed a high degree of impunity, while the directors engaged in a relentless and time-consuming battle for power. Equally, there is very little trace of correspondence from the psychiatrists to the director. This too confirms the impression of a two-tier institution, where the director left psychiatrists to carry on undisturbed and psychiatrists had no intention of engaging in a dialogue with management. It would reinforce the feeling of San Salvi as an institution in certain ways still anchored to the past, where medical professionals were not reluctant to consider their work environment as a place for the detention and isolation of mentally ill patients, despite the few openings to modern trends and approaches, referred to earlier in the chapter. The impression of San Salvi as anchored to the past is also corroborated by the relatively high incidence of moral madness diagnoses.

Nurses' voices are unfortunately absent in the available documentation. This makes it impossible to compare their professional attitudes with that of their Santa Maria della Pietà colleagues. It is interesting to note, though, that in one instance, suggestion of punishment for promiscuous behaviour between male patients and male members of staff came from one of them. This would confirm that nurses felt entitled to enter the moral sphere of patient behaviour and, as they were increasingly employed on the grounds of a fascist political faith rather than professional merits, on issues of sexuality they followed the PNF directives very strictly.

An almost complete lack of scientific interest for issues of sexuality and for homosexuality can be observed at San Salvi. The absence of directives from the two documented directors in office during the fascist regime, Amaldi and Simonelli, on how to handle these patients complements a general absence of interest in homosexuality on the part of medical staff, as can be deduced from their notes. In fact, the two cases where male homosexuality was ascertained did not seem to attract particular interest, cures or comments. The only woman whose bisexuality appeared in medical notes was referred to the psychiatric system before Fascism by her mother, who clearly perceived her attraction towards women as one of the many behavioural problems that had to be solved through psychiatry. In this case, the doctors seem to have aligned with the girl's mother and the carer in the countryside. They did not challenge reports on the girl's scandalous conduct and character, they believed the mother's description of her turbulent adolescence and the caretaker's accounts of her immorality and promiscuity. As her internment stretched out to the fascist years, psychiatrists did not update the initial description and diagnosis, based on moral judgement. They carried on siding with her family and acted in order to detain and isolate this young woman from society. The interest in this case seems to be primarily aimed at fulfilling a moralizing duty. Her homosexual attraction did not worry them any more than other aspects of her personality and behaviour, such as promiscuity with her boyfriend and rebelliousness. This is in line with what could be observed in other female patient cases, where moral judgement on the part of doctors is much harsher compared to attitudes towards their male counterparts.

Psychiatrists eventually managed to persuade the bisexual patient, P.M., that she had a problem and that she was different and 'wrong', but only after a considerable number of months. Initially, the girl resisted their moralizing pressure and seems to have been unbothered by the stigma of lesbianism, immorality or eroticism she was aware of carrying. As mentioned in the previous chapter, it is evident that some young women openly contested the impositions of family and regime. They 'resisted', trying to assert their right to live as they wanted to, despite the known negative consequences of their choice.

While the young woman was interned following a request of her family, the two cases of male homosexuality were referred to the psychiatric system by the security forces and the legal system. However, in both cases, the element of danger was not particularly underlined in their medical files and, in fact, in the case of the man convicted for indecent behaviour, both the security forces and the hospital psychiatrists agreed he was fit to be discharged. Male homosexuality was observed with a considerable lack of scientific interest and moral concern, it was seldom punished and it was never commented upon as deserving specific attention or cures.

The only case of suspected hermaphroditism that could be retraced received doctors' attention only before the regime. The patient was examined and studied in his physical appearance, as the photographs in his file confirm, in the clinic, and his sexuality was the subject of questioning on the part of the doctors. No further examination ensued, though, and no specific therapy, surgical operation or hormone treatment, is mentioned in the patient's asylum file for the fascist period. N.N. was assigned to ergotherapy activities, like any other patient judged to be fit and sufficiently interested in carrying out these duties. He was studied also when he was transferred to the Castel Pulci branch of San Salvi, the hospital for chronic but not dangerous patients. However, while he was in the asylum, attention concentrated on several aspects of his psychic infantilism, on his behaviour, prior and during internment, but not on his sexuality.

There is consistency with the Rome asylum in that San Salvi contradicts the theoretical psychiatric trends as much as Santa Maria della Pietà. While theory expanded on issues such as sexual inversion, hermaphroditism and intersexuality, in the routine psychiatric practice these conditions were not high on the agenda during the *Ventennio*. San Salvi's lack of scientific interest in homosexuality is perhaps not so surprising, given that Florence was a city known for its relatively visible gay and lesbian community during Fascism, compared with most other Italian towns. In the capital of Tuscany lived a relatively large group of intellectuals and artists, some of them foreigners and upper class, who made no secret of their sexual inclinations. The regime tacitly accepted them. Writer and poet Radclyffe Hall (1880–1943), author of the scandalous *The Well of Loneliness*, lived in Florence during the *Ventennio*.[83] She frequented a crowd of lesbian artists, intellectuals and socialites, Italian and from other European countries, among them Romaine Brooks (1874–1970) and Nathalie Barney (1876–1972), who lived in the Tuscan capital or visited it regularly. In Florence, Radclyffe Hall lived her lesbianism very openly, often wore men's clothes, co-habited with her female partner, Una Troubridge (1887–1963), nicknamed Vincenzo, in a central apartment and scandalously had other female lovers at the same time. Among the Italian artists' community, there was painter Ottone Rosai (1895–1957), whose nude portraits of male prostitutes were known to the police.[84] The regime kept a discreet eye on him, but never intervened to censor him. Besides, the existence of a vast scene of male prostitution was also known to the authorities, as recent studies prove.[85] It is plausible that this relatively higher level of tolerance and acceptance of homosexuality could have influenced the local asylum's psychiatrists.

In addition, given that psychiatrists at San Salvi were accustomed to using abusive language to describe patients, their respect for the male homosexual patients is even more noticeable. Confronted with the way they described other patients, when they wrote notes on interned homosexual men, they never revealed an abusive attitude towards them. Homosexuality was never mentioned in the Admissions Registers as a diagnosis. It appeared only inside the individual patient files and it seems to have been considered an aggravating factor, one of the several aspects that signalled degeneration, but not the most worrying and certainly not a dangerous condition for the patient or others. In the case of the patient referred to the asylum by the Court, only the generic word 'perversion' appeared on his internment diagnosis.

To conclude, San Salvi reiterates the impression that Italian families had no doubt that psychiatry was at their service. The amount of pressure from P.M.'s mother on doctors is a clear example of this attitude. However, opposite to what was observed at Santa Maria della Pietà, the San Salvi psychiatric staff seem not to have resisted this kind of pressure and, when a relative demanded it, internment of a homosexual relative, in this case a bisexual girl, took place without further questions or doubts. However, it is certainly relevant to note C.D.'s father's willingness to have his son back home, showing he had a complete lack of moral concern about his son's homosexuality. Also, interestingly, P.M.'s boyfriend was reported to not be too worried or scandalized by the girl's previous internment, probably considered a routine type of punishment for young women with licentious conduct. The research carried out in the Florence asylum's archives confirms that, while in the women's cases, the aspect of repression on the part of families emerges clearly, attitudes towards male homosexuality attracted a very different response from relatives. Equally, Florentine psychiatrists did not refuse internment to male homosexual individuals referred by the security forces, but in these cases, professionals seem to have acted much more half-heartedly and their moral judgement was far more lenient.

In certain ways, San Salvi was innovative and projected itself in the future of psychiatry, anticipating several new therapeutic and diagnostic facets. Its directors were anxious to emphasize this aspect of the institution. In other ways, this asylum remained anchored to old approaches and to a moralizing and punitive function, especially directed at women, which belonged to the past and to a heritage difficult to shake off. Therefore, the regime's pressures to act as a disciplining institution seem to have generated less adverse reactions here compared with Rome. Within this context, however, it is interesting to note that attitudes towards male homosexuality were relatively more open-minded while women's immorality, let alone lesbianism or bisexuality, was severely judged, in accordance with the ingrained misogynistic context that characterized the *Ventennio,* but not the *Ventennio* alone.

5

The Girifalco asylum: 'A grave for the living'[1]

After having observed the psychiatric hospitals of two major Italian towns, Rome and Florence, different in size and from several other points of view, but both with an international reputation and famous tradition, I turn to analyse the asylum of a small provincial town, Girifalco, situated on the hills of central Calabria, in the south of Italy. The purpose is to compare structures of different size and located in different regions of Italy, so that it will be possible to draw comparisons, emphasizing similarities and differences between their practices and approaches.

Girifalco is equidistant from the Tyrrhenian and the Ionian Sea, and from the towns of Cosenza and Catanzaro, although it belongs to the Catanzaro province. Nowadays, its population is around 5,700 inhabitants, roughly the same as during the fascist period. For the *Ventennio* we have in fact the results of two population censuses, carried out in 1931 and 1936, when the population was, respectively, 5,744 and 6,299.[2] It is no surprise that the variation is minimal between the time of the dictatorship and the present day, despite the sharp demographic increase in post-war Italy. In fact, migration from Calabria to northern Italy, Europe, North and South America played a large part in maintaining almost constant the number of inhabitants. The Girifalco mental health hospital, still in use in part as a residence for the mentally ill and in part for the elderly, is situated at the borders of what was the ancient town and is now its historical centre. It is the perfect embodiment of the concept of psychiatric patient exclusion and segregation.

In this chapter, I sketch briefly the history of Girifalco and outline its structure and activity, although primary sources such as internal correspondence, registers and administrative documentation are absent. The available documentation, consisting of secondary sources and some primary sources chosen and quoted in the historiography, cannot be considered completely impartial, and allows only a partial reconstruction, as I highlight later in the chapter.

Brief history of the institution

The Girifalco asylum was founded in 1878, after undergoing some restructuring to make it suitable for its new use. In this case, like in many other cases in Italy, the building chosen to host the asylum was a seventeenth-century convent. Initially it was designed to host forty to fifty patients and it was created in response to the overcrowding of other southern Italian psychiatric hospitals and hospices, mainly from the entire region of Calabria, Campania and Sicily.

This mental health institution presents several peculiarities with consequences for the type of care it provided and its specialists' approaches to mental illness, diagnosis and treatment. First, it is situated in a region where, during Fascism, there were no major cities. Calabria was mostly a rural area. This, for instance, might partially explain why its psychiatrists were not interested in issues connected with degeneration, usually associated with the lifestyle in large urban centres and whose causes were identified in the typical urban routine, its chaotic rhythm, vices and temptations.[3] Degeneration as a mental health condition seldom appears in the patient files examined for the purpose of this research.

Secondly, like in most asylums at the time, in Italy and elsewhere, poverty was the main reason for internment, but in Calabria poverty was probably worse than elsewhere in the country, and the Girifalco asylum had to act as a *chronicarium* and a shelter for derelicts to a higher degree than other Italian psychiatric institutions of the time. Most of the internees were described as malnourished, vagrancy and homelessness were widespread, patients' homes were said to be dirty, insalubrious and not fit for habitation. This situation undoubtedly fed into the Lombrosian school's stereotypical portrayal of southern Italians.[4] The Girifalco psychiatrists, firmly anchored to Lombrosian theories, looked upon the rural Calabrian population as an underdeveloped, starving, ignorant and derelict mass of individuals, prone to excesses, overexcitement, jealousy and crime. They pathologized it *a priori*. Patient files offer to the historian endless variations of this stereotypical image, even before accurate observation and examination of the patient.

Fascist times: The asylum structure, its directors and staff

As both Oscar Greco and Ennio Passalia note, the Girifalco institution offers a unique perspective to evaluate Lombrosian thought. Most of its directors and psychiatrists of the initial phase of activity, until the First World War, came from northern Italy and were well rooted in the Lombrosian tradition, which considered southern Italians, and particularly Calabrian people, as racially inferior.[5] Significantly psychiatrists from the *Mezzogiorno* worked in the Girifalco asylum during Fascism. However, in terms of the perpetuation of Lombrosian thought and traditions, the origin of psychiatrists made little or no difference; most psychiatrists at Girifalco, whether from the north or the south, were influenced by Lombroso.[6]

The Girifalco asylum had a couple of illustrious names among its first directors and specialists. One was Silvio Venturi (1851–1900), twice director, first between 1882 and 1883, and then from 1887 to 1900. He was one of the most authoritative and well-known Italian psychiatrists of his time, with a long list of publications and several university teaching posts in his curriculum. Between 1903 and 1907, Marco Levi Bianchini (1875–1961), another important psychiatrist, worked in the Girifalco asylum as an assistant director. He is generally remembered as one of the few pioneers of psychoanalysis in Italy.[7] Compared to other asylums in the country, in the *Ventennio* there was a considerable turnover of directors, which is another peculiarity of the Girifalco asylum. Directors were appointed, and then resigned, psychiatrists acted temporarily as directors while public competitions for the post were announced. Bernardo Frisco, in charge from 1913, was replaced by Vincenzo Fragola in 1926. In 1929, there was joint 'regency' of two psychiatrists, Carmelo Ventra and Annibale Puca. In 1930 a public competition for the post of director was announced and Puca won. He left Girifalco in 1934 and his post was assigned to Fragola again, who acted as director *ad interim* for seven years, until 1941, when he won the competition and was officially appointed. From this point of view too, the nomination of Girifalco asylum directors was not transparent. Regencies and *ad interim* directors are rare in the other Italian psychiatric hospitals examined. The unofficial appointments and procedures, together with the long gaps between one official director and the next, leave the impression of an institution that had considerable freedom because it was so secluded and distant from central government, or even from the region's capital, Reggio Calabria.

In addition, the sequence of directors and psychiatrists of the institution in the *Ventennio* shows that such a small and provincial hospital did not attract the best names in the profession. Bernardo Frisco was not among the most prestigious psychiatrists in Italy. In charge of the hospital from 1913 until the first few years of the fascist regime, he was primarily a criminal pathologist. The Girifalco asylum journal published several of his articles that were in fact his official psychiatric assessments, used in court cases. He was a strong adherent to Lombrosian theories. An apt example to illustrate the extent to which Frisco considered the inborn or inherited genetic aspects to be decisive in a human being's behaviour is an article in which he argued that menstruation was a predisposing factor for committing crime and for developing psychiatric pathological conditions, from erotic and religious delirium to suicidal tendencies.[8] Coherently, he therefore concluded that menstruation had to be looked upon as an attenuating factor in court, as it was a condition similar to mental infirmity and would subtract conscience or free will when committing a criminal action. This was a way to say that women were inherently and genetically predisposed to crime, a concept that sanctioned legally their diminished responsibility. Equally, he thought that even war trauma depended to some extent on pre-existing inherited pathological factors, as Greco emphasizes.[9] Frisco, remembered for pioneering the Girifalco *dispensario*, the health care prevention centre in 1914, went on to direct the Agrigento asylum in 1931.

Annibale Puca is better known because he was appointed as director of the infamous Aversa criminal asylum, a post he held between 1949 and 1966. He published in several psychiatric journals, such as *Rassegna di Neuropsichiatria* and *Il Pisani*. He also wrote on epilepsy in Calabria, drawing from his experience at Girifalco.[10]

Very little is known about Carmelo Ventra and Rocco Cerra; even Vincenzo Fragola, director for many years during the fascist regime, is absent from all major encyclopaedias or biographical dictionaries consulted.[11] The Girifalco asylum psychiatric journal, the *Annali del Manicomio Provinciale di Catanzaro in Girifalco*, (referred to as *Annali* from now on) published from 1914, did not attract any prestigious collaboration other than from the Girifalco directors and members of its medical staff and there is little mention of the Calabrian institution and its directors in articles written and published by other Italian colleagues.

In a long article published in 1931 by the *Annali*, Puca accurately described how the hospital was designed and organized.[12] The asylum was divided into three sections: the observation unit, the hospital itself and a third section dedicated to patients affected by chronic conditions. In 1931, a separate women's observation section was still under construction. The scientific laboratory, part of the asylum, included a radiology section, and there was an infirmary inside the hospital as well. In addition, there were three *dispensari*: anti-rabies, anti-tuberculosis and mental health. The latter acted as a general medicine drop-in clinic for all sorts of health-related issues, from headache to appendicitis, and was open to the local residents. Puca underlined that psychiatrists 'were no longer prison warden-philosophers, but therapists who do not despair', claiming again a medical and scientific role for his profession, and went on to describe all the pharmacological therapies available to Girifalco's patients.[13] These were in line with what was offered to patients in the two institutions analysed earlier, and included malariotherapy, insulin-induced shock, fever provoked by injections of sulphur, to quote a few.

Despite the optimistic tone of the entire essay, Puca could not avoid pointing out that there was a constant problem of overcrowding, although the asylum patients increased by only roughly twenty per year. Given the extent of this problem during the fascist years, overcrowding in Girifalco does not seem particularly exceptional. The institution reached a peak of 455 patients in 1916, while in 1929, by Fragola's calculations, there were 392 internees, twenty-six less compared with the previous year. At the end of 1930, as calculated by Puca, the Girifalco psychiatric institution hosted 426 patients, while at the end of 1931 the number reached 439, but in the meantime the structure had been expanded and new building work was under way, so that the effects of overcrowding were probably less dramatically felt than before.[14]

In 1931, the medical staff, numerically insufficient in his opinion, consisted of a director, a vice director, also in charge of the men's section, two assistant doctors also in charge of the women's section and of the radiology laboratory. By 1930, a third doctor had joined the team. Puca stressed that there were weekly informal staff meetings and that such a small institution offered the advantage of having little bureaucracy, thus allowing friendly relationships among members of staff, although, he hastily added, hierarchy was not overlooked. The twenty-six male nurses, sixteen female nurses and five nuns, also judged to be numerically insufficient, were coordinated by a chief inspector and two head nurses. The nursing staff was also considered not to be up to the task from a qualitative point of view and was therefore given a three evenings a week course for six months a year, to improve their professional and ethical standards. The internal permanent staff were integrated with external professionals, such as a carpenter, a mechanic and so forth, who led the ergotherapeutic work. The asylum included a library, which subscribed to all the major psychiatric journals of the time, and a music school.

Annibale Puca was as keen as his predecessor, and successor, Vincenzo Fragola to stress that he was careful with money, that the asylum was well administered and that its prevention schemes worked in the direction of efficiency and cost reduction. He provided a chart where he calculated the average cost of a patient per day in most Italian asylums of the time. The Girifalco asylum, according to his calculations, was the least expensive in the country, with a mere five Lire twenty-eight to four Lire eighty-two average daily cost per internee, approximately equivalent to five Euros (just over four UK pounds), compared with the nineteen Lire of Rome or the roughly twelve Lire of Florence.

It is difficult to reconstruct the daily practice of this asylum for the years Mussolini was in power. First, the administrative documentation is not available for consultation.[15] Secondly, the available sources cannot be considered impartial. They consist of the history of the institution written by Domenico Marcello, a psychiatrist at the Girifalco asylum in the post-war years, and several *Annali* articles written by the institution's directors, consisting of detailed reports on the asylum's activities and aimed at the provincial authorities.[16]

Marcello, one of the few historians of the Girifalco mental health hospital, and the only one who has also analysed the fascist years, belongs to the Italian tradition of psychiatrists who ventured into the history of mental health. His work is significant because he had access to documentation that is now unavailable to historians and because of his privileged 'from-within' perspective. However, his view is influenced by his role within the institution. For instance, he describes the 1930s as a period when the general world economic crisis was reflected in the psychiatric hospital's lethargic routine. In his view, during that time, the asylum 'remained still, in an immobility of values that had to last with shocking monotony until the Second World War and until the immediate post-war period', but this might be a judgement influenced by his intention to show that the 1950s and the following decades were highly innovative and lively.[17] Not much seems to have happened in the fascist years, according to his account, other than a reallocation of two hundred patients transferred to Girifalco from the Sicilian asylums of Catania and Palermo in 1933, who were sent back in 1938. He also mentions the arrival of several patients from the Dodecanese islands, who were transferred to Girifalco during Fascism.[18]

Marcello's book contains several photographs and, most importantly, transcripts of internal correspondence, although he does not note where the originals can be found.[19] From the few documents he chose to transcribe and publish in his book, one can see that Annibale Puca, when he was the director of the Girifalco asylum, insisted on the particular role of doctors, their duties, the necessity to write notes on patients if and when they developed different symptoms or, in any case, every month. Puca also stressed that the medical personnel had to be reachable during breaks, that none of the doctors on duty could take leave, and he listed all the bureaucratic duties allocated to psychiatrists. Clearly, professional standards at Girifalco were below Puca's expectations. For example, he thought it was necessary to emphasize that no person external to the asylum was to be allowed to visit patient quarters. He blamed the psychiatrists for breach of protocol; during an official visit by the *Rettore*, a reference to the head of the provincial authority, the psychiatrists were absent. This incident, defined by Puca as '*gravissimo*', most serious, called for psychiatrists' mandatory signature for acceptance of the doctors' rota and attendance timetable. In addition, the hospital had to have a doctor in attendance between 9.00 am and 8.00 pm, if the director was absent and the psychiatrists had to be reachable at all times during the night.[20] This rare material reveals that the director not only addressed nursing staff, he issued directives to medical staff as well. The tone of his communications was authoritative. He called for discipline, rigour and strict observance of rules. However, Marcello's choice of documents might be influenced by the fact that he, as a psychiatrist who worked at Girifalco, liked to recall the old days, underlining the difference between the psychiatric professional standards of past and present, and praising the rigour of the asylum tradition. In any case, from what can be deduced, working conditions for those employed as doctors at the Girifalco mental health hospital in the *Ventennio* must have been tough and their commitment to the job and the institution was expected to be exclusive. Only from 1 April 1935 were they allowed to take one day off per week.[21]

In addition, Marcello's evidence reveals that strict instructions were given by the director to nurses too, on what had to be avoided, such as giving ward keys to patients, and what had to be done, such as counting patients when they went to bed, making sure that their clothes and shoes remained outside the dormitories.[22] Puca underlined that all nurses had to be body-searched before re-entering patient wards, a measure that was aimed, he explained, at 'avoiding dangerous objects being taken' into the wards.[23] In another startling note he specified that nurses and workers who came into contact with patients could not keep weapons on them or in their lockers, otherwise they would be sacked. As observed in Rome and Florence, these internal communication notes between the director of an asylum and his nursing staff give a clear sense of the low professional standards he had to confront. As in Rome and Florence, also in Girifalco nurses were probably recruited locally and were usually not trained for the task, as these frequent reprimands invariably confirm.

Interestingly, in an *o.d.s.* dated 6 December 1931, Puca also spelled out his resentment at having to impose these strict regulations:

> The new Penal Code equates the director to a prison warden, therefore I arrange as follows: 1 – Work is of consolation to the spirit of normal patients only;

> condemned convicts who were released [and interned] must live in idleness
> and be kept under strict surveillance as they must be considered dangerous
> convicts; 2 – For no reason must these released convicts leave their wards; 3 –
> All released convicts are placed in the under-surveillance patient section; 4 –
> Every patient who goes out of the hospital to carry out work must be assigned
> to a nurse who is directly responsible of his/her behaviour; a patient's evasion
> is punished with imprisonment of the person who is responsible for it (art. 321
> of the Penal Code).[24]

The asylum director's sarcastic remarks are aligned with the opinions of most
of his Italian colleagues, according to which current legislation had diminished
the director's authority and scientific merits, expecting him to act as a public
security officer. Puca's bitter irony shows he was also extremely critical of the
decision to isolate patients who had committed crimes, not allowing them to
work like the other interned patients. In other words, he strongly believed these
people could be rehabilitated through cures, such as ergotherapy, and that an
asylum could not operate as a prison.

Puca was also in favour of no-restraint, as he stated several times and
confirmed in one of his *o.d.s.*, dated 25 February 1932, which demonstrates that
his views were not always shared by his staff:

> I found a female patient tied up and I had not been informed about it. I fined
> the nurses …. I order that no patient is tied up without a written authorisation
> by the director or, in his absence, by the vice-director. … This is not a director's
> decision, but an order contained in the State Asylum Regulations.[25]

The tone and content of the director's *o.d.s.* strengthens the impression that an
old-fashioned hierarchical system was in place at the Girifalco asylum, and that
serious disciplinary problems were addressed in an authoritarian manner.

A further source of information on the Girifalco structure and practice is
its journal, the *Annali*, which published some of the annual technical and
administrative reports written by the director in charge and addressed to
the provincial authority. In the absence of other documentation available for
consultation, these are extremely important documents, although, as highlighted
earlier, they cannot be considered impartial. Obviously, the director's aim was to
prove the asylum's efficiency and to underline its achievements. In 1924, Vincenzo
Fragola photographed the psychiatric hospital whose direction he was about to
officially inherit.[26] His concern was to prove to the Catanzaro province that the
asylum management was careful not to overspend. He therefore offered tangible
proof to show how he had organized things so that there would be a considerable

reduction in expenditure. His report contains a very detailed description of the new patient diet, for instance, which was substantially reduced, so that there would be savings, while making sure that the internees were not deprived of the necessary intake of vitamins, proteins and other essential nutritional substances.

The overcrowding of the asylum, in Fragola's opinion, depended on several factors, such as the over-prescription of internment and the delay in dismissing those whose madness was not medically confirmed. Another aggravating factor, in his view, was the absence of effective cures, which determined not only longer internment periods but in some cases chronic mental illness. Fragola insisted to the province on ergotherapy as an effective way to save money, while providing care. The Girifalco institution was not only self-sufficient in many ways, as the patients produced most of what they consumed, he noted with pride, but it also provided an income. Patients worked in the fields; fed cows, pigs and hens; baked their own bread; and washed, ironed and mended their clothes and bedlinen, thus contributing to their own subsistence, but they also produced shoes, brooms, bricks, cloth, soap, honey, mattresses and tablecloths. They worked in the internal printshop, or as carpenters, cobblers, blacksmiths and embroiderers. They even fed silkworms and produced silk. Fragola asserted firmly that patients' work was not exploitative; on the contrary, he argued, it was one of the most valid therapies the asylum could offer. More than half of the internees, 66.50 per cent of the men and 65 per cent of the women, worked.

In some ways, Fragola's views were modern for his times. He thought that early release would be conducive to recovery because he recognized that the presence of the family and the freedom patients enjoyed at home would act as positive factors. He rightly observed that long internments would often worsen a mental health condition, making it become chronic. His contestation of over-prescription of internment was an open critique to GPs who thought asylums were hospices or shelters for the indigent. At the same time, implicitly, he criticized the security forces, and their idea of psychiatric hospitals as a solution to homelessness, alcoholism and other social or public order problems. He strongly believed in prevention and underlined that the three *dispensari* helped a great deal in saving money, as they reduced the number of internments. He compared the successes of these free, drop-in health care centres with similar experiments carried out in Sweden, Switzerland and France, showing he kept up to date with what happened beyond Calabria and Italy's borders, and reiterated the importance of prophylaxis, a modern concept that he embraced thoroughly.[27] As an example, he quoted the 1,010 people affected by syphilis who were cured by the Girifalco *dispensario*. Rightly, he underlined that at least three hundred of them would have ended up in the asylum had they not been cured in a timely fashion. The drop-in health care centres dealt not just with mental health problems but with all sorts of pathologies, from stomach ulcers to cardiopathy. From Fragola's reports, it is possible to see how the local population from the entire region, not just the Girifalco area, took full advantage of these free clinics, whose meritorious action went well beyond its original task.

In other ways, Vincenzo Fragola was firmly anchored to the past. For instance, in his view, one method to save money was to prolong the eight-hour day for nurses – the eight-hour day was a recent right won by workers – and his idea of ergotherapy was exploitative by today's standards. He saw prophylaxis in terms of eugenics, identifying mental health care as a suitable tool to improve the 'stock', and considered mental illness merely from a medical and scientific perspective.

In 1931, the *Annali* published a long article by the director, Annibale Puca, who was asked to retrace the history of the institution in its fiftieth year.[28] Puca too highlighted the importance of prophylaxis from a eugenics perspective: 'The stock takes advantage of anything that is prophylactic foresight …. The patients' families … are the seedbed of madness. … in some of its manifestations, madness represents an index of race impoverishment and extinction.'[29] He insisted on the consequent need to carry out detailed investigations of patients' families and to monitor their children. Among the main acquired causes of mental health problems, he picked out alcoholism, syphilis and even tuberculosis. The last condition was in strict relation to immorality and crime, in his view, as it presented the patient with a conflict between a vigilant conscience and visions of the end.[30] In other words, it would produce serious depression which might induce a person to commit crimes. He thought alcohol was an additional trigger factor of psychiatric illnesses, as it multiplied the delirium caused by other pre-existing conditions. In addition, he considered alcoholism to be one of the main eugenic problems of his time: 'Alcoholics' children are the army of frenasthenics, epileptics, psycho and ethical deficient people, the poor of spirit and inborn, violent and impulsive criminals.'[31] Puca attempted a sociological explanation for the relative absence of women among the Girifalco's internees, another peculiarity of this asylum. It was due, in his opinion, to their segregation at home, which protected them from alcoholism, tuberculosis and other predisposing factors. Yet, he thought that, because of their segregation and subordination to men, they were generally incapable of reactions and were resigned to their enslavement, but when they did develop psychiatric issues, these would be of an extremely serious nature.

Women are subjugated, insensitive, hyporeactive, meio-thymic; more servile than men, therefore less numerous and less curable [than interned men]. But these women, who have been historically so repressed, when they explode, they are ferocious beasts.[32]

He also offered a succinct anthropological analysis of the Calabrian popula-tion, 'a race in which contrasts are especially dominant', a clear tribute to Lombrosian theories.[33] In his report he also provided a detailed study, based on the Girifalco asylum's admissions, on how certain factors had an influence in determining psychiatric conditions, such as age, profession and marital status. His considerations on the connection between unmarried status and madness mirrored Mussolini's campaign slogans and were a perfect manifesto of the regime's demographic campaign.[34] He stated that single people were, by definition,

unbalanced individuals, predisposed [to crime and madness], often dominated by an inferiority complex and by the inability to deal with life. The unmarried man, through his renunciation, declares that he is escaping his duty and denounces his inborn tendency both towards isolation, and therefore, he remains solitary, and towards a spontaneous exclusion from the social mechanism, and therefore he places himself at the margins of normal, hard-working, prolific and reproductive mankind. ... The unmarried person is an anachronism.[35]

Interestingly, single women are only mentioned in passing, as the practice of forced marriages would make them total exceptions not worthy of specific analysis.

Listing and discussing the pathologies present in the Girifalco asylum, Puca included the twenty-five cases of moral madness interned in the fifty years of the institution's life. He inserted them in the broad category of psycho-degeneration, underlining that these were 'diagnoses dear to some of our predecessors'.[36] This statement partially explains why the diagnosis of moral madness is almost absent in this mental health hospital's documentation. It was considered old-fashioned, a mere tribute to the old schools of thought. However, there is an important proof that Puca was aware that homosexual patients were interned and that a sort of standard procedure was in place. In an article on spinal injuries and the observed consequent male impotence, published in the Palermo asylum's journal, *Il Pisani*, he illustrated several cases.[37] Among them was the case of a young man who presented what he described as the typical characteristics of effeminacy, both in his somatic secondary traits and in his gestures and behaviour. Leaving aside the main topic of his essay, that of impotence, he only noted that this man had a funnel-shaped anus, thus revealing that the patient was subjected to anal examination to ascertain his 'passive' homosexuality. The comment on this patient is the only one that testifies that the director of an asylum was aware of homosexual patients present in his institution. It is also extremely interesting to note that Puca referred to stereotypes and added that the young man was known as a homosexual in his town, but he refrained from moral judgement on the patient. The fact that he included him in an observational essay on patients with impotence problems is also revelatory of the fact that he did not think homosexuality deserved a separate, in-depth and *ad hoc* discussion.

To summarize, Puca embraced several aspects of fascist propaganda and its demographic campaign, such as considerations of eugenics, the belief that certain individuals were genetically predisposed towards mental health problems, such as unmarried people, although he remained critical of the role assigned to psychiatry by the regime, like most of his contemporaries. His rejection of the diagnostic category of moral madness can be read in line with the contemporary attempts to disentangle psychiatry from morality and to give it the same scientific relevance enjoyed by other branches of medicine. The strong element of continuity with Fragola's opinions is immediately evident. Like him, Puca rejected the idea that psychiatry had something to do with public order issues and optimistically believed that mental illness was a curable disease and could be cured through advances in science and medicine. Like Fragola, he too thought that psychiatry's mission was to improve the 'stock'.

Two years later, it was Fragola's turn to update the authorities on the institution's activities.[38] He made some interesting remarks on the changes that had taken place in terms of the population of internees. He emphasized that the number of schizophrenics had sensibly increased and that this diagnostic category was now in the majority. The average age of patients had drastically changed too, he pointed out, and the highest number of those interned in the year 1932–3 was between twenty-one and forty years of age. Among them, the majority of men were unmarried. Echoing Puca, Fragola asserted:

> Unmarried men, as stated in the previous reports, are doubtlessly more prone to contracting mental illnesses because, as they do not have the responsibility of a family, they lead a more dissolute life, full of adventures and of all kinds of vices, so that they dedicate themselves, much more than others, to alcohol, tobacco, sexual excesses, to solitary Venus, to prowling at night, and are therefore more prone to contracting syphilis and tuberculosis, etc.[39]

This rapid change of scenario is interesting, although it is difficult to understand why schizophrenia suddenly became such a frequent diagnosis. The lowering of the average internee's age, also difficult to explain without consulting the relevant internal documentation, meant that the Girifalco asylum had quickly become less similar to a *chronicarium* for the elderly. Maybe it indicates that public order–related internment had risen, in accordance with the role psychiatrists were increasingly asked to fulfil. In fact, Fragola lamented that the local GPs only stated the aspect of danger related to referred patients, omitting personal and family details, which would be of great help to psychiatrists. This is an important indication of how, like Puca and most of his Italian contemporaries, he wanted to underline the primacy of medical reasons for internment, rather than public order offences. It could also point to his acknowledgement that the Girifalco asylum, like most of its equivalent institutions in the country, increasingly dealt with public order issues and therefore interned a higher percentage of younger people. The relatively high mortality rate, he added, although it had decreased compared to previous years, still depended on the high percentage of older patients, whose families refused to take them back home because of their indigence and who were therefore left in the hospital, which had to act as a hospice. This statement too was a reiterated critique of the role assigned to asylums, as a shelter for those who were not mentally ill, but simply in need of care that their families and other institutions could not offer.

Fragola was keen to confirm that a new pavilion was almost finished. It could host up to 150 patients. He listed all the refurbishment work carried out in the year, mostly by patients, who he patronizingly referred to as the 'internees' family', insisting they were not exploited at all.[40] He added that Emilio Rizzatti, director of the Racconigi asylum, in the distant Piedmont province of Cuneo, had praised the Calabrian asylum and its therapeutic approaches and activities.[41] It is a further proof of Fragola's connection with the external world, his network of contacts both in Italy and abroad, his efforts to keep updated with contemporary psychiatric practice and his comparison with therapies adopted elsewhere.

Annibale Puca too demonstrated he was well informed, although more in terms of psychiatric theory than hospital practice. He quoted Marañon in stating that the environment could dent inherited conditions and inborn genetic traits, for instance, and that only the 'integral Man and Woman generate the pure race'.[42] In another article he voiced his support for Pende's theories on inborn attitudes, and on the importance of hereditary factors in a person's health, behaviour and aptitude, although he added that some personality traits could be acquired and then transmitted.[43] In the same essay, he also quoted Giuseppe Vidoni and his studies on Genoese underage criminals.[44]

Specific methodological issues

In addition to the peculiarities of this asylum discussed above, its Admissions Registers did not specify patient diagnosis, unlike the Rome, Florence and other Italian asylums. This meant that I had to change approach and decided to sample-search, randomly choosing three years of the *Ventennio*. I chose 1924, 1933 and 1939, roughly the beginning, the middle and the end of the fascist regime, and opened all the patient files for these three years. I consulted a total of 538 files: 106 for the year 1924; 268 for the year 1933; and 164 for the year 1939.[45] They represent roughly 14 per cent of the 3,861 total internments at Girifalco during the fascist regime. The three years chosen are also representative from the point of view of the asylum directors, because in 1924 the post was covered by Frisco, in 1933 by Puca and in 1939 by Fragola. Files are kept in folders that follow a chronological order by date of admission, therefore in this case I provide the date of internment, which is the one the archivist and researchers need in order to locate a patient's file.

The different methodological approach meant that I consulted files I would have not considered if I had followed the method deployed in the other two psychiatric institutions analysed prior to Girifalco. In Rome and Florence, I concentrated on certain diagnostic categories connected with immorality, sexual inversion, perversion and degeneration, as explained in detail in the introduction, and in Rome I sample-searched other diagnostic categories that were mostly linked with excitement and lack of self-control. Here I took into consideration all patients' files, without choosing specific diagnoses. After having consulted all patient files for the three years I selected, I found two cases with some direct relevance to the topic of my research, and both had a diagnosis that was not connected with either morality or sexuality. If I had followed my previous research criteria, I would not have come across them. Ennio Passalia observes that, in the 1881–1920 period he investigated, some loose omni-comprehensive diagnostic terms, such as *stato maniacale*, manic status, were widely used in the Girifalco asylum. In his view, this implies its psychiatrists' inability to formulate a clear-cut diagnosis. The two patients I found were diagnosed with such broad non-committal terms, one with frenasthenia, the other with *dementia praecox*, both categories that belong to this group of vague and non-committal definitions. The word frenasthenia comes from the Greek and literally means weakness of mind, so it is the vaguest term available to refer to any psychiatric problem. It was widely used in the Girifalco asylum patient files, in the three years of the *Ventennio* I considered, together with other broad diagnoses such as delirium and mental confusion. In any case, under these loose definitions, homosexuality was mentioned only once in the three years examined, and it was never mentioned in the diagnosis or as the main reason for internment.

Furthermore, in the three years analysed, there were no diagnoses of moral madness, immorality, perversion or amorality. Only a few cases of erotic tendencies or erotic manias were noted, together with other diagnoses vaguely related to sexuality such as psychosis induced by the climacteric or menopause. Annibale Puca, in his long commemorative article to mark the fiftieth anniversary of the institution, mentioned the internment of only eleven cases of sexual psychopathies, and twenty-five cases of moral madness, included in the broader psycho-degeneration category, without specifying in which year they were interned.[46] He also added that this type of diagnosis was a tribute to the old school, as mentioned earlier. In other words, he considered it old-fashioned.[47]

However, although moral madness, morality and sexuality were almost never mentioned in the diagnosis, the patient's moral conduct prior to interment was always commented upon by the GP because the form that accompanied a patient to the asylum, the *Modula Informativa*, asked for many details, starting from family history, and including the patient's behaviour and moral conduct before internment. The judgement on these aspects was therefore an integral part of the reasons why a person was interned and reinforced the mental health illness diagnosis, although it rarely appeared to be the main reason for interment. Psychiatrists relied heavily on GP evaluations and on corroborating documents issued by the police or witnesses. The *Modula Informativa*'s descriptions were often just copied into the patient's medical history file and there is no proof that psychiatrists ever contested any of them. Furthermore, as Passalia rightly stresses, the *Modula Informativa* was formulated in such a way that it strongly influenced doctors in their pathologizing certain behaviours, such as onanism, for example.

Issues connected with morality and sexuality were frequently mentioned in the *Modula Informativa* and appeared, in an identical formulation, in medical notes. Several patients, especially women, were said to be dominated by erotic delirium or to be erotomaniac, have erotic tendencies and similar definitions. Among them, there was, for instance, C.E., a single thirty-four-year-old primary schoolteacher, who was referred to the psychiatric system on request of the *Carabinieri* Marshal in 1939 because she was said to be affected by

> massive hysteria fits based on obscene ideas and on exhibitionism of some parts of her body, mental confusion, logorrhoea and persistent desire for men. For these reasons Miss C. with her obscene ideas can be damaging and give the bad example of lack of shame in public, I therefore judge it necessary to urgently intern her in an asylum.[48]

Morality and sexuality did not appear in her diagnosis, though. She was in fact diagnosed as affected by 'serious delirium', a category that I would have not taken into consideration if I had followed my previous methodological criteria and that does not bear any immediate connection with morality or sexuality.

Frequently, the words 'scandal' or 'scandalous behaviour' or 'obscene acts' appear in the patient's file or in the accompanying witness statement, usually associated with exhibitionism or erotic tendencies, mostly in women. For instance, B.R., who was diagnosed with hallucinatory psychosis, was said to have lost 'every sense of shame thus giving public scandal';[49] or L.P.R., a widow, indigent, illiterate, affected by persecution delirium was also said to 'periodically suffer from phases of excitement with an erotic tendency and exhibitionism'.[50] Her medical certificate stated: 'She suffers from a sexual psychopathy, characterised by shameless exhibitionism, consisting in ostentatious show of her naked body in public, thus creating public scandal.' She was diagnosed with a manic-depressive psychosis. Her notes are one of the few instances where the sexual psychopathy is explained.

In the Girifalco asylum in the fascist period, and in previous decades, onanism was usually remarked upon as an aspect of pathological male behaviour.[51] When it was observed in a patient, it was usually attached to a picture of general symptoms, and the diagnosis rarely mentioned anything to do with sexuality or morality. For instance, in the case of Z.S., onanism was associated with a diagnosis of epilepsy with frenasthenia.[52] In this sense, the case of L.B. is an exception. He was said to have the habit of having sex with prostitutes, demonstrating he was affected by erotic delirium and a 'delirium of self-accusation', as he felt guilty of abandoning his wife to seek sexual gratification elsewhere.[53] As an appendix to his situation, he was also described as having a tendency towards auto-eroticism. In this case, a vague explanation of the patient's mental state was attempted and onanism was related to his general moral conduct. Even in this case, however, the diagnosis was schizophrenia.

In all cases, when moral deficiency or immoral conduct of a patient was mentioned, it was not detailed further. Often very generic terms and expressions were used to allude to sexual behaviour, immorality and so forth. This way of leaving things unsaid can be exemplified by many cases. Among them, there was R.M., an unmarried housewife, indigent, illiterate, mother of a child, who was diagnosed with senile dementia, and whose *Modula Informativa* spoke about 'moral perversion'.[54] The Catanzaro head of police's note ordered her internment saying that she was 'affected by agitation and moral perversions'. No detail on her moral conduct was further explained, analysed during internment, diagnosed or commented upon by psychiatrists or by nurses.

The general impression is that morality and sexuality were not a priority in the Calabrian institution specialists' eyes. They were part of the patient's overall pathological picture and were included in the medical notes, as required by the pre-printed medical history form and medical file. They merely helped to complete the description of a patient's condition and were not the object of specific examination, in fact hardly any further detail emerged in relation to this during internment.[55] The other possible hypothesis to explain the silence is that specialists censored themselves and preferred to keep perversions or issues connected with sexuality unspoken, without spelling out the word homosexuality, for instance, so that the element of danger could be lessened or ruled out *a priori*, and internment could take place without having to follow special procedures. In other words, to sweep sexuality and homosexuality under the carpet was a way to avoid bureaucratic and care complications, such as extra-surveillance or patient isolation, which the few overworked doctors could not comply with. So, medical notes mentioning F.N.'s 'vices', L.A.'s 'moral and affective perversion', G.S.'s 'notable moral perversion', T.E.'s 'hallucinations with an erotic content and moral and affective perversion' could all be ways to refer to homosexuality, although this has to remain a mere hypothesis.[56] This could also apply to the several unmarried patients described as *disaffettivi*, a term that indicates emotional inability to feel affection, but could have been deployed to indicate that the patient was not interested in a love relationship with a heterosexual partner.

Girifalco psychiatrists followed Lombroso's guidelines and underlined any somatic anomaly which pointed to an evolutionary delay or degeneration. They diligently complied with routine practice requirements and measured skulls, hips, chests and limbs, in clear accordance with Lombrosian teaching. The forms did not ask any specific question on genitalia, but among the body measurements, the description of genitals was often volunteered by the psychiatrist who carried out the first patient assessment. Since such considerations were not specifically asked for, it seems that the Girifalco doctors had completely absorbed not only the Lombrosian school's thought but also Marañon's and his followers' theories, and considered it appropriate to routinely insert this type of information. They probably also shared Vincenzo Fragola's views who, when talking about alcoholism, a frequent condition among the Girifalco patients, stated that it affected sexual organs and consequently determined somatic degenerative characteristics, due to biochemical alterations, in alcoholics' children.[57] Nevertheless, this type of information was not elaborated on or commented upon in subsequent notes or in the *Annali*. Interestingly, in fact, the asylum journal never published articles on specific cases encountered in asylum practice, like other similar journals did, but either simply made public the directors' official reports on the asylum from an organizational and administrative perspective, or offered essays on broad subjects, such as the connection between tuberculosis and a tendency to commit crime. In this case too, concrete examples taken from the Girifalco asylum interned population were not offered.

In conformity with this Lombrosian context and with its idea of the connection between physical appearance and mental health, in the years analysed most patients were photographed, and their image was glued on to the front page of their file. According to Passalia, the habit of photographing each patient and inserting the image into his/her file was introduced in Girifalco in 1914, a time of hegemony of Lombrosian theories in Italian psychiatric practice.[58] The asylum documentation proves that in the 1920s and 1930s photographic evidence of body appearances was still considered important, here more than elsewhere. Almost every patient's file had a photograph in the first year examined, 1924, while the number of photographs only slightly decreased in the 1930s. However, even when a somatic anomaly was detected, the photographer seems to have contradicted the task he was called on to perform. While in Florence, for instance, N.N.'s case was documented by the image of a patient, naked, tense and uncomfortable, here patients were photographed in a respectful head-and-shoulder frontal shot that clearly reveals they were clothed.[59] The photographer, probably an acquaintance of most patients in such a small provincial context, managed to obtain a series of portraits that are remarkable because of the subjects' relatively relaxed attitude in front of the camera. His lens did not intrude further and did not document any physical fault.

In addition, the detailed observation of body anomalies also failed to draw the attention of the Girifalco psychiatrists, as the patient diagnosis or medical notes show. After the initial psychiatric assessment, considerations on somatic defaults never reappeared. For instance, C.N., an unmarried shepherd diagnosed with epilepsy in 1939, in his anthropological degenerative notes was described as having 'a cranial-facial asymmetry. An infantile aspect is in contrast with his normally developed genitalia. The body hair disposition is not normal (the disposition of hairs in the pubic area is slightly feminine) .... Excessive development of breast.'[60] After this remark, his file never concentrated on this aspect again or on the consequences that these physical traits were thought to have at the time.

The two Girifalco cases: Exceptions or tips of the iceberg?

In 1924, 1933 and 1939 only one Girifalco patient was described as a 'passive pederast'. T.R., unmarried, illiterate, indigent and without a profession, born in 1910, was interned on 23 January 1939.[61] His diagnosis was frenasthenia and in his file he was said to have no degenerative anthropological aspects worthy of notice, his organs were judged as healthy and no comment was formulated on his genitalia. The certificate issued by the local administration, part of the necessary documentation for discussion of the patient's internment, did not mention homosexuality at all. It stated only that T.R. was 'affected by serious frenasthenia since he was born, lately his actions were of public scandal and he became aggressive and dangerous'. The public scandal caused by the patient was only explained in the Girifalco asylum medical history form box, which asked, 'How long ago and in which way did the current illness start?' The psychiatrist replied, 'In the last few months he gave signs of psycho-motor excitement and was of public scandal for acts of pederasty.' This detail was probably revealed by the GP, in the *Modula Informativa*, which in this case was probably lost, as it is absent from his file. At admission, T.R. appeared to be 'calm. Oriented in time and space. Evident delay in mental development. Defective ideation and critical skills.' His measurements, both of body and skull, were marked, he was photographed, his perception and attention were judged as good, his intellectual patrimony as poor, his memory normal. He was described as tidy, respectful and clean. In the 'conscience and orientation' section of the psychic analysis part of the clinical file, the psychiatrist said: 'He has full knowledge of his psychic inferiority state.' If this was a way to say that he admitted his homosexuality and believed it was a problem or a factor that determined his inadequacy, it was certainly obscure. In the 'Feelings and affection' box, he was said to be *disaffettivo*, a term that implies a total emotional numbness. This too could be an ambiguous way to describe a homosexual patient, thought to be incapable of having a heterosexual family and therefore a recognized and approved world of affections. Clearly, it would be a very ambiguous way to infer it and, in any case, in the Girifalco asylum's files, the word *disaffettivo* was used in many patient descriptions. The word can be included in the list of vague and omni-comprehensive terms in use in this psychiatric hospital and referred to earlier in the chapter. Importantly, he was said to have no dangerous tendencies. In his file, all these comments and definitions resurfaced several times over the years and in different handwriting, including the absence of danger the patient presented.

Looking at the daily reports, we learn that, on 28 January 1939, a few days after internment, the patient stated, 'He passively obeyed, he says, to an act of "sodomy", but without eroticism.'[62] In other words, the patient tried to justify himself by stating that he was to some degree coerced into having sex with another man, and underlined that there was no willingness on his part to engage in same-sex sexual intercourse, ambiguously adding that he had felt no sexual pleasure from it. This remark is a tangible proof of how the medical and psychiatric discourse on homosexuality had been absorbed by the Italian population. This man knew the difference – and the importance given by psychiatrists to the difference – between habitual and occasional, inborn and acquired, passive and active homosexuality. He 'placed' himself in what he thought was the best possible situation in the eyes of the medical authorities. Outed by his GP, who described him as a passive homosexual, he knew that the weakness of his position could only be improved by stating that he was an occasional homosexual. In fact, in his case, as he had been forced into an act of sodomy, his sexual inversion would constitute an isolated exception. In addition, as he had felt no pleasure, the implication was that he was not an inborn homosexual at all.

T.R. was assigned to agricultural ergotherapeutic activities, and after a couple of months the person who wrote his notes commented, 'He never has either dangerous impulses or pederast tendencies.' Later described as cheerful but lacking in moral and critical skills, the absence of danger he presented was frequently remarked upon.

There is no indication of any pharmacological therapy or other treatments being prescribed or administered to T.R., although in other Girifalco patient files these were sometimes specified. There is also no trace of specific examinations being carried out to ascertain his 'passive' homosexuality.[63] The patient was simply kept in the institution, it seems, and although he presented no behavioural problem and was considered not dangerous, he was never discharged. In 1960, he contracted tuberculosis and was transferred to a sanatorium, where he died fourteen years later.

The aspect of danger was only mentioned in the official certificate that supported T.R.'s internment, and never again. Clearly, to justify internment, the element of danger had to be present, together with that of scandal, in observance of Article 1 of Law 104.[64] Homosexuality was depicted by the regime as a condition that would fulfil both requirements, but here it looks as if it were a sterile formula deployed to obey national guidelines. As this case shows, the Girifalco asylum psychiatrists disagreed with the automatic association between homosexuality and dangerousness and made sure that this was clear. The patient's homosexuality was always remarked upon, but no other negative aspect of T.R. was associated with it and danger was specifically ruled out. The case seems to illustrate Fragola's previously mentioned complaint that GPs only concentrated on the danger posed by patients, rather than providing details on their health and behaviour. During his internment, the patient was sometimes described as having poor or no moral sense or feelings, without further explanations.

The second case found in the archives is of a different nature. G.A., a twenty-seven-year-old cobbler, a widower with a basic education, was interned in the Girifalco asylum in 1933.[65] He had a long history of internments; he was first interned in Turin and Palermo, as stated on the cover of his file, and in the Aversa criminal asylum, probably only for an assessment, as stated in a Palermo asylum director's certificate. In Turin, according to his medical notes, he had shown delirium with a persecution content.[66] In this case too, the *Modula Informativa* is absent and G.A.'s Girifalco medical file starts with notes taken in Palermo, where he was admitted in December 1922, after a short period of time spent inside a hospice in the same town. At admission, in the 'psychic functions' section of his file, he was described as 'a fairly calm subject, with a depressive attitude, who presents persecution delirium. He lacks critical skills and feelings of affection.' The diagnosis was of *dementia praecox*, but surprisingly his clinical history form, started in Palermo and simply transferred to the Girifalco colleagues, was left mostly blank. His sensitivity was described as normal, so was his motility. Only the reflexes of his tendons were mentioned, and they were judged to be slightly exaggerated. However, no routine measurements were taken, no anomaly was noted and his file has no photograph on its cover. The daily reports too started in December 1922.[67] These notes from Palermo, all written by the same person until 1933, described him as a calm, quiet, oriented, depressed person with a persisting persecution complex. The patient was presumably asked to explain what had happened and why he was referred to a mental health hospital when he was in the north of Italy, and he replied that he thought that in Turin his landlady and neighbours tried to poison him. Apart from the persecution complex, his firm refusal to work in the shoe-mending workshop was the only sign that the nurse thought worthy of notice in an otherwise tidy and untroublesome patient, who only showed signs of depression and an unwillingness to cooperate.

However, on 23 November 1925, an unexpected gesture caught the Palermo hospital's personnel by surprise. G.A.

> was found in bed by the warden on night duty, he was covered in blood that came from a wound on his scrotum. When he was asked about it, he said that on the evening of 21st he had procured the wound on his scrotum with a sharpened piece of tin, and had managed to tear off his <u>right testicle</u> [underlined in the original] and had swallowed it. As he could not bear the pain, he lay in bed, taking care to sew the wound up with waxed string. He was sent to the infirmary for the necessary medication.

Three days later, the notes reported that 'he was cleaned and medicated by the infirmary doctor and it was necessary to tie him because he manifested the delirious purpose to tear his other testicle off'. G.A. was said to have recovered roughly over a month later. He was sent back to the mental health hospital main building, and later was always described – as usual – as docile, tidy, although still incongruous in his reasoning. After this period of apparent calm, again, on 23 July 1928, he was sent to the *consegnati* section because the previous day he had tried to cut off his other testicle with a piece of sharpened tin.[68] The same routine procedure followed. Roughly six months later, the Palermo notes report that 'he has not tried to commit any other self-harming action again'. He was then transferred from one section to another of the Palermo asylum, sometimes ending up in the ward where self-harming people were kept. These frequent transfers suggest the staff's difficulty in placing this patient from a diagnostic point of view.

Finally transferred to the Girifalco asylum in 1933, one of the two hundred patients coming from Sicily, G.A. was always described as calm and tidy, and his self-harming tendencies were said to have subsided. However, he was judged to be unsuitable for any type of work and his thinking continued to be considered incongruous. His persecution complex was observed to persist, and in 1934 it appeared to have sensibly worsened, as it was combined with some 'sensory-delirious problems' and 'ideas with a religious content'. He died in the Girifalco asylum of a brain haemorrhage on 17 October 1939.

The case was catalogued as a self-harming patient affected by dementia. Given the importance assigned to anything to do with genitalia, primary and secondary anatomical details of the opposite sex such as hair disposition, presence of breasts, hip width and so on, it is surprising that the specialists did not think this case called for detailed observation, especially after the first castration attempt had taken place. On the contrary, no comment was noted on his gesture at all, the two self-inflicted surgical operations were only described in the Palermo daily reports section, but they did not attract any further specialist attention. His file contains no mention on any therapy prescribed, his genitalia and physical traits were never commented upon, either in Palermo or in Girifalco, and the patient was never asked why he attempted to castrate himself or questioned about his sexuality.[69]

Conclusions

Despite being an institution situated at the periphery of Italy, geographically distant from the main Italian asylums where psychiatric thought was formulated and discussed, the Girifalco directors demonstrated they were not isolated from theory. They kept informed on what happened elsewhere, in the country and abroad. The Girifalco asylum presented certain aspects of modernity, such as drop-in health care centres and early release followed by home care. Its directors were in line with the psychiatrists' rejection of their role as an extension of the security forces and strongly asserted the medical and scientific stature of psychiatry, like most of their colleagues at a national level. They embraced the national trend that saw mental health problems as curable through pharmacological remedies or ergotherapy, and in fact there is very little mention in patient files or *Annali* articles of psychotherapy or anything that vaguely resembled it. Freud and Krafft-Ebing were never mentioned, and patients were seldom interrogated, from what can be deduced from daily reports. The Girifalco psychiatrists and directors also followed current trends in terms of eugenics, which inspired their preventative work. Consistent with this, they backed some of the regime's theories, especially those connected with the demographic campaign, and considered unmarried people to be predisposed to mental health conditions, for instance. Despite the rapid turnover, there was a high degree of continuity between the main directors of the *Ventennio*, Bernardo Frisco, Vincenzo Fragola and Annibale Puca.

However, the Girifalco directors and doctors, like their Rome and Florence colleagues, did not show any particular interest in sexuality and all the theories connected with studies on sexuality, that were so relevant at the time, in Europe and in Italy. The Calabria asylum specialists continued, following the Lombrosian tradition, to see a connection between body and mind, believed that hereditary factors were of paramount importance, and even saw genital malformations and the existence of features peculiar to the opposite sex as relevant in assessing psychic problems and delay of development of a patient, but did not expand on it. The concept of degeneration did not interest them at all; sexual inversion, somatic or psychic hermaphroditism and all related subjects were never given specific attention, either at a theoretical level or in patients' observation notes.

A possible explanation for this lack of interest is that the Girifalco psychiatrists did not have the time to investigate further, as the medical staff consisted of only three doctors, a director and a vice director that dealt with a patient population of more than four hundred in the 1930s, and was lumbered by multitasking and bureaucratic duties. This might explain why they copied most of what the GP had written in the *Modula Informativa*, added body measurements and other clinical considerations, as required by the medical assessment form, and did not go more in depth. There is no sign that they ever asked many questions of patients, probably in observance with the idea that mental illness was to be addressed and cured only through medicine, or because the patient accounts were discredited in the general anti-psychotherapy positions, but maybe also because they had no time to do so.

In addition, as mentioned earlier in the chapter, the Girifalco specialists had other priorities. The institution was situated in an area characterized by extreme economic depression, most of the patients were described as indigent, malnourished, living in unsuitable conditions, often without a permanent address or in insalubrious homes. The majority of them were illiterate, alcoholism was widespread and their general health was often described as poor. Besides, as the asylum functioned as a hospice, the older age of the average internee might have pushed aside considerations of sexuality even more, at a time when the male and female *climacteric* were considered to bring an end to sexual activity, always perceived in Catholic terms as finalized to procreation. Probably, the Lombrosian stereotype of the patients the specialists encountered daily did not stimulate any further investigation on their part and pushed them to discredit patient accounts.

Despite all these considerations, the Girifalco psychiatrists' lack of interest in sexuality remains difficult to explain. It is plausible that in the three years examined there were more cases of homosexuality but that they remained hidden behind vague terms such as scandalous behaviour, absence of moral feelings, lack of affection, vices and similar ambiguous definitions, as observed earlier. It is possible that psychiatrists avoided the word homosexuality so that internal procedures would be smoother and bureaucratically less complex. To admit a patient was homosexual would imply that he was dangerous, had to be given special attention, perhaps had to be kept in isolation or under separate surveillance, and this would constitute an additional problem in a small and overcrowded mental health institution. In other words, what appears to be lack of interest could simply be a way to cut corners and costs. However, this complete silence remains partially inexplicable.

Equally, the absence of diagnoses of moral madness remains enigmatic. In an era that still favoured it, within a context strongly influenced by Lombrosian thought, it is curious that this formulation was almost completely absent in the Girifalco asylum, in the years analysed. On the contrary, the use of loose and vague diagnostic terminology confirms national trends, but its much wider deployment in the Girifalco asylum restates the impression that psychiatrists opted for the fewer committal definitions that allowed for second thoughts, easy and frequent transfers of a patient from one ward to another, no special care issues or exceptional procedures. Passalia argues that, in the decades preceding Fascism, most of the medical file notes were taken when the patient was discharged or when he or she died inside the institution, as they often appear to have been written in the same handwriting.[70] This might be true for a good percentage of patients' files for the three years of the fascist regime here analysed.

The only two Girifalco asylum cases directly connected with homosexuality and sexuality that were found for the years 1924, 1933 and 1939 are cases where the patients' pathologized behaviours were signalled elsewhere, and their history had been recorded in the first case by the GP, and in the second case by the Palermo asylum staff. In both cases, it would have been impossible to ignore. In the first case, homosexuality was probably clearly stated by the GP on the *Modula Informativa* and had to be taken as it was, although it was not associated with danger and was judged as unproblematic. G.A. came from another institution, the Palermo asylum, where his castration attempt took place and was described in detail. Nevertheless, since mentions of the patient's sexuality were never pronounced, the Girifalco asylum specialists could pretend they did not see anything other than self-harm. Although the case could have been read as unequivocally pointing at an issue connected with sexuality, they refused to investigate further.

The research in the Calabria mental health hospital's archives confirms that, during the *Ventennio*, homosexuality, hermaphroditism and sexuality in general attracted considerable attention from a theoretical point of view that was not matched by the routine practice of mental health hospitals. It was generally considered one of the various evident symptoms of a composite psychic pathological situation. This does not mean that homosexuals were not interned during the fascist regime's years. On the contrary, they were, and their homosexuality counted when their internment was judged as necessary. However, the words homosexuality or sexual inversion were rarely spelled out. This was not only a time-saving strategy, it also confirmed Mussolini's public statements where he asserted that in Italy homosexuality did not exist, as it was a problem only affecting northern Europe and the large islands, by which he meant England primarily. Italian 'stock' consisted only of virile men and of feminine women, the dictator kept shouting. Denying the existence of homosexuals, not pronouncing even the word sexual inversion, or overlooking it, was therefore completely in line with the regime's propaganda. This is probably the reason why, at the Girifalco asylum, nobody felt the need to investigate and discuss the issue. It was not just easier and faster, it was also in line with *fascistizzazione*.

Conclusions

This book has investigated whether psychiatric internment was a tool used by the fascist regime to repress homosexuality. It first analysed psychiatric theory of the time in materials produced during the *Ventennio*, and illustrated the main influences on them, to show how homosexuality, hermaphroditism and connected topics were approached and categorized and which therapies were proposed as an effective cure for these conditions. The second part of the book is based on archival research carried out in three different Italian mental health institutions whose size, geographical location, tradition and level of national and international reputation varied. The intention was to give a wide spectrum of practical attitudes and approaches towards homosexual patients in fascist Italy and to ascertain to what extent psychiatric practice implemented theoretical thinking.

This research demonstrates that in the few cases where homosexuality was among the main causes for internment, it was brought to the attention of the psychiatric system by patients' families, members of the patients' local communities or the security forces, who thought psychiatry was the most appropriate discipline to address and correct out-of-the-norm sexual behaviour when other coercive methods had failed. The general assumption was that psychiatry had a duty to intervene when such cases were brought to its attention. Relatives of sexually non-conforming individuals asked psychiatrists to play the moralizing and social control role that the 1904 internment law had assigned to their profession.

When solicited by relatives, security forces and community representatives, psychiatry agreed to offer its knowledge and services, and interned sexually non-conforming individuals. Relatives and figures of authority show that they expected psychiatry to intervene and they thought it was its duty to intern non-conforming individuals. When they encountered psychiatrists' doubts on the need to intern, they felt entitled to pressurize them. However, there was a high degree of reluctance and resentment among psychiatrists when they interned these patients. In fact, in most cases, they dissented with families and the security forces who had referred them to an asylum in the first place and strongly disagreed with the idea that internment was a suitable cure for homosexuality. Therefore, while homosexuality was a concern for families, imbued with the regime's propaganda, and for the security forces, who implemented the regime's call for moralization, mental health professionals disagreed but did not refuse to do what the law prescribed. Psychiatrists did what they were expected to do and interned sexual 'deviants' and, among them, homosexuals, but only to state that homosexuality was not the main cause of a mental health problem, that these cases were not particularly interesting from a scientific point of view, that homosexual patients were not to be isolated from the other internees and that their early release was desirable.

In particular, in the study of the Rome asylum it emerges that psychiatrists consistently refuted the idea that homosexual patients constituted a danger, as their notes invariably prove, thus openly contravening the clear directives imposed on Santa Maria della Pietà staff. In Florence and Girifalco asylums too, psychiatrists seem to have shared this view. This confirms the existence of a discrepancy between what was imposed from above and how Italians implemented it, already identified by scholars as a distinctive trait of Mussolini's dictatorship, whose orders were often partially disobeyed or disregarded. This widespread non-alignment between the regime's directives and their effective implementation has recently been interpreted as a form of passive resistance to Fascism.[1] Psychiatry had fought for its autonomy since the introduction of the 1904 law, and it continued to do so under the dictatorship, showing boldness and professional pride. The more it felt pressurized and forced to act as a social dumping ground, the more it tried to establish clear boundaries, asserting the dignity of the profession and its importance as a medical and scientific discipline, rejecting its role as ancillary to the security forces. This type of contrast to the regime's directives in terms of medical practice is coherent with the documented presence of several psychiatrists in the Italian *Resistenza*.[2] Despite their reluctance and dissent, however, psychiatrists in the institutions I examined did not exert any open opposition to external pressures.

Rome and Florence asylum directors were eager to prove they implemented *fascistizzazione* in the institution they managed, and open contestation of the regime's impositions was carefully avoided. The image psychiatry wanted to convey was that of obedience to the dictatorship's guidelines and beliefs. The asylum directors' written communications to staff emphasized the necessity to adopt all the new fascist rites, words and expressions; the rhetoric of internal correspondence was geared towards leaving no doubt on their acceptance of fascist dogma. The eyes of the regime, through its authorities and representatives, were constantly checking asylums, their practices and procedures, therefore appearances had to be commendable. It was the price to pay for a considerable degree of autonomy. This superficial adherence to fascist impositions proved convincing not only to the authorities and the regime's representatives but also to the Italian population at large, who perceived psychiatry as the *longa manu* of the regime. With few exceptions, those who referred sexually non-conforming relatives, fellow citizens, neighbours and acquaintances to the psychiatric system had no doubt that psychiatry would raise no objection and would implement the regime's clear indications on matters of sexuality, morality, eugenics and the demographic campaign. Asylum directors are very likely to have known about the attitudes of their medical staff towards homosexual patients, which was in disobedience with directives, but they chose not to intervene. They ensured that appearances were satisfactory, that episodes of misconduct were addressed, but they seem to have concentrated their attention on nurses rather than psychiatrists. A considerable amount of time went into implementing *fascistizzazione*, while they also spent a great deal of their efforts in engaging in a relentless struggle for power with the provincial authorities and security forces.

The fact that psychiatrists who worked in the three mental health institutions I analysed unanimously seem to consider homosexuals not dangerous indicates that the idea of the contagiousness of sexual inversion, through seduction or coercion, was gradually fading away. In accordance with psychiatric theory, homosexuality was increasingly considered to be mostly congenital by medical professionals and acquired homosexuality was believed to be a possibility only in certain circumstances of vulnerability and when a congenital predisposition was present. The depiction of external factors and influences as a possible trigger of homosexuality does not seem to have had a real impact on psychiatric practice. Isolation of patients whose homosexuality was ascertained and noted in their patient's file was therefore considered unnecessary. Homosexual patients were kept in pavilions together with the rest of internees; punishment was inflicted only when episodes of sexual violence on patients unwilling to have a sexual rapport was detected.

As psychiatry did not refuse to intern homosexuals referred to the psychiatric system by relatives and public order forces, internment worked as an effective deterrent for them as much as *confino* did. To paraphrase Emilio Lussu's famous statement, it was a punishment that hit very few, but that everybody feared because it could happen to anyone.[3] It was a known fact that, despite its diverging opinions, psychiatry responded favourably to the call of families and police to intern homosexuals, something that contributed to the constant fear the Italian population experienced during the dictatorship. The absence of cases connected with sexuality in the *Storie Cliniche dei Ricoverati* in Florence, consisting of notes on patients who were not interned, confirms it. This is the most important finding in this research, and it is completely in line with recent studies on the type of repression that the fascist regime put in place. Relying on spies, informants and zealous members of the public, the coercive action of the dictatorship introduced terror in everyday life.[4] Punishment was unpredictable, discretionary, disproportionate and constantly hung over everyone's heads, and this produced a level of fear that influenced every citizen's action and decision, as observed by Michael Ebner, among others.[5] Therefore, the repression of homosexuality through psychiatry also consisted of LGBT people living in perennial fear of being referred by relatives, colleagues, neighbours or the security forces, to whom psychiatry never refused its services. Aware of the impending and constant danger of being interned, fined, sent to *confino* or kept in a prison cell without clear charges, homosexuals self-censored, lived underground lives, contracted cover-up marriages, remained silent and in the closet.

Furthermore, the Rome, Florence and Girifalco asylum psychiatrists' choice not to analyse the cases of homosexual patients in great detail, of not even mentioning their sexual inversion on the cover of their files and of omitting most details of their sexuality whenever possible was also coherent with Fascism's denial of the existence of homosexuality in Italy. To consider sexual inversion as a secondary and accessory aspect of mental illness was a way to dismiss it, to look at it as an insignificant presence within Italian society, thus reinstating the virility of the Italian 'stock'. It was politically impossible to criticize, and at the same time it served another purpose. As psychiatrists were aware of the implications that a homosexual patient was supposed to have, in terms of extra surveillance or detailed observation, for instance, the choice not to mention sexual inversion was also an effective way to cut costs and simplify procedures. Given the regular overcrowding of asylums, the lack of adequate nursing staff and the chronically low resources, doctors chose the easiest way to handle this type of patient, which consisted in not acknowledging their homosexuality whenever possible, making them equal to all the rest of the internees and avoiding the problems the new directives created. When the patient's homosexuality was impossible to ignore because it was signalled by relatives or external figures of authority, to underline that the patient was not dangerous meant that s/he was not considered worthy of internment, according to article 1 of the 1904 internment law.

It must be highlighted that a gender imbalance clearly emerged from this analysis. The number of homosexual men exceeded by far that of lesbians. Out-of-the-norm women's sexuality was often remarked and commented upon, and exhibitionism, 'eroticism' and sexual promiscuity were included both in the diagnoses and in the description of several female patients. However, the absence of comments on female patients' lesbianism seems to be a deliberate choice to avoid the subject. The ambiguous medical descriptions of the many women interned during the *Ventennio* because of their generic rebellious behaviour and out-of-the-norm sexuality make lesbians invisible and undetectable. In other words, lesbians were presumably interned in higher numbers than those this research found, but in some cases, they were probably referred to psychiatric care with diagnoses that did not mention sexuality or morality at all, while in other cases, they were interned because of their non-conforming sexuality or immorality, but their lesbianism was not mentioned. In any case, this aspect is coherent with psychiatric theory of the time. During the years of the fascist regime lesbianism attracted less interest than in the previous decades, where, as observed by scholars, it was always present at least in theoretical psychiatric work. During the *Ventennio*, as shown in Chapter 2, Italian theoreticians seem to have focused mostly on male homosexuality and so did asylum psychiatrists, as observed in several circumstances in three asylums here examined. Lesbianism was hardly ever mentioned. This finding is completely in line not only with psychiatric theory but also with the regime's propaganda and the general repression of women's sexuality in all of its aspects, as femininity had to signify modesty, associated with lack of desire or ambition and with innate maternal feelings.

In a minority of instances, psychiatrists still judged the moral conduct of the homosexual patients, or did not question the moral judgement formulated by GPs, nurses, families and witnesses, but in the majority of cases they maintained a distance from moral accusations. In the overall evident attempt to disentangle psychiatry from Roman Catholicism, and to transform it into a modern scientific and objective discipline, psychiatrists insisted on considering homosexuality just one of the manifestations of a mental condition and refrained from formulating moral judgements. Negative remarks by relatives, nurses and GPs were not totally discredited, though, and they were often transcribed in medical files, without being questioned, modified or changed. In certain cases, these notes written prior to internment bore a decisive weight on the formulation of the final diagnosis, probably not to contradict members of staff who were increasingly recruited because of their political ideas, rather than merit. However, despite the effort to stay clear of moral judgements, these attitudes clearly persisted, especially towards women with out-of-the-norm behaviour.

The absence of scientific interest shown for homosexual patients in asylums, the evident suspension of judgement on these cases and the tendency not to prescribe specific therapies to cure homosexuality reinforce the idea of an existing and widening gap between psychiatric theory and practice. While in fact during Fascism, psychiatric theory continued to concentrate its attention on sexual inversion and its possible somatic evidence, signs of hermaphroditism, congenital and inherited homosexual tendencies, connecting them with endocrinology or neurology, studying radical approaches that could alter the patient's sexuality, such as brain surgery and genital transplants or experimental opotherapy, psychiatrists who worked every day at the forefront of mental health care had taken a completely different approach.

Effectively, psychiatric theory followed its own path and had a relatively low impact on daily routine practice. In the much more conservative context of fascist academia, theoreticians remained firmly rooted in the 'glorious past' of Lombrosian tradition. They continued expanding these old theories in new directions, but never radically enough as to abandon them completely. Most Italian theoreticians in fact tried to show the validity of past theories, even when they espoused medical disciplines such as neurology and endocrinology as an explanation for homosexuality. Lombrosian theory was sometimes challenged. For instance, it was generally accepted that in a considerable number of cases of sexual inversion, physical appearance was deceptive, as many homosexuals showed no evident somatic sign of their condition. However, even when links were established between homosexuality and inborn neurological or glandular dysfunctions, theoreticians deployed some efforts to discover the visible somatic aspects of these flaws, in Lombrosian terms. Psychiatric practice seems to have gradually given less importance to somatic elements. Measurements were often absent, or only given to fill the relevant pre-printed forms' boxes. Few comments on measurements appear to have been noted and photographs of patients also seem to have been gradually abandoned. Theoretical thought did not exclude that environment; education, promiscuity and bad example could interfere and play a role in the development of sexuality or in the awakening of latent sexual inversion. Psychiatric practice did not share the same concern. The outcome of theoretical conceptual elaborations of the *Ventennio* was often ambiguous, but theory in Italy insisted on the congenital nature of homosexuality, on an inborn predisposition. Therefore, it appeared confirmed by observation that homosexuality could not just simply be cured. A more radical intervention was called for. These individuals now appeared to be re-programmable through the newest scientific research achievements, genetic hormonal patrimony could be radically altered or genitals and/or brain conformation surgically modified in order to obtain results. Practitioners, on the contrary, were probably aware of new techniques and approaches, but seem to have believed that behaviour correction was possible, and a second chance should be given to homosexual patients, especially if young. They favoured early release and underlined their behaviour improvement, change of views – even when it was too sudden to be plausible – or lack of interest in sex, in their notes, to show that the patient was capable to control his/her instincts. This was coherent with what psychiatric practice encouraged. As available cures, in general, often appeared inadequate, the best results that could be achieved through internment were thought to be self-censorship, gaining inhibitions that had been lost, acquire awareness of behaviour inadequacies and be able to control oneself. Homosexuals, like other psychiatric patients, were observed, and the psychiatrists' hope was that, through the institution discipline, they would learn how to behave in a socially acceptable way. This translated into a very strong message: visibility, open rebelliousness and scandal called for internment by law. If one avoided attracting public attention in the first place, or once interned s/he demonstrated s/he could control his/her instincts, this would be interpreted as a sign of normality and regained sanity. The fascist regime punished homosexuals who were visible, as amply demonstrated by those who analysed the topic, while it was often prepared to turn a blind eye when the issue did not surface. Hypocrisy was encouraged and, in psychiatric terms, was read as proof of sanity.

Theory insisted on the aspect of danger posed by homosexuals to society and believed that pederasts could pervert adolescents, as admitting an inborn bisexuality meant that the 'wrong' part of it could be awoken if solicited. It felt it was imperative to indicate ways to prevent negative influences on young and vulnerable individuals. Arguably, this admission of the influence played by environmental factors in determining an individual's homosexuality represented a regression and reversal of psychiatric theorization in Italy. Its concerns were in line with the moralization campaign launched by the regime, framing the discipline in the defence of traditional values, but this meant moral condemnation of certain behaviours and the pathologization of onanism, for instance, positions that belonged to earlier decades. In other words, theory found itself trapped in the nineteenth-century Roman Catholic–inspired moralizing approach that it wanted to surpass and transcend. Coherently, theoreticians went back to advocating censorship, segregation of sexes, abstinence prior to marriage and old-fashioned remedies such as imposed intercourse with a person of the opposite sex as a valid cure for sexual inversion.

As mentioned, the attempt to cure or correct homosexuality with the most scientific approach possible, advocated by Italian psychiatric theory, led to the complete discredit of psychoanalytic methodology. With few exceptions, psychoanalysis in Italy at the time was generally believed to be unreliable because it was not based on science but on patients' accounts and memories, judged to be, by definition, not objective. In addition, as observed earlier, homosexuals were considered, in Lombrosian terms, to be inherently liars and with a tendency to deceive. This decision put Italian psychiatry at the margins of Europe's most advanced psychiatric thought, relegating it to a debate characterized by provincial isolation. It forced psychiatry in Italy to look to countries such as Spain and France, and to the most traditionalist of German theoreticians, many of whom were strongly rooted in eugenics and degeneration theories. And despite all the best efforts to show the lack of validity in psychoanalytic approaches, Italian psychiatric theoreticians failed to reach a convincing scientific approach to homosexuality, a method that could be applied in all cases in order to detect it, and a valid and widely accepted medical therapy to correct it or prevent it. The terrain proved slippery. The subject always called for exceptions to be added, it escaped a rigid classification based on symptoms or causes and it was difficult to slot into a category. If psychoanalysis was believed to be questionable, science did not offer a clear-cut answer either.

In addition, in the practical psychiatric routine, the contrast with psychoanalytical approaches was to a certain extent disregarded. Patient accounts of their feelings and past lives played a considerable part in the diagnosis and medical description, in clear contradiction with psychiatric theory. The importance of nurses' *diari* is interesting proof of how psychiatrists valued patients' confessions. Nurses had the specific task to gather patients' impressions and comments, and to mark them in their files so that the doctors could be informed on what the patients thought. The general assumption was that a more informal situation of a dialogue with a nurse, usually from a working-class context as much as most asylum patients, could induce patients to recount intimate recollections or personal opinions that were judged useful to formulate a diagnosis. So, psychiatric theory in Italy stayed clear of psychoanalysis and discredited patients' confessions, often judged as mendacious or manipulative, and hands-on psychiatrists did not dare to openly challenge this essential theoretical trend. Yet at the same time, they found a suitable *escamotage* to introduce an innovative approach into asylum routine practice, putting the patient and his/her narrations at the centre of the attention. They clearly thought that patients' voices had to be heard and believed. In P.G.B.'s case, for instance, they learnt from nurses about his cross-dressing, his adventures and his 'feeling he was a woman'. They did not comment on his lifestyle, but they duly noted it. The patient's narrative of his situation and of his past was clearly thought to be relevant and psychiatrists did not want to overlook it. In some instances, judgemental comments were added next to these reported speeches by patients, but the importance given to them was a clear prelude to future developments.

The analysis of the Rome, Florence and Girifalco asylums sheds light not only on doctors' attitudes towards homosexual patients but on nursing practices and professional conduct too. From the available documentation it is possible to see that nursing staff was a constant concern for asylum directors. Their professional misconduct required continual disciplinary action, to the extent that in certain cases it was necessary to call for an 'amnesty' because reprimands and punishments had reached an unmanageable level. The inadequacy of nurses' training was often remarked on by directors, who devised specific courses to partially fill the all-too-evident *lacunae*. However, nurses' misconduct went well beyond professional inadequacy, as it even included theft and exploitation of patients. Their daily reports also reveal that there was often a problem of illiteracy. As observed, the recruitment of nurses was increasingly based on their political background and their proven acceptance of fascist dogma. The adherence of nursing staff to fascist precepts is likely to be one of the reasons why doctors did not question the nurses' daily reports; on the contrary, they took them into consideration and often repeated without criticism in their patient's assessment what the nurse had noted earlier. In a few instances, the nurses' moral judgement on patients' moral conduct was much more aligned with the PNF directives than with doctors' opinions, which shows even more clearly how nursing staff were recruited on the grounds of political belief. Nurses' fascist beliefs are also probably the explanation for the lenient fines and disciplinary measures inflicted on them when their misconduct was punished.

From the analysis of the Rome, Florence and Girifalco asylums, more points of contact and similarities emerged, rather than differences. All three institutions shared the same concerns in terms of nurses' misconduct, regular overcrowding, lack of funding, interference by local authorities and several other aspects of their daily routine. All directors engaged with the authorities and took every opportunity to emphasize psychiatry's dignity as a science, contesting the role of social control increasingly assigned to asylums. The exchange of correspondence with the provincial authority is very similar in the two asylums where it was consultable. Directors reiterated their alignment with government directives and implemented measures to comply with the required *fascistizzazione.* They persisted in showing that the institution under their direction was cost-effective, innovative and that its staff disciplined. In exchange, they insisted on their autonomy and on freedom of movement, drawing attention to any intrusion or trespassing into their sphere of action. From the available documentation, it seems that the three asylums analysed were never officially inspected or reprimanded by the fascist authorities. In each of them, psychiatric practice yields evidence of being more in touch with the rest of the world than its theoretical counterpart. Asylum directors were informed of what went on beyond the Alps, they compared their achievements with results obtained by similar institutions in other countries in terms of prevention, for instance. They generally tried to adopt no-restraint approaches, favoured early release and pioneered drop-in prevention medical centres, strongly believing in the validity of home care. Among the few aspects of Italian theory that left some trace in the daily psychiatric care routine was the somatic measurements box in the standard asylum admission forms. As observed, this section of the forms was often not even filled in by asylum doctors. Moral madness and degeneration had become broad and non-committal descriptions that were increasingly considered old-fashioned, although sometimes they were still regarded as useful as they were sufficiently elastic categories to include all sorts of different symptoms and conditions. There is also consistency in the use of other broad and non-committal diagnostic categories to describe patients, which would allow for subsequent changes of diagnosis and reallocation to different pavilions, in contradiction with theory's effort to categorize and sub-divide the symptoms and causes of mental illness. From the comparative analysis of these three Italian asylums comes a confirmation that psychiatric theory and practice on several issues and approaches had effectively divorced on most issues.

Most homosexual patients interned during the fascist regime and identified in this research had been intercepted by the security forces and referred to the psychiatric system, or were interned at the request of their families. Despite the social stigma that internment implied, the segregation they endured and, in some cases, the forced labour they were subjected to, they somehow reacted, within the limits the situation allowed. Many remained in contact with supportive family members and friends, such as E.C. and P.G.B. in Rome, and showed they could count on a social network and on the understanding of some of their relatives. C.D. in Florence did not leave any correspondence, but had an equally supportive father, despite his conviction for indecency (*oltraggio al pudore*) and his homosexuality. Some patients stubbornly contested their internment and wrote to the director of the institution to have their opinion heard, such as P.M. in Florence. B.P., interned at Santa Maria della Pietà, had fiercely rebelled against brutal and homophobic prison staff. The two patients who were described as active homosexuals, E.C. at Santa Maria della Pietà and D.B.E. at San Salvi, attempted to have a sexual life within the walls of the asylum and continued to do so, despite being reprimanded. Some patients remained silent, or at least their files do not hold any letters written by them, but their obstinate behaviour both in the outside world and inside the asylum, as we learn from their reported statements in their patient's file, is testimony that they did not capitulate, such as the case of L.A., who was interned in Rome. He tried to come out to his family and lived in a steady homosexual relationship that, in the intentions, was to become public and, *ante-litteram*, recognized and legally sanctioned. P.M. in Florence admitted her bisexuality, her liking alcohol and other aspects of her lifestyle, although she probably knew they would be considered negatively by doctors. The voices of the few homosexuals that could be retraced in asylum documentation leave the strong impression of a certain degree of boldness, courage and, if not pride, at least dignity. Their testimony echoes some patient accounts that psychiatrists collected and published in journals at the time, where homosexual patients were negatively judged for refusing to repent, for being happy to remember their lifestyle outside the institution.[6] The psychiatric system did not manage to silence and annihilate them completely.

None of the psychiatric hospital patients whose homosexuality was noted by psychiatrists in the years 1922–43 that my research could identify appear to have received any specific pharmacological or shock treatment. Only in three cases, that of T.R. and of G.A., both in the Girifalco asylum, and N.N. in Florence San Salvi, is there evidence that ergotherapy was assigned, although one of the two Girifalco patients was said to have refused to carry it out. Keeping in mind that sedation was not always marked on the patient's medical notes, the general impression, however, is that doctors were uncertain on a correct and valid therapy for this type of patient or they thought there was no valid cure for their condition. In some cases, they clearly stated that isolation from society and family, together with the asylum discipline, generally thought to be apt measures in most cases, on these patients proved unnecessary and useless. The experience of being interned, for most of these homosexual men and women, translated into mere incarceration and exclusion from society, and psychiatrists were often not convinced these would work. If mental health institutions' doctors believed that other, more drastic cures such as brain surgery or testicle transplants would be more appropriate – which cannot be excluded, although there is no trace of this view in their notes – it would have been impossible to implement them, given the inadequate structure, means and budget of the asylums I analysed. There is no retraceable indication that proves that any of these patients were ever sent to hospital to receive specific medical treatment or to be subjected to surgical operations elsewhere.

To conclude, the analysis of the three chosen Italian mental health hospitals shows that during Fascism, very few homosexual patients were interned because of their sexual inversion, and usually, when they were, they had a diagnosis that had nothing to do with their sexual orientation. In most cases, homosexuality was clearly stated only inside the patient's file and was treated almost as a collateral symptom, one of the many manifestations of a mental health condition. However, since psychiatry always reacted positively when a homosexual was referred to a mental health institution because of his or her sexuality, internment was a tangible and omnipresent risk for homosexuals in fascist Italy. Fear of internment, rather than internment itself, was a powerful tool of repression of homosexuality used not only by the regime and its representatives but also by members of Italian society. Mussolini's propaganda worked effectively in transforming every citizen into a collaborator and a consistent part of the Italian population agreed to play a role in the moralization campaign the regime promoted. Families, together with the security forces and other figures of authority, had the certainty they could count on psychiatry as a reluctant, but ultimately obedient ally. Psychiatric practice, under pressure and with no backing from its theoreticians and academics, accepted this social control and moralizing role at a formal level, while, under the surface, it tried to impose a shift of mentality and approach. Psychiatrists of the *Ventennio* could not completely subvert the rules, but considering the level of pressure they were subjected to, and the fact that theory had adhered in a compact way to central government directives, their professional conduct shows a degree of courage that cannot be underestimated.

The fear of internment remained ingrained in the Italian LGBT community for many decades after the *Ventennio*, as homosexuals continued to be referred and interned in the following decades. Psychiatry was clearly identified as the most dreaded tool of repression of homosexuality in the years of the Sexual Liberation Movement. The fact that mostly visible homosexuals were reprimanded, incarcerated or interned left a powerful legacy in Italy, where invisibility continued to be considered an essential condition for survival for several decades after Liberation.

Notes

Introduction

1 Dall'Orto Giovanni, 'Manicomi e Omosessualità in Italia (1880–1978)', www. wikipink.it, 20 December 2017.

2 Nerina Milletti, 'Analoghe Sconcezze. Tribadi, saffiste, invertite e omosessuali: categorie e sistemi sesso/genere nella rivista di antropologia fondata da Cesare Lombroso (1848–1949)', *DWF* 24 (1994): 50–122.

3 I put in brackets the dates of birth and death of psychiatrists and theoreticians only the first time I mention them. When dates of birth and death are not written in brackets, it means that these could not be found.

4 Gabriella Romano, *The Pathologisation of Homosexuality in Fascist Italy: The Case of G.* (Basingstoke: Palgrave Macmillan 2019).

5 Vinzia Fiorino, *Le Officine della follia. Il frenocomio di Volterra, 1888–1978* (Pisa: ETS, 2011); Mimmo Franzinelli and Nicola Graziano, *Un'Odissea Partigiana: Dalla Resistenza al Manicomio* (Milano: Feltrinelli, 2015); Annacarla Valeriano, *Ammalò di testa: Storie del Manicomio di Teramo (1880–1931)* (Roma: Donzelli, 2014); Annacarla Valeriano, *Malacarne: Donne e Manicomio nell'Italia Fascista* (Roma: Donzelli, 2017). I analyse these books later in the chapter.

6 For instance, Massimo Tornabene, *La Guerra dei Matti: Il Manicomio di Racconigi tra fascismo e Liberazione* (Boves: Araba Fenice, 2007).

7 Richard Cleminson and Francisco Vasquez Garcia, *Los invisibles: A History of Male Homosexuality in Spain 1850–1940* (Cardiff: University of Wales Press, 2007).

8 Alvar Martinez-Vidal and Adam Antoni Donat, 'Homosexuality, psychiatry and legal medicine in Franco's regime and democratic transition in Spain, 1936–1979', in *Citizens, Courtrooms, Crossings*, edited by Astri Andresen, Tore Grønlie, William Hubbard, Teemu Ryymin, and Svein Atle Skålevåg (Bergen: Bergen University Press, 2008), 107–18.

9 Runar Jordåen, 'Concepts of same-sex sexuality in Norwegian forensic psychiatry, 1930–1945', in *Citizens, Courtrooms, Crossings*, Astri Andresen, Tore Grønlie, William Hubbard, Teemu Ryymin, and Svein Atle Skålevåg (Bergen: Bergen University Press, 2008), 95–106.

10 In particular: Florian Mildenberger, *Kulturverfall und Umwandlungsmännchen: die Psychiatrie und die Homosexuellen im Dritten Reich am Beispiel München* (München: Forum Homosexualität und Geschichte München, 2000); Florian

Mildenberger, 'Kraepelin and the "urnings": Male homosexuality in psychiatric discourse', *History of Psychiatry* 18, no. 3 (2017): 321–35.

11 Malick Briki, *Psychiatrie et homosexualité. Lectures médicales et juridiques de l'homosexualité dans les sociétés occidentales de 1850 à nos jours* (Besançon: Presses Universitaires de Franche-Comté, 2009).

12 Janet Weston, *Medicine, the Penal System and Sexual Crimes in England, 1919–1960s* (London: Bloomsbury, 2017).

13 Ira Rodulgina, 'Why are we the people we are? Early Soviet homosexuals from the first-person perspective', *Ab Imperio* 2 (January 2016): 183–216.

14 Ferruccio Giacanelli, 'Note per una ricerca sulla psichiatria italiana tra le due guerre', in *Passioni della mente e della storia*, edited by Filippo Maria Ferro (Milano: Università Cattolica del Sacro Cuore, 1989), 567–75; 567.

15 Ibid., 568.

16 Giorgio Bignami, 'L'unione degli insegnamenti di Neurologia e Psichiatria nella riforma fascista dell'università', in *Passioni*, edited by Ferro, 577–84.

17 For a full concise biography of Franco Basaglia, see www.treccani.it. Among the most recent publications: John Foot, *The Man Who Closed Asylums: Franco Basaglia and the Revolution in Mental Health Care* (London: Verso, 2015).

18 Law n. 180, 13 May 1978.

19 Gianni Rossi Barilli, *Il movimento gay in Italia* (Milano: Feltrinelli, 1999).

20 Patrizia Guarnieri, *La Storia della Psichiatria. Un secolo di studi in Italia* (Firenze: Olschki, 1991), followed by an article on the same subject: Patrizia Guarnieri, 'The history of psychiatry in Italy', *History of Psychiatry* 7, no. 2 (September 1991): 289–301.

21 Laura Benadiba, 'The persistence of silence after dictatorships', *Oral History Review* 39, no. 2 (2012): 287–97.

22 Among the texts consulted: Eugenio Borgna, 'La psichiatria negli anni del fascismo', in *Novara fa da sé: Atti del Convegno di Belgirate – 1993*, edited by Adolfo Mignemi (Novara: Provincia di Novara, 1993), 285–7; Sante De Sanctis, *Autobiografia* (Bologna: Zanichelli, 1937); Giulio Cesare Ferrari, 'Autobiografia', *Rivista di psicologia* (1933): 2–91; Pasquale Giordano, *Storia di uno psichiatra: viaggio critico attraverso la psichiatria italiana di ieri e di oggi* (Firenze: L'Autore Libri, 2012); Giacomo Pighini, *Vita di psichiatra* (Parma: Maccari, 1968); Mario Tobino, *Le libere donne di Magliano* (Milano: Mondadori, [1953] 1963); Fabio Visintini, *Memorie di un cittadino psichiatra (1902–1982)* (Napoli: Edizioni Scientifiche Italiane, 1983).

23 Among the many publications in this field, I consulted: Marilena Massasso, 'I Reparti Femminili di Collegno per "Lavori Donneschi: 1972–78"' (BA diss., University of Turin, academic year 1996–7); Vinzia Fiorino, *Matti, Indemoniati e Vagabondi* (Venezia: Marsilio, 2002); Fiorino, *Le Officine*; Barbara Galligani, 'La storia di Villa Azzurra' (BA diss., University of Turin, academic year 2001–2); Oscar

Greco, *I Demoni del Mezzogiorno: Follia, Pregiudizio e Marginalità nel Manicomio di Girifalco (1881–1921)* (Soveria Mannelli: Rubbettino, 2018); Antonino Iaria, Tommaso Losavio and Pompeo Martelli, *L'Ospedale Santa Maria della Pietà*, vol. I, II, III (Roma: Dedalo, 2003); Massimo Moraglio, *Costruire il manicomio. Storia dell'ospedale psichiatrico di Grugliasco* (Milano: Unicopli, 2002); edited by Massimo Moraglio, *Effimeri entusiasmi, quotidiane sofferenze. La fondazione del manicomio di Racconigi* (Boves: Araba Fenice, 2007); Francesco Cassata and Massimo Moraglio, eds, *Manicomio, società e politica: storia, memoria e cultura della devianza mentale dal Piemonte all'Italia* (Pisa: BFS, 2005); Andrea Scartabellati, *La 'questione follia' in Italia tra fine Ottocento e inizio Novecento e il caso del Manicomio Provinciale di Cremona* (Milano: Franco Angeli, 2001); Tornabene, *La Guerra dei Matti*; Valeriano, *Ammalò*; Valeriano, *Malacarne*.

24 Bignami, 'L'Unione', 584.

25 Such as: Francesco Cassata, *Building the New Man: eugenics, racial science and genetics in XX century Italy* (Budapest: Central European University Press, [2006] 2011); Delia Frigessi, *Cesare Lombroso* (Torino: Einaudi, 2003); Claudia Mantovani, *Rigenerare la società: L'eugenetica in Italia dalle origini ottocentesche agli Anni Trenta* (Soveria Mannelli: Rubbettino, 2004); Claudio Pogliano, *L'Ossessione della razza: antropologia e genetica nel ventesimo secolo* (Pisa: Edizioni Scuola Normale di Pisa, 2005); Claudio Pogliano, 'Bachi, Polli e Grani: Appunti sulla ricezione della genetica in Italia', *Nuncius* 14 (1999): 133–68.

26 I consulted: Valeria Babini, *La questione dei frenastenici. Alle origini della psicologia scientifica in Italia, 1870–1910* (Milano: F. Angeli, 1996); Valeria Babini, Fernanda Minuz and Annamaria Tagliavini, *La donna nelle scienze dell'uomo* (Milano: F. Angeli, 1986); Robert Castel, *L'ordine psichiatrico. L'epoca d'oro dell'alienismo* (Milano: Feltrinelli, 1980); Francesco De Peri, 'Il Medico e il Folle: istituzione psichiatrica, sapere scientifico e pensiero medico tra Otto e Novecento', in *Storia d'Italia, Malattia e Medicina*, Annali 7, edited by Franco della Peruta (Torino: Einaudi, 1984), 1057–140.

27 Among them: Robert Aldrich, *The Seduction of the Mediterranean: Writing, Art and Homosexual Fantasy* (London: Routledge, 1993); Valeria Babini, Chiara Beccalossi and Lucy Ryall, eds, *Italian Sexualities Uncovered, 1789–1914* (Basingstoke: Palgrave Macmillan, 2015); Chiara Beccalossi, *Female Sexual Inversion: Same-sex Desire in Italian and British Sexology, c 1870–1920* (Basingstoke: Palgrave Macmillan, 2012); Sean Brady, *Masculinity and Male Homosexuality in Britain, 1861–1913* (Basingstoke: Palgrave Macmillan, [2005] 2009); Giovanni Dall'Orto, 'I matti son matti: Psichiatria, "normalità", omosessualità', in *Dentro e Fuori*, edited by R. Mauri (Milano: Edizioni Dell'Arco, 2005); Dagmar Herzog, *Sexuality in Europe: A Twentieth Century History* (Cambridge: Cambridge University Press, 2011); Dagmar Herzog, ed., *Sexuality and German Fascism* (New York: Berghahn Books, [2002]

2005); Milletti, *Analoghe Sconcezze*; Florence Tamagne, *A History of Homosexuality in Europe: Berlin, London, Paris 1919–1939* (New York: Algora, [2000] 2006); 'Italy: Sexuality, Morality and Public Authority', in *Sexual Cultures in Europe*, Franz Eder, Leslie Hall and Gert Hekma, eds (Manchester: Manchester University Press, 1999), 114–37; P. F. Bruno Wanrooij, *Storia del pudore. La questione sessuale in Italia 1860–1940* (Venezia: Marsilio, 1990); Perry Wilson, ed., *Gender, Family and Sexuality: The Private Sphere in Italy 1860–1945* (Basingstoke: Palgrave Macmillan, 2004).

28 Matteo Fiorani, *Bibliografia di storia della psichiatria italiana* (Firenze: Firenze University Press, 2010).

29 Romano Canosa, *Storia del manicomio in Italia dall'Unità a Oggi* (Milano: Feltrinelli, 1979); Michael Donnelly, *The Politics of Mental Health in Italy* (London: Routledge, 1992); Franco Silvano, *Legislazione e politica sanitaria del fascismo* (Roma: APES, 2011); Ada Lonni, 'Pubblica Sicurezza, Sicurezza Pubblica e Malato di Mente. La Legge del 1904', in *Follia, Psichiatria, Società*, edited by Alberto De Bernardi (Milano: F. Angeli, 1982), 264–83.

30 Romano Canosa was a magistrate who dedicated himself to historical research. He initially investigated issues related to Italian laws, social history and sexuality. Among his books in these fields: *Storia della criminalità in Italia, 1845–1945* (Torino: Einaudi, 1991); *La Restaurazione sessuale: per una storia della sessualità tra Cinquecento e Settecento* (Milano: Feltrinelli, 1993); *Storia di una grande paura: la sodomia a Firenze e a Venezia nel Quattrocento* (Milano: Feltrinelli, 1991); *Sessualità e Inquisizione in Italia tra Cinquecento e Seicento* (Roma: Sapere, 1994). In more recent years he wrote extensively on Fascism, and among his many titles on the subject, it is worth mentioning: *I servizi segreti del Duce: persecutori e vittime* (Milano: Mondadori, 2000); *La voce del Duce: l'agenzia Stefani, l'arma segreta di Mussolini* (Milano: Mondadori, 2002); *A caccia di ebrei: Mussolini, Preziosi e l'antisemitismo fascista* (Milano: Mondadori, 2006); *Mussolini e Franco: amici, alleati, rivali* (Milano: Mondadori, 2008; *Farinacci: il superfascista* (Milano: Mondadori, 2010). Given his knowledge of the law and his interest in Fascism, his book, *Storia del manicomio in Italia dall'Unità a oggi* (Milano: Feltrinelli, 1979), is considered one of the most valid texts available on the history of psychiatric health institutions in Italy and their evolution from the second part of the nineteenth century to the 1970s. It is also one of the few texts that analyses in depth psychiatric institutions during the fascist period.

31 The Rocco Code of Law was introduced in 1930 and became fully operational in 1931. It substituted the Zanardelli Code.

32 Canosa, *Storia del Manicomio*, 166. 'Constitutional' theories see mental illness as a consequence of an illness or malfunction of a part of the body.

33 Benadiba, 'The persistence'.

34 Francesco Paolo Peloso, *La Guerra Dentro: La Psichiatria Italiana tra Fascismo e Resistenza 1922–1945* (Verona: Ombre Corte, 2008).

35 Ibid., 32.

36 Italy had already invaded part of Libya after the Italo-Turkish conflict of 1911–12, but it renewed its efforts in 1922. The Libyan territory became an Italian *Governatorato* in 1934. The colonization of Ethiopia and part of Somalia, then called *Eritrea*, was a totally fascist enterprise. The territories were declared A.O.I. (Africa Orientale Italiana) in 1936.

37 Massimo Moraglio, 'Dentro e fuori il manicomio: L'assistenza psichiatrica tra le due guerre', *Contemporanea* 9, no. 1 (January 2006): 15–34.

38 Valeria Babini, *Liberi Tutti: Manicomi e psichiatri in Italia. Una Storia del Novecento* (Bologna: Il Mulino, 2009).

39 Zbigniew Kotowicz, 'Psychosurgery in Italy, 1936–1939', *History of Psychiatry* 19, no. 4 (2008): 476–89; Zbigniew Kotowicz, *Psychosurgery: The Birth of a New Scientific Paradigm. Egas Moniz and the Present Day* (Lisbon: Centre for Philosophy of Science, University of Lisbon, 2012).

40 Mariopaolo Dario, Giovanni Del Missier, Ester Stocco and Luana Testa, *Psichiatria e psicoterapia in Italia dall'unità a oggi* (Roma: L'Asino D'Oro, 2016). The book was preceded by an article specifically of the topic: Andrea Piazzi, Mariopaolo Dario, Giovanni Del Missier, Ester Stocco and Luana Testa, 'The history of Italian psychiatry during fascism', *History of Psychiatry* 22, no. 3 (2011): 251–67.

41 *Enciclopedia Italiana* (Roma: Treccani, 1925–38).

42 Maria Antonietta Coccanari De' Fornari, Andrea Piazzi, Gioia Piazzi and Luana Testa, 'La rappresentazione della psichiatria italiana nell'Enciclopedia Italiana Treccani degli anni Trenta', *Medicina nei Secoli, Arte e Scienza* 25, no. 2 (2013): 541–64.

43 The last volumes of the *Enciclopedia Italiana* project were published by Treccani in 1937.

44 Matteo Petracci, *I Matti del Duce* (Roma: Donzelli, 2014).

45 Franzinelli and Graziano, *Un'Odissea*.

46 Ibid., 29.

47 Valeriano, *Ammalò*.

48 Valeriano, *Malacarne*.

49 Fiorino, *Le Officine*.

50 Ibid., 196.

51 Ibid., quoted 197.

52 Tornabene, *La Guerra dei Matti*.

53 Ibid., 51.

54 Among them: Giovanni De Luna, *La Repubblica del Dolore. Le Memorie di un'Italia divisa* (Milano: Feltrinelli, 2011); Richard Ned Lebow, Wulf Kansteiner and Claudio

Fogu, eds, *The Politics of Memory in Postwar Europe* (Durham: Duke University Press, 2006); John Foot, *Italy's Divided Memory* (Basingstoke: Palgrave Macmillan, 2009); Silvana Patriarca, *Italian Vices. Nation and Character from the Risorgimento to the Republic* (Cambridge: Cambridge University Press, 2010).

55 S. C. Robert Gordon, *The Holocaust in Italian Culture, 1944–2010* (Stanford: Stanford University Press, 2012); Foot, *Divided*.

56 Primo Levi, *Se Questo è un Uomo* (Torino: De Silva, 1947).

57 Giovanni Dall'Orto, 'Ci furono femminelle che piangevano quando venimmo via dalle Tremiti!', *Babilonia* 50 (October 1987): 26–8; Giovanni Dall'Orto, 'Credere, Obbedire, Non Battere', *Babilonia* 36 (May 1986): 13–17; Giovanni Dall'Orto, 'Per il bene della Razza al Confino il Pederasta', *Babilonia*, 35 (April– May 1986): 14–17; Giovanni Dall'Orto, ed., *La pagina strappata* (Torino: Gruppo Abele, 1987); Giovanni Dall'Orto, 'La "Tolleranza Repressiva" dell'Omosessualità', *Quaderni di Critica Omosessuale* 3 (1987): 37–57.

58 Gianni Rossi Barilli and Paolo Hutter, *Novecento* (1983), [radio programme series] Radio Popolare.

59 *L'altro Ieri* (2001), [documentary] Director Gabriella Romano, Italy; *Ricordare* (2003) [documentary] Director Gabriella Romano, Italy; Gian Franco Goretti, 'Il periodo fascista e gli omosessuali: il confino di polizia' and 'Un "pederasta" catanese al confino', in *Le ragioni di un silenzio. La persecuzione degli omosessuali durante il nazismo e il fascismo*, edited by Circolo Pink (Verona: Ombre Corte, 2002): 64–74 and 124–7.

60 Circolo Pink, ed., *Le ragioni di un silenzio*; Romano, Gabriella. 'Talking about silence', *EUI Working Papers HEC* 1 (2020): 1–16. Available online: http://hdl.han dle.net/1814/66587. I base my observations on the response and debates I obtained at the end of my film's screenings, together with LGBT associations' replies to my solicitation of interest in my projects.

61 Among them: Babini, Beccalossi, Ryall, eds, *Italian Sexualities*; Sandro Bellassai and Maria Malatesta, eds, *Genere e Mascolinità. Uno sguardo storico* (Roma: Bulzoni, 2000); Lorenzo Benadusi, *Il nemico dell'uomo nuovo. L'omosessualità nell'esperimento totalitario fascista* (Milano: Feltrinelli, 2005); Giovanni Dall'Orto, *Tutta un'altra storia. L'omosessualità dall'antichità al secondo dopoguerra* (Milano: Il Saggiatore, 2015); Michael Ebner, *Ordinary Violence in Mussolini's Italy* (Cambridge: Cambridge University Press, 2011); Michael Ebner, *The Persecution of Homosexual Men under Fascism* in *Gender, Family*, edited by Wilson, 139–56; Tommaso Giartosio and Gian Franco Goretti, *La Città e l'Isola* (Roma: Donzelli 2006); Umberto Grassi, Vincenzo Lagioia and Gian Paolo Romagnani, eds, *Tribadi, sodomiti, invertite e invertiti, pederasti, femminelle, ermafroditi: per una storia dell'omosessualità, della bisessualità e delle trasgressioni di genere in Italia* (Pisa: Ets, 2017); Herzog, *Sexuality*; Cristoforo Magistro, *Adelmo e gli altri. Confinati omosessuali in Lucania* (Verona: Ombre Corte, 2019); Nerina Milletti and Luisa Passerini, eds, *Fuori dalla*

Norma. Storie lesbiche nell'Italia del primo Novecento (Torino: Rosenberg & Sellier, 2007); Andrea Pini, *Quando eravamo froci. Gli omosessuali nell'Italia di una volta* (Milano: Longanesi, 2011); Laura Schettini, *Il Gioco delle Parti. Travestimenti e Paure Sociali tra Otto e Novecento* (Firenze: Le Monnier, 2011); Florence Tamagne, *A History of Homosexuality in Europe. Berlin, London, Paris 1919-1939* (New York: Algora, 2006); Maya De Leo, *Queer. Storia culturale della comunità LGBTQ+* (Torino: Einaudi, 2021).

62 Benadusi, *Il Nemico.*

63 George Mosse, *The Image of Man. The Creation of Modern Masculinity* (Oxford: Oxford University Press 1996).

64 Dall'Orto, *Tutta un'altra.*

65 Grassi and Lagioia and Romagnani, eds, *Tribadi.*

66 Donatella Lippi, *San Salvi. Storia di un manicomio* (Firenze: Olschki, 1996).

67 Magistro, *Adelmo.*

68 Wendy Mitchinson and Franca Iacovetta, *On the Case: Explorations in Social History* (Toronto: University of Toronto Press, 1998). Quoted in Cora Salkovskis, '"They cannot reason, they can only feel". Positioning and experiencing the "insane body" and its perversions of feeling in Britain, c. 1840-1914' (PhD diss., Birkbeck College, University of London, academic year 2020-1).

69 Romano, *The Pathologisation.*

70 There is a procedure, through the *Prefettura*, which in some cases allows consultation of files that were closed less than seventy years ago, but it is a very long process.

71 Greco, *I Demoni.*

72 Lucia Sandri, 'Le cartelle cliniche e i ricoverati di San Salvi del 1941', in *Il contributo della Toscana alla psichiatria*, Paola Benvenuti and Esther Diana, eds (Firenze: Polistampa, 2018), 91-6.

1 Main influences on Italian psychiatric theories on homosexuality during the fascist regime

1 Fabio Stok, *La formazione della psichiatria* (Roma: Il Pensiero Scientifico, 1981).

2 Philippe Pinel, *Trattato medico-filosofico spora l'alienazione mentale* (Lodi: Orcesi, [1801] 1830).

3 On the importance of the *perizia psichiatrica* in Italy, Roberto Villa, 'Perizie psichiatriche e formazione degli stereotipi dei devianti: note per una ricerca', in *Follia, Psichiatria, Società*, edited by Alberto De Bernardi (Milano: F. Angeli, 1982), 384-401.

4 Fabio Stok, 'Kraepelin in Italia', *Il Piccolo Hans* 46 (1985): 89-108.

5 Alberto Cavaglion, *La filosofia del pressapoco: Weininger, sesso, carattere e la cultura del Novecento* (Napoli: L'Ancora del Mediterraneo, 2001).

6 Otto Weininger, *Geschlecht und Charakter* (Wien: Barumüller, 1903).

7 Oswald Bumke, *Trattato di Psichiatria* (Torino: Unione Tipografico-Editrice Torinese, [1919] 1927).

8 Florian Mildenberger, "Kraepelin" and the "urnings": Male homosexuality in psychiatric discourse', *History of Psychiatry* 18, no. 3 (2007): 321–35.

9 Felice Mondella, 'Il Concetto di malattia mentale nell'opera di Emil Kraepelin', *Sanità, Scienza e Storia* 1 (1986): 83–110.

10 Emil Kraepelin, *Trattato di psichiatria* (Milano: Vallardi, [1903] 1906).

11 Emil Kraepelin, *Psichiatria Speciale, Volume II* (Milano: Vallardi, 1907). The essay mentioned is: Mildenberger, 'Kraepelin'. A comment on this second volume by Emil Kraepelin in Schettini, *Il Gioco*.

12 Clear explanation of Hirschfeld's theories and Steinach's experiments in Chandak Sengoopta, 'Glandular politics: Experimental biology, clinical medicine, and homosexual emancipation in fin-de-siècle Central Europe', *Isis* 89, no. 3 (September 1998): 445–73.

13 Kraepelin, *Trattato*, 658.

14 Ibid., italics in the original.

15 Mildenberger, 'Kraepelin'.

16 Wilhelm Weygandt, *Atlante e Manuale di Psichiatria* (Milano: Società Editrice Libraria, [1902] 1908).

17 Ibid., 286.

18 Pietro Benassi and Salvatore Luberto, 'Evoluzione del concetto di pericolosità sociale', in *Passioni*, edited by Ferro, 507–18, quoted 513.

19 Eugen Steinach and Joseph Löbel, *Sex and Life. Forty years of medical experiments* (London: Faber & Faber, 1940); Chandak Sengoopta, *The Most Secret Quintessence of Life. Sex, Glands and Hormones, 1850–1950* (Chicago: University of Chicago Press, 2006).

20 Kotowicsz, 'Psychosurgery'; Kotowicsz, *Psychosurgery*.

21 Augusto Mario Coen, 'Contributo alla conoscenza della pazzia morale', *Rivista Sperimentale di Freniatria* (1923): 141–227.

22 Egas Moniz, quoted in Kotowicsz, *Psychosurgery*, 33.

23 Romano, *Pathologisation*, 100.

24 Luigi Scremin, 'Problemi sessuali e morale cattolica', *Rassegna di Studi Sessuali* (January–June 1932): 1–24.

25 Ibid., 16.

26 *Rassegna di Studi Sessuali* (May–June 1924): 168–75.

27 Ibid., 171.

28 Marc André Raffalovich, *L'Uranismo, inversione sessuale congenita. Osservazioni e consigli* (Torino: Bocca, [1896] 1896).

29 Ibid., 31. The concept has been investigated by Zuccarello U., *Omosessualità maschile e modelli di virilità*, edited by S. Bellassai and M. Malatesta, 225–42, *Genere e Mascolinità*.

30 No mention of C. Bruni could be found in *Dizionario degli Italiani* (Roma: Treccani, 2008); *Chi è* (Roma: Formiggini, 1928, 1931, 1936, 1940); *Enciclopedia Italiana*, www.treccani.it; www.aspi.unimib.it.

31 Jean Baptiste Félix Descuret, *La Medicina delle Passioni, ovvero le Passioni considerate relativamente alle malattie, alle leggi e alla religione* (Napoli: S. Romano, [1841] 1906).

32 Descuret, *La Medicina delle Passioni*.

33 Gregorio Marañon, *L'evoluzione della sessualità e gli stati intersessuali* (Bologna: Zanichelli, [1930] 1934).

34 Ibid., 167 of English translation (London: Allen and Unwin, 1932).

35 Ibid., 166.

36 Ibid., 188.

37 Ibid., 190.

38 Ibid., 192. The concept of homosexuality as a response to negative heterosexual first experiences is echoed by, among others, Paul Garnier, *Nevrastenia sessuale. Cause e rimedi* (Milano: R. Quintieri, [1895] 1915).

39 Ibid., 193.

40 Cleminson and Vasquez Garcia, 'A history'. On the subject see also Geoffrey Huard, 'Spain from Franco's Repressive Regime to Same-Sex Marriage', in *From Sodomy Laws to Same-Sex Marriage*, edited by Brady and Seymour, 95–109.

41 Luigi Pasolli, 'Sessualità maschile e sessualità femminile', *Rivista di Studi Sessuali* (1930): 1–2. This is how the journal is quoted, but the correct journal's title is *Rassegna di Studi Sessuali*.

42 As defined by Mario Canella in his preface to Marañon, *L'Evoluzione*, 2 of Italian edition.

43 Mario Canella, *Razze Umane estinte e viventi* (Firenze: Sansoni, 1940).

44 As explained in Chiara Volpato, 'Mario Canella e la psicologia razziale. Un caso di conformismo al potere universitario', www://aipass.org, Associazione Italiana di Psicologia (accessed January 2020). This article is the main source utilized on Mario Canella.

45 As highlighted in Romano, *The Pathologisation*; Beccalossi, *Female*; Schettini, *Il Gioco*, among others.

46 Herzog, *Sexuality*.

47 Beccalossi, *Female*.

48 James Cowles Pritchard, *A Treatise on Insanity and Other Disorders Affecting the Mind* (Sherwood: Gilbert and Pieper, 1835).

49 Cesare Agostini, *Manuale di Psichiatria* (Milano: Vallardi, 1897).

50 Beccalossi, *Female*, 10 and 49–50.

51 Leonardo Bianchi, *Eugenica, igiene mentale e profilassi delle malattie nervose e mentali* (Napoli: Idelson, 1925); Leonardo Bianchi, *Contributo alla conoscenza dell'isterismo* (Milano: Vallardi, 1912).

52 Leonardo Bianchi, *Trattato di psichiatria ad uso dei medici e degli studenti* (Napoli: Idelson, [1900] 1924).

53 Ibid., 239.

54 Ibid., 508.

55 Ibid., 504.

56 Ibid., 508.

57 Beccalossi, *Female*.

58 Ibid., 161.

59 Paolo Mantegazza, *Gli Amori degli Uomini* (Milano: P. Mantegazza, [1886] 1892).

60 Ibid., 93.

61 Ibid., 85. By 'character's prostitution' he meant immorality.

62 Paolo Mantegazza, *Igiene dell'Amore* (Milano: Treves, 1891).

63 Quoted by Charlotte Ross, 'Italian medical and literary discourses around female same-sex desire, 1877–1906', in *Italian Sexualities*, edited by Babini and Beccalossi and Ryall, 228–48.

64 Eugenio Tanzi, *Trattato delle malattie mentali* (Milano: Società Editrice Libraria, 1905), 619.

65 Ibid.

66 Angelo Matteo Caglioti, 'Race, Statistics and Italian Eugenics: Alfredo Niceforo's trajectory from Lombroso to Fascism (1876–1960)', *European History Quarterly* 47, no. 3 (2017): 461–89.

67 Alfredo Niceforo, *Le psicopatie sessuali acquisite* (Roma: Capaccini, 1897).

68 Alfredo Niceforo and Scipione Sighele, *La malavita a Roma* (Torino: Roux Frassati, 1898).

69 Alfredo Niceforo, *Antropologia delle classi povere* (Milano: Vallardi, 1908); Alfredo Niceforo, *Forza e Ricchezza: studi sulla vita fisica ed economica delle classi sociali* (Torino: Bocca, 1906); Alfredo Niceforo, 'The cause of inferiority of physical and mental character in the lower social classes', *International Eugenics Congress and Eugenics Education Society* (1912): 193–4, to cite a few examples.

70 Caglioti, 'Race', 467.

71 Milletti, 'Analoghe Sconcezze'. The journal changed its name several times over the years, as Milletti explains.

72 Milletti, 'Analoghe Sconcezze'.

73 Paolo Giovannini, *La psichiatria di guerra. Dal fascismo alla seconda guerra mondiale* (Milano: Unicopli, 2015).

74 Giacomo Pighini, 'Per la eliminazione dei degenerati psichici dall'esercito combattente', *Giornale di Medicina Militare* (1918): 977–94.

75 Ibid., 989.

76 Paul Ginsborg, *Famiglia Novecento. Vita famigliare, rivoluzione e dittature, 1900–1950* (Torino: Einaudi, 2013).

77 Paul Ginsborg, *Storia d'Italia 1943–1996. Famiglia, società, Stato* (Torino: Einaudi, [1989] 1998).

78 Alessandro Scurti, 'Gli esordi della medicalizzazione degli omosessuali', *Società e Storia* 108 (2005): 283–317.

79 See Chapter 4.

80 As observed in the second part of the book.

81 On the ambiguous and difficult relationship between Fascism and the Catholic Church, the *Concordato*, the figures of Pope Pio XI and Pio XII, there is a vast literature that cannot be fully accounted for in this book. In addition to publications that focus on this issue, all books on the history of Fascism touch on the subject.

82 Ginsborg, *Storia d'Italia*.

83 Ibid.; Luisa Passerini, *Torino Operaia e Fascismo* (Bari: Laterza, 1984).

84 Egilberto Martire, 'Elogio della famiglia', *Politica Sociale* 6 (September 1929): 615–18.

85 Ibid., 616.

86 Charlotte Ross, 'Dalla patologizzazione all'amore per gli "anormali": la rappresentazione del desiderio dissidente tra donne in testi (pseudo-) scientifici del tardo Ottocento e del primo Novecento', in *Tribadi*, edited by Grassi and Lagioia and Romagnani, 155–71.

87 Alberto Orsi, *Lussuria e castità. Saggio di psicologia* (Milano: La Brodierie, 1913); Nice Fowell, *La masturbazione nella donna: cause e forme, casistica e rimedi (con illustrazioni)* (Firenze: Il Pensiero, 1914). Both are quoted in Ross, 'Dalla Patologizzazione'.

88 Martin Laurent, *L'Amore, la Lussuria e il Libertinaggio* (Roma: Capaccini, [1865] 1897); Louis Martineau, *Le Deformazioni vulvari e anali prodotte dalla masturbazione, dal saffismo, dalla deflorazione e dalla sodomia* (Roma: Capaccini, [1884] 1898); Auguste Ambroise Tardieu, *I Delitti di Libidine, psicopatia sessuale, oltraggi pubblici al pudore, pederastia e sodomia* (Roma: Capaccini, [1857] 1898); Thésée Pouillet, *L'onanismo nella donna* (Roma: Capaccini, [1877] 1898).

89 Giulio Cesare Ferrari, *Per la storia della psichiatria. Recensioni 1893–1907* (Bologna: Pitagora, 1984), 86.

90 John Gerard Champagne, *Queer Ventennio: Italian Fascism, Homoerotic Art, and the Nonmodern in the Modern* (Pieterlen: Peter Lang, 2019); Francesco Gnerre,

L'Eroe negato. Omosessualità e letteratura nel Novecento italiano (Roma: Rogas, [1981] 2018).

91 Marcella Leone De Andreis, *Capri 1939. L'isola in bianco e nero* (Capri: La Conchiglia, 2002); Lea Vergine, ed., *Capri 1905–1940. Frammenti postumi* (Milano: Il Saggiatore, 2018).

2 Italian psychiatric theories on homosexuality published during the fascist regime

1 Biographical information on Enrico Morselli is taken from the Treccani Encyclopaedia's entry written by Patrizia Guarnieri, available online: www.treccani.it/encliclopedia/enrico-morselli.

2 Enrico Morselli, *Psicoanalisi* (Torino: Bocca, 1926).

3 Enrico Morselli, *Sessualità umana* (Torino: Bocca, 1931).

4 Ibid., 139.

5 Ibid., 49.

6 Ibid., 164.

7 Giuseppe Vidoni, *I valori e i limiti dell'endocrinologia nello studio del delinquente* (Torino: Bocca, 1923). On Giuseppe Vidoni in the fascist regime years see Peloso, *La Guerra Dentro*; Paolo Francesco Peloso, 'Psychiatry in Genoa', *History of Psychiatry* 15, no. 1 (2004): 27–43; Martina Salvante, 'La prostituzione maschile nel discorso scientifico della prima metà del Novecento in Italia', in *Nuove Frontiere per la Storia di Genere*, vol. III, edited by Laura Guidi and Maria Rosaria Pelizzari (Padova: Webster Press, 2013), 533–9.

8 Mario De Paoli, 'Contributo allo studio della omosessualità passiva', *Quaderni di Psichiatria* (August 1925): 239–52.

9 Sengoopta, *The Most Secret*.

10 Salvante, 'La Prostituzione'.

11 Giuseppe Vidoni, *Prostitute e prostituzione* (Torino: Lattes, 1921), quoted in Salvante, 'La Prostituzione', 534.

12 Giuseppe Vidoni, 'Per lo studio della prostituzione maschile', *Il Manicomio* 3 (1922): 225–46.

13 Nicola Pende, *Dalla medicina alla sociologia* (Palermo: Coop. Editrice Prometeo, 1921). Most details on Nicola Pende were taken from José Mottola, *Gente di razza. Così parlò Nicola Pende, tutore della stirpe e pupillo dei Gesuiti* (Foggia: Bastogi, 2010).

14 Nicola Pende, *La Biotipologia umana* (Palermo: Coop. Editrice, 1924).

15 Carlo Foà and Nicola Pende, *La fisiologia e la clinica degli increti* (Milano: Istituto Biochimico Italiano, 1927).

16 Chiara Beccalossi, 'Optimizing and normalizing the population through hormone therapies in Italian science, c. 1926–1950', *British Journal on the History of Science* 53, no. 1 (2020): 1–22.

17 Ibid., 2.

18 Nicola Pende, 'Per l'educazione biologica della femminilità', *Le Opere e i Giorni* (July 1931) 88–96; Nicola Pende, 'La Donna secondo la scienza', *L'Illustrazione Medica* (1931): 3–4.

19 Nicola Pende, 'Psicologia individuale e psicologia di razza', *Rivista di Psicologia* 1 (January–March 1930): 22–6.

20 *Dizionario Biografico degli Italiani* (Roma: Treccani, 2008).

21 Giuseppe Mariani, *La Questione Sessuale. Fisiopatologia, Sociologia e Legislazione Sessuale* (Milano: Istituto Editoriale Scientifico, 1926).

22 Ibid., 354.

23 Ibid., 46.

24 Giulio Moglie, *Manuale di psichiatria ad uso dei medici pratici e degli studenti* (Roma: L. Pozzi, 1940).

25 No mention of Giulio Moglie could be found in *Dizionario degli Italiani* (Roma: Treccani, 2008); *Chi è* (Roma: Formiggini, 1928, 1931, 1936, 1940); *Enciclopedia Italiana*, www.treccani.it; www.aspi.unimib.it. From a prescription written by him on headed paper, found in the SMPA, I could deduct that he co-directed, together with Augusto Giannelli, the Clinic for Nervous and Mental Illnesses situated in via Angelica 2, Rome.

26 Moglie, *Manuale*, 67.

27 Ibid., 234–5.

28 Alfredo La Cara, *La base organica dei pervertimenti sessuali* (Milano: Bocca, [1902] 1924). No mention of Alfredo La Cara could be found in *Dizionario degli Italiani* (Roma: Treccani, 2008); *Chi è* (Roma: Formiggini, 1928, 1931, 1936, 1940); *Enciclopedia Italiana*, www.treccani.it; www.aspi.unimib.it.

29 Joanny Roux, *Psicologia dell'istinto sessuale* (Roma: Capaccini, [1899] 1900).

30 Babini, *Liberi Tutti*.

31 Emilio Servadio, 'Sessuologia', in *Encliclopedia Treccani* (Roma: Treccani, 1936), 494–500. There is no entry for '*omosessualità*', the word sends the reader to the entry '*sessuologia*'.

32 My main sources on *Rassegna di Studi Sessuali* were: Lorenzo Masi, 'Rassegna di Studi Sessuali, 1921–1932: Autonomia di un periodico' (BA diss., University of Pisa, academic year 2014–15); Benadusi, *Il Nemico*; Dall'Orto, *Tutta un'Altra Storia*.

33 Aldo Mieli, 'Review of Havelock Ellis', *Studies in the Psychology of Sex, Eonism and other supplementary studies, vol. VII*, *Rassegna di Studi Sessuali* (April–May 1928): 52; Aldo Mieli, 'Review of Schulte-Vaerting, 'Der homosexuelle als staatlicher typus', *Rassegna di Studi Sessuali* (January–March 1928): 53.

34 Aldo Mieli, 'La discussione sull'omosessualità al Reichtag', *Rassegna di Studi Sessuali* (March–April 1922): 125–6.

35 Aldo Mieli, 'Patologia sessuale', *Rassegna di Studi Sessuali* (1921): 81–94.

36 Aldo Mieli, Review of Vidoni, 'Prostitute', *Rassegna di Studi Sessuali* (1921): 209–10.

37 Pr, 'Review of Kurt Blum, 'Omosessualità e ghiandola puberale', *Rassegna di Studi Sessuali* (January–February 1923): 69; Pr, 'Review Ferdinand Adalbert Kehrer, 'Considerazioni critiche sulla cura dell'omosessualità col metodo di Steinach', *Rassegna di Studi Sessuali* (September–October 1923): 364; Pr, 'Review of M. Bondy, *Cura chirurgica dell'omosessualità*, *Rassegna di Studi Sessuali* (January–February 1922): 52.

38 Proteus, 'Review of Gregorio Marañon, *Problemas actuales de la doctrina de las secreciones internas*', *Rassegna di Studi Sessuali* (March–April 1923): 150.

39 Proteus, 'Per l'insegnamento universitario della Sessuologia in Italia', *Rassegna di Studi Sessuali* (March–April 1922): 80–3; Proteus, 'Moralità e Sessualità', *Rassegna di Studi Sessuali* (1922): 332–49.

40 Ferdinando De Napoli, 'La bisessualità latente come carattere individuale costante e consecutiva opoterapia antiomosessuale', *Rassegna di Studi Sessuali* (1923): 229–44.

41 Raimondo Villano, 'Farmaci di Sintesi: origini e sviluppo', *puntoeffe*, 61–2, https://www.researchgate.net/ publication/ 332736022_Farmaci_di_sintesi_origine_e_ sviluppo (accessed February 2021).

42 Ernani (or Hernani) Mandolini, 'Il Contagio delle Psicopatie Sessuali', *Rassegna di Studi Sessuali* (1923): 169–72. It was published again by the *Rassegna di Studi Sessuali, Biblioteca dei Curiosi* (Roma: Tinto, 1926).

43 Ernani (or Hernani) Mandolini, 'Amicizia ed Omoerotismo', *Rassegna di Studi Sessuali* (1923): 393–9.

44 Aldo Mieli, 'Per la lotta contro la delinquenza collegata a manifestazioni omosessuali', *Rassegna di Studi Sessuali* (September 1926): 256–61.

45 Aldo Mieli, 'Review of Alfredo La Cara, *La base organica dei pervertimenti sessuali e la loro profilassi sociale*', *Rassegna di Studi Sessuali* (January–February 1924): 58–9.

46 Aldo Mieli, 'Review of Piero Pesce Maineri, *I pericoli del cinematografo*', *Rassegna di Studi Sessuali* (May–June 1922): 178–9.

47 Masi, 'Rassegna'.

48 For instance, in 1930, Giovanni De Nigris referred to the case of a mattress maker who could be described as a hermaphrodite from a physical point of view but was not homosexual in his sexual behaviour. His article was aimed at proving that physical observation might lead the specialist astray. Giovanni De Nigris, 'Pseudoermafroditismo femminile e mascolinismo psichico in soggetto degenerato', *Archivio Generale di Neurologia, Psichiatria e Psicoanalisi* (1930): 373.

49 Moraglio, 'Dentro e fuori'; Canosa, *Storia del Manicomio*; Silvano, *Legislazione*; De Bernardi, ed., *Follia, psichiatria*.

50 Paolo Giovannini, *La psichiatria di guerra. Dal fascismo alla Seconda guerra mondiale* (Milano: Unicopli, 2015); Peloso, *La Guerra Dentro.*
51 Moraglio, 'Dentro e fuori'.

3 The Rome asylum, Santa Maria della Pietà: Quiet disobedience

1 Paul Corner, *The Fascist Party and Popular Opinion in Mussolini's Italy* (Oxford: Oxford University Press, 2012). Version consulted: *La dittatura fascista. Consenso e controllo durante il Ventennio.* Roma: Carocci, 2017.
2 The first were issued by Augusto Giannelli, from 1934 until 1937. The *Libretti* of 1938 and 1939 were issued by his successor, Francesco Bonfiglio.
3 For instance, in Collegno: Romano, *The Pathologisation.*
4 Peloso, *La Guerra dentro.*
5 Most information on the history of Santa Maria della Pietà was taken from www.cartedalegare.it; Augusto Giannelli, *Il Nuovo Ospedale Santa Maria della Pietà* (Roma: Tipografia Santa Maria della Pietà, 1937); Iaria and Lo Savio and Martelli, *L'Ospedale.*
6 SMPA, F 15. Files from F 1 to F 42 refer to the Director's correspondence and various internal affairs.
7 Ibid.
8 Giannelli, *Il Nuovo Ospedale.*
9 Ibid.
10 Ibid.
11 SMPA, F 17, 24 October 1940.
12 Ibid., 9 December 1940.
13 SMPA, F 24, 5.5.1939.
14 SMPA, D 453.
15 SMPA, F 2355 – 2360 Registri Prestazioni Chirurgiche.
16 SMPA, F 2.
17 Ibid.
18 See introduction.
19 Augusto Giannelli, *Studi sulla Pazzia nella Provincia di Roma* (Roma: Cecchini, 1905).
20 Giannelli, *Il Nuovo Ospedale.*
21 Ibid., 14.
22 Ibid., 40–1.
23 Ibid., 71.

24 Information on the hospital's directors was taken mainly from Iaria and Lo Savio and Martelli, *L'Ospedale*; Anna Lia Bonella and Franca Fedeli Bernardini, eds, *L'ospedale dei pazzi di Roma dai papi al '900. Fonti per la storia della follia: S. Maria della Pietà e il suo Archivio Storico (sec. XVI - XX)*, vol. I (Bari: Dedalo, 1994).

25 Francesco Bonfiglio, *Curriculum Vitae ed Attività Scientifica e Clinica Ospedaliera del dott. Prof. Francesco Bonfiglio* (Roma: Tipografia dell'Ospedale Santa Maria della Pietà, 1938).

26 Ibid., 13.

27 SMPA, F 6–7.

28 Iaria and Lo Savio and Martelli, *L'Ospedale*.

29 SMPA, F 5, Libretto I.

30 Ibid., Libretto XIX.

31 Ibid., Libretto XII.

32 SMPA, F 23. On the regime's demographic campaign see, among others, Victoria De Grazia, *Le donne nel regime fascista* (Venezia: Marsilio, [1992] 1993).

33 SMPA, F8, Concorsi 1935, 1937, 1939–40.

34 Fiorino, *Le Officine*; Petracci, *I Matti*; Ebner, *Ordinary Violence*.

35 SMPA, F 19.

36 SMPA, F 5, Libretto XVIII.

37 SMPA, F 19, 30 September 1940.

38 SMPA, F 10.

39 Ibid.

40 SMPA, F 36, 1943.

41 Ibid., circular to the staff, 23 March 1943.

42 SMPA, F 22.

43 SMPA, F 5, Libretto XV.

44 SMPA, F 1687–1688, Consigli di Disciplina. It is sometimes difficult to date documents, as, for instance, booklets of instructions to staff often contain documents with previous dates, probably inserted because they were still considered valid. Booklets of staff instructions are sometimes in the form of a series of typed pages, the printed final pamphlet is missing.

45 For instance: Massimo Moraglio, *Costruire*; Moraglio, ed., *Effimeri*; Petracci, *I Matti*; Romano, *The Pathologisation*; Scartabellati, *La 'questione follia'*; Tornabene, *La Guerra dei Matti*.

46 Both SMPA, F 1687, Consigli di Disciplina.

47 Ibid.

48 Ibid.

49 Ibid., SMPA, F 6, F 15.

50 Ibid.

51 Ibid.

52 Ibid.

53 SMPA, F 7, Libretto IV, dated 26 August 1942.

54 SMPA, F 1687, Consigli di Disciplina.

55 The '*campagna di epurazione*', as it was often referred to, implied an idea of national purification. It went hand in hand with toughened censorship on publications, films and theatre shows, closure of dancehalls and strict surveillance on places of entertainment. Most books on Fascism talk about censorship during the fascist regime. Among them: Guido Bonsaver, *Mussolini censore. Storie di letteratura, dissenso e ipocrisia* (Bari: Laterza, 2013); Valerio Castronovo and Nicola Tranfaglia, eds, *La stampa italiana nell'età fascista* (Bari: Laterza, 1980); Mauro Forno, *La stampa del ventennio. Strutture e trasformazioni nello stato totalitario* (Soveria Mannelli: Rubbettino, 2005); Giorgio Fabre, *Il Censore e l'editore. Mussolini, i libri, Mondadori* (Milano: Fondazione Arnoldo e Alberto Mondadori, 2018).

56 SMPA, F 5, Libretto XIX.

57 SMPA, F 15.

58 Ibid.

59 F 1687, Consigli di Disciplina.

60 In SMPA, F 5, Libretto II is missing.

61 SMPA, F 5, Prot. 11896, p. 13, 4 August Eleventh (i.e. 1935), Libretto III.

62 Aldrich, *The Seduction*.

63 SMPA, File 5, Libretto IV, no date, presumably 1935–6.

64 Beccalossi, *Female*; Milletti, 'Analoghe'.

65 SMPA, File 5, Libretto X.

66 SMPA, F 239, Invio alla clinica psichiatrica a scopo di studio 1924–1940; F 283, Invio alla clinica psichiatrica a scopo di studio, 1938–41; F 305, Invio alla clinica psichiatrica a scopo di studio 1942.

67 SMPA, F 2355–2360, Registro Prestazioni Chirurgiche; F 2366–2367 Registri Rapporti del Chirurgo.

68 SMPA, F 2355–2360, Registro Prestazioni Chirurgiche: Operazioni Medicature 1927–9.

69 SMPA, F 2355–2360, Registro Prestazioni Chirurgiche 1930–3.

70 SMPA, F 9.

71 Giartosio and Goretti, *La Città*.

72 P.G.B.'s case is described later in the chapter.

73 SMPA, Donne F 2019, mixed dates, consulted 28 October 1922–4; Donne F 2021, 1925–7; Donne F 2023, 1927–9; Donne F 2025, 1935–9; Donne F 2027, mixed dates, consulted from January 1940 until 29 September 1943; Uomini F 2020, mixed dates, consulted 28 October 1922–4; Uomini F 2022, 1926–9; Uomini F 2024, 1927–9; Uomini F 2026, 1935–9; Uomini F 2028, mixed dates, consulted from January 1923 until 29 September 1943.

74 SMPA, F 2355–2360, Registro Prestazioni Chirurgiche (Register of Surgical
    Operations) 1930–33; F 2366–2367, Registro dei Rapporti del Chirurgo (Surgeons'
    Reports Register); F 239, Invio alla clinica psichiatrica a scopo di studio 1924–40
    (Patients sent to the psychiatric clinic for study purposes 1924–40); F 283, Invio
    alla clinica psichiatrica a scopo di studio 1938–41 (Patients sent to psychiatric clinic
    for study purposes 1938–41); F 305, Invio alla clinica psichiatrica a scopo di studio
    1942 (Patients sent to the psychiatric clinic for study purposes 1942); F 236, Pre-
    osservazione alla clinica psichiatrica (Pre-observation at the psychiatric clinic).

75 SMPA, F 1687–8, Consigli di Disciplina; F 2154 a and b, Registro Rapporti Sanitari;
    D 445–453, Ordini e commesse, pagamenti, appalti ….; F 216, Ricoverati criminali
    (detenuti o prosciolti); F 316, Ricoverati Criminali (Detenuti o prosciolti) 1944–5;
    E 137, Registro di protocollo 1923–4; F 2098, Trasferimenti from 1931 onwards,
    consulted up to 1943; F 1–39, Corrispondenza del Direttore e Affari Diversi.

76 Luca Des Dorides, 'Scemi, derelitti e degenerati. Strategie di potere e contrattazione
    del sapere nell'ospedale dei matti di Roma, 1918–1938' (PhD diss., La Sapienza,
    Rome, academic year 2009–10). Luca Des Dorides identifies a few more patients
    because his analysis followed all diagnostic categories and took into consideration
    a much longer period of time. He too highlights that homosexuals were interned
    under different descriptions and diagnoses, and that their homosexuality often
    appears only inside the patient file. He concentrates on the case of P.G.B. that
    I discuss at length, which he analyses from the point of view of power relations
    within the family and between the family and the institution. He then talks about
    three other cases of patients whose homosexuality was noted inside their files: B.G.,
    interned in 1922 for a state of excitement, who was said to have tried to commit
    obscene acts on fellow male patients; T.U., who was interned seven times, the last
    during Fascism, for various reasons, such as drunkenness, aggressive behaviour,
    threats, disturbance and pederasty (the official patient file diagnosis is not quoted);
    D.V.O., whose persecution complex involved his feeling insulted because of his,
    true or suspected, homosexuality. As Des Dorides does not provide details of these
    patients' internment files or other identifying elements, I could not retrace their
    files. Des Dorides does not analyse any case of hermaphroditism or lesbianism.
    His work was of vital importance in identifying P.G.B.'s file, which I would not
    have located using the diagnostic categories I decided to examine, and to focus on
    the power relationships between internees, doctors, asylum directors and patients'
    relatives.

77 SMPA, E.C.'s file, died in hospital 9 March 1929.

78 Des Dorides, 'Scemi, derelitti'.

79 This is the reason why I could find this file. Although the patient was interned
    much earlier than 1922, he was also listed in the Admissions Register when he was
    transferred to Santa Maria della Pietà.

80 Aldrich, *The Seduction*.

81 SMPA, P.G.B.'s file, discharged on 8 October 1935.

82 The ambiguous term *compagno d'arte*, literally translatable as 'colleague in the same art', could imply a tongue-in-cheek comment on the part of the professional who wrote the notes. Alternatively, it could be a term used by the boy to describe a fellow-actor.

83 *Ricordare* (2003) [documentary] Dir. Gabriella Romano.

84 On Neapolitan 'Femminielli' there is a vast literature. Among the many books on the subject: Paolo Valerio and Eugenio Zito, *Corpi sull'uscio. Identità possibili* (Napoli: Filema, 2010); Paolo Valerio and Eugenio Zito, eds, *Femminielli. Corpo, genere, cultura* (Napoli: Edizioni Libreria Dante & Descartes, 2019).

85 Sandro Bellassai, 'The masculine mystique: Antimodernism and virility in fascist Italy', *Journal of Modern Italian Studies* 10 (2005): 314–35; Bellassai and Malatesta, eds, *Genere e Mascolinità*; Benadusi, *Il Nemico*; Mosse, *The Image*.

86 For instance: Marañon, *The Evolution of Sex*; Leonidio Ribeiro, *Omosessualità e endocrinologia* (Milano: Bocca, [1938] 1940).

87 At the time Francesco Bonfiglio was still a psychiatrist at Santa Maria della Pietà.

88 SMPA, P.G.B.'s file, letter dated 6 August 1932.

89 SMPA, D.P.F.P.'s file, discharged on 11 May 1927.

90 SMPA, D.B.R.'s file, died in hospital on 7 August 1930.

91 SMPA, P.G.B.'s file, letter to the director dated 20 August 1935.

92 SMPA, B.P.'s file, discharged on 20 June 1923.

93 SMPA, D.P.V.'s file, discharged for the last time on 7 August 1944.

94 SMPA, M.P.'s file, retraceable as discharged on 20 July 1942, although reported as present on 3 October 1942.

95 SMPA, L.A.'s file, discharged 8 June 1936.

96 SMPA, B.E.'s file, deceased while interned on 18 May 1947.

97 Among the many articles published in fascist times on the subject: Giuseppe Bianchi, 'Un caso di eunucoidismo', *Rivista Sperimentale di Freniatria* (1930): 559–66; Giulio Agostini, 'Su di un caso di pseudo-ermafroditismo esterno femminile', *Annali dell'Ospedale Psichiatrico di Perugia* (January–December 1929): 31–53; Michele Levi, 'L'origine dell'intersessualità', *Archivio di Antropologia Criminale, Psichiatria e Medicina Legale* (1929): 496–502; Angelo Vanelli, 'Un caso di eunucoidismo', *Rassegna di Studi Psichiatrici* (1931): 949–58; Gaetano Boschi, 'In tema di impotenza sessuale', *Rassegna di Studi Psichiatrici* (1931): 1257–66. Some interesting considerations on the subject in ed. Grassi and Lagioia and Romagnani, *Tribadi*.

98 SMPA, P.D.'s file, discharged on 23 August 1929 because he was transferred to Volterra.

99 SMPA, L.E.'s file, transferred to the Rieti hospital branch on 29 August 1932.

100 SMPA, A.B.'s file, discharged on 15 June 1951.

101 De Gratia, *Le Donne*, 76 of Italian translation.

102 Giannelli, *Il Nuovo Ospedale*.

103 For instance: Mario De Paoli, 'Contributo'; Luigi Tomellini, 'Alcuni casi di pazzia morale studiati in rapporto all'imputabilità secondo il nostro codice', *Bollettino dell'Accademia di Genova* (1906): 147–75.

104 Des Dorides, 'Scemi, Derelitti'.

105 Ginsborg, *Family Politic*.

106 Paul Corner, 'Corruzione di sistema? I 'fascisti reali' tra pubblico e privato', in *Il fascismo dalle mani sporche. Dittatura, corruzione, affarismo*, edited by Paolo Giovannini and Marco Palla (Bari: Laterza, 2019): 3–26.

107 Paul, 'Dictatorship'.

108 Melis, *La Macchina*, 236.

4 The Florence asylum, San Salvi: Precarious balance

1 Data of Florence census is taken from www.treccani.it.

2 Data on Rome's census is taken from www.comune.roma.it. In 1931, the residents in Rome were 942,657.

3 Florence was the capital of Italy between 1865 and 1871.

4 My main sources to reconstruct San Salvi's history and its directors' profiles are: www.aspi.unimib.it; www.siusa.archivibeniculturali.it; www.cartedalegare.it; Lippi, *San Salvi*; Paola Benvenuti and Esther Diana, eds *Il contributo della Toscana alla psichiatria* (Firenze: Polistampa, 2018).

5 See later in the chapter.

6 Lippi, *San Salvi*.

7 Ibid.

8 Carlo Ferrio was an authoritative psychiatric theoretician and practitioner during Fascism who collaborated with several important journals. His major publications, however, date to after the war: Carlo Ferrio, *La Psiche e i Nervi* (Torino: Utet, 1948); Carlo Ferrio, *Trattato di psichiatria clinica e Forense* (Torino: Unione Tipografica-Editrice Torinese, [1959] 1970).

9 FSA, Ospedale Neuropsichiatrico Provinciale Vincenzo Chiarugi, Manicomio San Salvi; from now cited as Manicomio. Direzione 1939, Affari Diversi, article draft, p. 2.

10 Ernesto Lugaro was widely published and taught at several Italian universities. A detailed biography can be found in: www.treccani.it.

11 FSA, Manicomio, Direzione 1939, Affari Diversi, 3.

12 FSA, Manicomio, Direzione 1942–3, Affari Diversi, article draft, 270.

13 Eugenio Tanzi, *Trattato delle Malattie Mentali* (Milano: Società Editrice Libraria, 1905). During the *Ventennio*, it was reprinted twice.

14 FSA, Manicomio, Direzione 1939, Affari Diversi.

15 www.aspi.unimib.it.

16 FSA, Manicomio, Direzione 1942–3 and Affari Diversi, 18 September 1942.

17 FSA, Manicomio, Direzione 1935, Affari Diversi.

18 FSA,, Manicomio, Direzione 1939, Affari Diversi, 25 September.

19 FSA, Manicomio, Direzione 1942–3 and Affari Diversi, 5 June 1943.

20 Ibid., 18 September 1942.

21 Ibid.

22 Both FSA, Manicomio, Storie Cliniche dei Ricoverati, Donne 5801–6300, anno 1942.

23 FSA, Manicomio, B.U.'s file, died while interned 8 March 1929.

24 FSA. Manicomio, P.G.'s file, discharged 30 September 1937.

25 FSA, Manicomio, G.D.'s file, discharged for the last time 14 August 1938.

26 FSA, Manicomio, Circolare 26.7.1935, Direzione 1935, Affari Diversi.

27 FSA, Manicomio, Direzione 1935, Affari Diversi, 3 October 1935.

28 FSA, Manicomio, Direzione 1938, Affari Diversi, 2 May 1935.

29 FSA, Manicomio, Commissione Amministrativa, F 154, f 4, n. 214, dated 6 May 1936.

30 FSA, Manicomio, Direzione 1939, Affari Diversi, 28 February 1939.

31 FSA, Manicomio, Direzione 1939, Affari Diversi, Letter dated 9 February 1939.

32 FSA, Manicomio, Commissione Amministrativa, F 139, f 5, n. 337.

33 See introduction.

34 FSA, Manicomio, Direzione 1938, Affari Diversi.

35 Petracci Matteo, *op. cit.*

36 FSA, Manicomio, Commissione Amministrativa, F 180, f, 2, n. 113.

37 Ibid.

38 Ibid., as reported by the *Prefettura* itself in the same file.

39 FSA, Manicomio, Direzione 1935, Affari Diversi.

40 Ibid.

41 Ibid.

42 Ibid.

43 FSA, Manicomio, Direzione 1939, Affari Diversi.

44 Ibid.

45 Ibid.

46 Ibid.

47 FSA, Manicomio, Commissione Amministrativa, F 60, f, 2, n. 90.

48 FSA, Manicomio, Direzione 1935, Affari Diversi, 9.5.1935 and Direzione 1938, Affari Diversi, 14 May 1935.

49 FSA, Manicomio, Direzione 1938, Affari Diversi.

50 Ibid. and FSA, Manicomio, Direzione 1939, Affari Diversi.

51 FSA, Manicomio, Direzione 1939, Affari Diversi, 25 February 1939.

52 FSA, Manicomio, Direzione 1942–3, Affari Diversi.

53 For instance, FSA, Manicomio, Direzione 1938, Affari Diversi.

54 FSA, Manicomio, Direzione 1938, Affari Diversi.

55 FSA, Manicomio, Direzione 1939, Affari Diversi.

56 Some of the old San Salvi premises are now part of the University of Florence, Faculty of Psychology.

57 For San Salvi, there are two types of Admissions Register, one by date that does not mention patient diagnoses, and a second one that shows patients present in the institution, year by year, in alphabetical order, where diagnoses are marked. This second type of register is the one I refer to. I consulted registers for the years 1922–43.

58 FSA, Manicomio, Commissione Amministrativa, F 60 f 2 n. 90. According to Lippi, Personnel Regulations were issued in 1921 (Delibera 9 May) and 1930 (Delibera del cons. prov. 25 April), but despite the archivist's best efforts, these could not be found in the State Archives when I consulted the San Salvi documentation.

59 FSA, Università degli Studi di Firenze, Clinica Psichiatrica; from now on cited as Storie Cliniche. Uomini e Donne 1924–25–26; Donne morte nel 1924; Donne morte nel 1925; Donne morte nel 1926. Uomini morti nel 1924; Uomini morti nel 1925; Uomini morti nel 1926; Uomini dal 3501 al 3850 year 1933; Uomini dal 5731 al 6160, years 1938–9; Uomini e Donne morti – Ammessi prima dallo schedario 1927, 1928, 1930, 1931; Uomini e Donne morti 1932, 1933, 1934; Donne dal 5801 al 6300, year 1942.

60 FSA, Manicomio, G.D.'s file, discharged the last time in April 1939, day not readable. The quoted diagnosis is dated 1 May 1935.

61 FSA, Manicomio, P.M.'s file, discharged for the last time on 2 July 1929.

62 For instance, Valeriano, *Ammalò*; Fiorino, *Le Officine*; Romano, *The Pathologisation*.

63 The most accurate analysis of this concept is in Klaus Dörner, *Madness and the Bourgeoisie. A Social History of Insanity and Psychiatry* (London: Basil Blackwell, [1969] 1981).

64 Silvia Mazzoleni, one of my previous oral history interviewees, told me a similar story about her sister, who was exorcized as she was believed to have nourished excessive affection for a female schoolmate. Her interview is part of *L'Altro Ieri* (2001), [documentary] Dir. Gabriella Romano.

65 On the history of hysteria as a psychiatric diagnosis there is a vast literature. Among the many texts on the subject, I consulted: Giuseppe Roccatagliata, *Riflessioni sulla decadenza dell'isteria* (Napoli: Liguori, 1992); Mark Micale, *Approaching Hysteria, Disease and Its Interpretations* (Princeton: Princeton University Press, 2019).

66 FSA, Manicomio, C.L.'s file, discharged on 21 September 1926.

67 FSA, Storie Cliniche Uomini e Donne Morti – Ammessi prima dallo schedario 1927, 1928, 1930, 1931, Cartella Clinica of 26 July 1917; Cartelle dei pazienti, D.M., deceased while interned on 12 September 1931.

68 FSA, R.L.'s file, mentioned in FSA, Manicomio, Direzione 1939, Affari Diversi, 16 June 1939.

69 FSA, Manicomio, C.D.'s file, discharged on 11 June 1927.

70 FSA, Cartella del Tribunale di Firenze. Decreto di Ammissione al Manicomio di D.C.

71 Des Dorides, 'Scemi, Derelitti'.

72 SSA, D.B.E.'s file, discharged for the last time 12 August 1943.

73 Carlo Spartaco Capogreco, *I campi del Duce* (Torino: Einaudi, 2004).

74 Giovanni Dall'Orto reports some of these cases. See Dall'Orto, *Tutta un'altra*.

75 FSA, Storie Cliniche Ricoverati 1924–25–26, Z.T.'s file, the date the patient was discharged is not mentioned.

76 FSA, Storie Cliniche Ricoverati, dal 5731 al 6160, 1938–9, P.G., date he was discharged not available; Storie Cliniche Ricoverati, dal 5731 al 6160, 1938–9, B.B. discharged on 4 August 1955.

77 FSA, Storie Cliniche Ricoverati, Morti nel 1932, 1933, 1934, B.A., date he was discharged not available.

78 FSA, Storie Cliniche Ricoverati, Morti – Ammessi prima dallo schedario 1927, 1928, 1930, 1931, B.U., his file is present in the Patient's Files series. He died while interned on 8 March 1929.

79 See note 66.

80 FSA, Storie Cliniche Uomini e Donne Morti 1924–25–26, F.O., date he was discharged not available. FSA, Storie Cliniche Uomini 3501–3850, 1933, R.G., discharged on 14 October 1932.

81 FSA, Storie Cliniche Ricoverati, 1924–25–26. N.N., died while interned on 24 July 1925. *Acromegalia* means overgrown limbs or other parts of the body due to glandular disfunction.

82 FSA, Manicomio, N.N.'s file, died while interned on 27 July 1925.

83 Radclyffe Hall, *The Well of Loneliness* (London: J. Cape, 1928).

84 Vincenzo Patanè, 'Ottone Rosai. Firenze di Notte', *Babilonia*, 135 (July–August 1995): 36–40. On the gay artists and writers in fascist Italy, also see Gnerre, *L'Eroe*; Champagne, *Queer Ventennio*.

85 Several Tuscan men were sent to *confino* to San Domino delle Tremiti, Ustica and to small villages in Basilicata or other southern regions. From their confessions to the police, part of the gay life in Florence has been reconstructed. Some hints that allow partial reconstruction of the existence of a gay circuit in Florence in the fascist years can be found in: Benadusi, *Il Nemico*; Magistro, *Adelmo*; Giartosio and Goretti, *La Città*; Ebner, *Ordinary Violence*.

5 The Girifalco asylum: 'A grave for the living'

1 GAA's file, number 4455, Letter to the director from a patient's sister, dated 15 March 1925. Here I can mention the file number because there is no connection between the patient and issues of sexuality.

2 Data from www.ugeo.urbistat.com and www.tuttitalia.it.

3 See Daniel Pick, *Faces of Degeneration: A European Disorder, c. 1844–c. 1918* (Cambridge: Cambridge University Press, 1989).

4 Salvatore Inglese, 'Razza tellurica, razza criminale: il carattere calabrese nella mitologia scientifica della prima metà del Novecento', *Dedalus* 4 (January–June 1990): 113–27; Greco, *I Demoni*.

5 Greco, *I Demoni*; Ennio Passalia, 'Frammentari ricordi di esistenze scomparse. Storie dal manicomio di Girifalco (1881–1920)' (PhD diss., University of Genova, academic year 2009–10).

6 See later in the chapter.

7 Babini, *Liberi Tutti*.

8 Bernardo Frisco, 'I disturbi nervosi e le psicosi mestruali nei rapporti colla imputabilità della donna', *Annali del Manicomio Provinciale di Catanzaro in Girifalco* (1922–3): 3–123.

9 Greco, *I Demoni*.

10 Annibale Puca, *L'epilessia riferita ad alcune zone calabresi* (Nicastro: La Calabria, 1933).

11 No mention of Vincenzo Fragola, Carmelo Ventra, and Rocco Cerra in *Dizionario degli Italiani* (Roma: Treccani, 2008); *Chi è* (Roma: Formiggini, 1928, 1931, 1936, 1940); *Enciclopedia Italiana*, www.treccani.it; www.aspi.unimib.it.

12 Annibale Puca, 'Il 50° Anniversario dell'Ospedale Provinciale', *Annali del Manicomio Provinciale di Catanzaro in Girifalco* (October–November 1931): 1–222.

13 Ibid., 94.

14 Ibid.

15 The State Archives in Catanzaro and Cosenza confirmed they hold no documentation on the Girifalco asylum, whose archives hold only patient medical files and patient admissions registers.

16 Domenico Marcello, *Un Secolo di Manicomio. Storia del Manicomio di Girifalco* (Catanzaro: Ursini, 1995).

17 Ibid., 276.

18 The Dodecanese islands were conquered in 1911 and were part of Italian territory. During Fascism there was a renewed interest in 'Italianizing' them.

19 Marcello, *Un Secolo*.

20 Ibid., 277–8.

21 Ibid., 282.

22 Ibid., 278–9, *o.d.s.* of 15 December 1929 and of 23 June 1930.

23 Ibid., 277, *o.d.s.* of 26 November 1929.

24 Ibid., 280.

25 Ibid., 280–1.

26 Vincenzo Fragola, 'I nuovi orizzonti dell'Assistenza Psichiatrica nei Manicomi Provinciali e l'andamento amministrativo e tecnico del Manicomio di Catanzaro in Girifalco in rapporto ai malati di mente della provincia durante l'anno 1923–1924', *Annali del Manicomio Provinciale di Catanzaro in Girifalco* (1924): 3–160.

27 A concept he reiterated in an article devoted to the subject, Vincenzo Fragola, 'La Istituzione degli Ambulatori gratuiti per le malattie nervose e mentali nei rapporti della gestione economica nei Manicomi Provinciali', *Annali del Manicomio Provinciale di Catanzaro in Girifalco* (1924): 172–82.

28 Puca, 'Il 50° Anniversario'.

29 Ibid., 15.

30 Ibid., 27. The idea circulated and the Girifalco asylum journal had published an article on the subject: Rosolino Colella, 'Tubercolosi e Delinquenza. Perizia medico-legale', *Annali del Manicomio Provinciale di Catanzaro in Girifalco* (1920): 163–207.

31 Puca, 'Il 50° Anniversario', 29.

32 Ibid., 42. Meio-thymic: with epithelial gland deficiency.

33 Ibid.

34 Ibid., 62.

35 Ibid.

36 Ibid., 73.

37 Annibale Puca (1933), 'Sessualità e lesioni vertebrali', *Il Pisani*, 53 (1): 65–108.

38 Vincenzo Fragola, 'Relazione Tecnico-Sanitaria sull'andamento dell'Ospedale Psichiatrico provinciale di Catanzaro in Girifalco durante l'anno 1933', *Annali dell'Ospedale Provinciale di Catanzaro in Girifalco* (1933): 8–39.

39 Ibid., 12. *Venere solitaria* (solitary Venus) is a euphemism for masturbation.

40 Ibid., 37.

41 Ibid., 38.

42 Annibale Puca, 'Conversazione con la mamme', *Annali del Manicomio Provinciale di Catanzaro in Girifalco* (1933): 230–50.

43 Annibale Puca, 'Che cosa diventerà mio figlio', *Annali del Manicomio Provinciale di Catanzaro in Girifalco* (1934): 227–45.

44 See Chapter 2.

45 Files from 4,349 to 4,455, from 5,500 to 5,768, from 6,906 to 7,072. Two files of year 1939 are missing.

46 Puca, 'Il 50° Anniversario'.

47 Ibid., 73.

48 GAA, C.E.'s files, interned on 19 February 1939.

49 GAA, B.R.'s file, interned on 5 August 1939.
50 GAA, L.P.R.'s file, interned on 13 February 1933.
51 Passalia highlights that onanism was only mentioned when referring to male patients for the period he examines, Passalia, 'Frammentari ricordi'.
52 GAA, Z.S.'s file, interned on 12 December 1933.
53 GAA, L.B.'s file, interned on 14 June 1933.
54 GAA, R.M.'s file, interned on 25 January 1933.
55 Passalia specifies that, also for the period he examined, 'homosexual behaviour is never filed as the cause for internment, but as a further proof of the illness that is monitored during the hospitalisation period. In particular, the "passive pederasty" practice is juxtaposed to criminality and to an artistic predisposition, as in Krafft-Ebing's and Lombroso's theories. A higher degree of interest is reserved for a body's anomalies, [read as] signs of an incomplete sexual differentiation', Passalia, 'Frammentari Ricordi', 19.
56 GAA, F.N.'s file, interned on 14 April 1939, L.A.'s file, interned on 25 June 1939, G.S.'s file, interned on 5 August 1933, T.E., file, interned on 27 December 1933.
57 Vincenzo Fragola, 'I nuovi orizzonti dell'Assistenza Psichiatrica nei Manicomi Provinciali e l'andamento amministrativo e tecnico del Manicomio di Catanzaro in Girifalco in rapporto ai malati di mente della provincia durante l'anno 1923–1924', *Annali del Manicomio Provinciale di Catanzaro in Girifalco* (1924): 3–160.
58 Passalia, 'Frammentari Ricordi'.
59 See Chapter 4.
60 GAA, C.N.'s file, interned on 12 April 1939.
61 GAA, T.R.'s file, interned on 23 January 1939.
62 The *diari*, daily reports, in this patient's case seem to have been written by the doctors.
63 Routine anal examination to ascertain passive homosexuality has been proved to be a common practice in several historical studies on homosexuality during the Italian fascist regime, such as Giartosio and Goretti, *La Città*.
64 See introduction.
65 GAA, G.A.'s file, interned on 9 November 1933.
66 A search of his file in the Collegno (Turin) psychiatric hospital archives was fruitless, his file is missing.
67 In this case too, from the language used it seems more plausible that the notes were written by doctors rather than nurses.
68 This military term usually refers to soldiers who are reprimanded and punished through isolation. Dictionaries translate it with 'confined to barracks'. Here it might refer to the section of the hospital where the agitated patients were kept, and it might imply they were tied up.

69 Initially, I interpreted this gesture as a gender reassignment attempt, but I asked two consultancies on this issue, one by a urologist and one by a psychiatrist who both confirmed that nowadays they would consider this type of gesture as a sign of self-harm or paraphilia. However, at the time, given the extreme importance conferred by doctors to genitals, in my opinion the gesture should have attracted the attentions of psychiatrists on the patient's lifestyle and biography, soliciting some interest aimed at clarifying the causes of his self-harming actions.

70 Passalia, 'Frammentari Ricordi'.

Conclusions

1 Corner, 'Dictatorship'; Corner, *La dittatura fascista*.

2 Peloso, *La Guerra Dentro*.

3 Emilio Lussu, quoted in Benadusi, *Il Nemico*, 131.

4 Ebner, *Ordinary Violence*.

5 Ibid.

6 De Paoli, 'Contributo'.

Bibliography

Unpublished primary sources

Santa Maria della Pietà Archives documentation, Rome.

San Salvi 'Vincenzo Chiarugi' mental health hospital documentation, Faculty of Psychology Library, Florence.

San Salvi 'Vincenzo Chiarugi' mental health hospital documentation at the State Archives, Florence.

Girifalco mental health hospital archives documentation, Girifalco (Catanzaro).

Published primary sources

Agostini, Cesare. *Manuale di Psichiatria*. Milano: Vallardi, 1897.

Agostini, Giulio. 'Su di un caso di pseudo-ermafroditismo esterno femminile', *Annali dell'Ospedale Psichiatrico Provinciale di Perugia* (January–December 1929): 31–53.

Anfosso, Luigi. *La legislazione italiana sui manicomi e sugli alienati: Commento alla Legge 1904*. Torino: Unione Tipografico-editrice Torinese, 1907.

Antonini, Giuseppe. *Nozioni pratiche sull'assistenza dei malati di mente negli ospedali psichiatrici e nelle famiglie*. Milano: Coop Farmaceutica, 1928.

Bianchi, Giuseppe. 'Un caso di eunucoidismo', *Rivista Sperimentale di Feniatria* (1930): 559–66.

Bianchi, Leonardo. *Trattato di psichiatria ad uso dei medici e degli studenti*. Napoli: Pasquale, 1900. Consulted version: Napoli: Idelson, 1924.

Biffi, Serafino. *Opere complete*, vols. I, II, III. Milano: Hoepli, 1902.

Bonaparte, Marie. *Educazione e sessualità: La profilassi infantile delle nevrosi*. Roma: Cremonese, 1935.

Boschi, Gaetano. 'In tema di impotenza sessuale', *Rassegna di Studi Psichiatrici* 20 (1931): 1257–66.

Brugia, Raffaele. *I problemi della degenerazione*. Bologna: Zanichelli, 1906.

Bumke, Oswald. *Lehrbuch der Geisteskrankenheiten*. Berlin: 1919. Version consulted: *Trattato di Psichiatria*, vols. I and II. Torino: Unione Tipografica-Editrice Torinese, 1927.

Cassinelli, Bruno. *Storia della Pazzia*. Milano: Corbaccio, 1936.

Cerra, Rocco. 'I dispensari antirabici. Appunti di profilassi mentale', *Annali del Manicomio Provinciale di Catanzaro in Girifalco* (1933): 144–9.

Chavigny, M. 'Un Cas d'Homosexualité Feminine', *Annales médico-psychologiques* (1930): 7–41.

Coen, Augusto Mario. 'Contributo alla conoscenza della pazzia morale', *Rivista Sperimentale di Feniatria* (1923): 141–227.

Cristiani, Andrea. 'Psicopatie sessuali in donne con affezioni ginecologiche', *Rivista Italiana di Neuropatologia, Psichiatria ed Elettroterapia* (1910): 356–60.

Cucchi, Aldo. 'Sull'Omosessualità', *Note e Rivista di Psichiatria* (1940): 173–81.

Daneo, Luigi, and Ciro Batisti. 'Un ventennio di funzionamento del reparto "criminali" a Cogoleto. Gli immorali costituzionali. Casistica', *Neuropsichiatria, Annali dell'ospedale psichiatrico della Provincia di Genova* 10–11 (1932): 17–22.

De Napoli, Ferdinando. 'La bisessualità latente come carattere individuale costante e consecutiva opoterapia antiomosessuale', *Rassegna di Studi Sessuali* (1923): 229–44.

De Nigris, Giovanni. 'Pseudoermafroditismo femminile e mascolinismo psichico in soggetto degenerato', *Archivio Generale di Neurologia, Psichiatria e Psicoanalisi* (1930): 373.

De Paoli, Mario. 'Contributo allo Studio dell'Omosessualità Passiva', *Quaderni di Psichiatria* (August 1925): 239–52.

De Sanctis, Sante. *Autobiografia*. Bologna: Zanichelli, 1937.

De Sanctis, Sante. *Neuropsichiatria infantile: patologia e diagnostica*. Roma: Stock, 1925.

Del Greco, Francesco. 'Sui rapporti tra "immoralità" e "delinquenza" negli individui umani', *Rivista Italiana di Neuropatologia, Psichiatria ed Elettroterapia* (July 1914): 289–95.

Descuret, Jean Baptiste Félix. *La médicine des passions ou Les passions considerées dans leur rapport avec les maladies, les lois et la religion*. Paris: no publisher, 1841. Version consulted: *La Medicina delle Passioni, ovvero le Passioni considerate relativamente alle malattie, alle leggi e alla religione*. Napoli: S. Romano, 1906.

Ferrari, Giulio Cesare. *Per la Storia della Psichiatria. Recensioni 1893–1907*. Reprinted. Bologna: Pitagora, 1984.

Ferrari, Giulio Cesare. *Scritti di Pedagogia e sulla Rieducazione dei Giovani*. Reprinted. Bologna: Pitagora, 1984.

Ferrari, Giulio Cesare. *Scritti di Psicologia*. Reprinted. Bologna: Pitagora, 1985.

Ferrio, Carlo. *La Psiche e i Nervi*. Torino: Utet, 1948.

Ferrio, Carlo. *Trattato di psichiatria clinica e Forense*. Torino: Unione Tipografica-Editrice Torinese, [1959] 1970.

Ferro, Filippo Maria, ed. *Passioni della mente e della storia*. Milano: Università Cattolica del Sacro Cuore, 1989.

Fragola, Vincenzo. 'La istituzione degli Ambulatori gratuiti per le malattie nervose e mentali nei rapporti della gestione economica nei Manicomi Provinciali', *Annali del Manicomio Provinciale di Catanzaro in Girifalco* (1924): 172–82.

Fragola, Vincenzo. 'I nuovi orizzonti dell'assistenza psichiatrica nei Manicomi Provinciali e l'andamento amministrativo e tecnico del Manicomio di Catanzaro in Girifalco in rapporto ai malati di mente della provincia durante l'anno 1923–1924', *Annali del Manicomio Provinciale di Catanzaro in Girifalco* (1924): 3–160.

Fragola, Vincenzo. 'Relazione Tecnico-Sanitaria sull'andamento dell'Ospedale Psichiatrico Provinciale di Catanzaro in Girifalco durante l'anno 1933, XI', *Annali del Manicomio Provinciale Catanzaro in Girifalco* (1933): 8–39.

Frati, Ludovico. *La donna italiana nei più recenti studi*. Torino: Bocca, 1928.

Frisco, Bernardo. 'I disturbi nervosi e le psicosi mestruali nei rapporti colla imputabilità della donna', *Annali del Manicomio Provinciale Catanzaro in Girifalco* (1922–3): 3–123.

Frisco, Bernardo. 'I nuovi orizzonti dell'assistenza psichiatrica nei Manicomi Provinciali e il mantenimento dei folli poveri', *Annali del Manicomio Provinciale Catanzaro in Girifalco* (1924): 7–157.

Frisco, Bernardo. 'Osservazioni cliniche e considerazioni medico-legali sulla imputabilità e sulla capacità civile dei dementi precoci, Parte Prima', *Annali del Manicomio Provinciale Catanzaro in Girifalco* (1920): 61–142.

Fuhrmann, Manfredo. *Diagnosi e Prognosi delle Malattie Mentali*. Milano: Società Editrice Libraria, 1908.

Garnier, Paul. *Epuisement nerveux genital: cause et remèdes*. Paris: Garnier Fréres, 1895. Version consulted: *Nevrastenia Sessuale. Cause e rimedi*. Milano: Quintieri, 1915.

Giannelli, Augusto. *Il Nuovo Ospedale Santa Maria della Pietà*. Roma: Tipografia Santa Maria della Pietà, 1937.

Giannelli, Augusto. *Studi sulla Pazzia nella Provincia di Roma*. Roma: Cecchini, 1905.

Giordano, Pasquale. *Storia di uno psichiatra: viaggio critico attraverso la psichiatria italiana di ieri e di oggi*. Firenze: L'Autore Libri, 2012.

Hesnard, Angelo Louis Marie. *Traité de Pychologie Normale et Pathologiche*. Paris: Payot, 1933. Version consulted: *Manuale di sessuologia normale e patologica*. Milano: Longanesi, 1962.

Kraepelin, Emil. *Ein Lehrbuch für Studierende und Ärtze*, Leipzig: Barth, 1903. Version consulted: *Trattato di psichiatria*. Milano: Vallardi, 1906.

La Cara, Alfredo. *La base organica dei pervertimenti sessuali*. 1902. Milano: Bocca, 1924.

Legueu, M. 'Hermaphroditisme', *Journal des Practiciens* 60 (1926): 646–47.

Levi Bianchini, Marco. 'La Rappresentazione fallica del genitale femminile nella ricerca sessuale del bambino', *Archivio Generale di Neurologia, Psichiatria e Psicoanalisi* (1929): 65–71.

Levi Bianchini, Marco. 'Virilismo prosopopilare e androfania nella donna alienata', *Archivio Generale di Neurologia, Psichiatria e Psicoanalisi* (1930): 121–33.

Levi, Ettore. *Il I Quadriennio di vita dell'Istituto Italiano di Igiene. Un centro di studi e di attività sociali*. Roma: Edizioni dell'Istituto di Igiene, Previdenza ed Assistenza Sociale, 1925.

Levi, Michele. 'L'origine dell'intersessualità', *Archivio di Antropologia Criminale, Psichiatria e Medicina Legale* (July–August 1929): 496–502.

Mandolini, Ernani (or Hernani). 'Il Contagio delle Psicopatie Sessuali', *Rassegna di Studi Sessuali* (1923): 169–72.

Mantegazza, Paolo. *Gli Amori degli Uomini*. Milano: Mantegazza, 1892.

Mantegazza, Paolo. *Igiene dell'Amore*. Milano: Treves, 1891.

Marañon, Gregorio. *La evolucion de la sexualidad y los estados intersexuales*. Madrid: J. Morata, 1930. Version consulted: *The Evolution and Intersexual Conditions*. London: Allen & Unwin, 1932.

Mariani, Giuseppe. *La Questione Sessuale. Fisiopatologia, Sociologia e Legislazione Sessuale*. Milano: Istituto Editoriale Scientifico, 1926.

Marro, Antonio. *I caratteri dei delinquenti*. Torino: Bocca, 1887.

Martire, Egilberto. 'Elogio della famiglia', *Politica Sociale* 6 (September 1929): 615–18.

Moglie, Giulio. *Manuale di psichiatria ad uso dei medici pratici e degli studenti*. Roma: L. Pozzi, 1940.

Morselli, Enrico. *Sessualità umana*. Torino: Bocca, 1931.

Niceforo, Alfredo. *Le psicopatie acquisite*. Roma: Capaccini, 1897.

Niceforo, Alfredo, and Scipione Sighele. *La malavita a Roma*. Torino: Roux Frassati, 1898.

Obici, G. and G. Marchesini. *Le amicizie del collegio. Ricerche sulle prime manifestazioni dell'amore sessuale*. Roma & Milano: Dante Alighieri, 1905.

Ottolenghi, Salvatore. *Trattato di Polizia Scientifica, vol. II. Identificazione psichica e biografica e investigazioni giudiziarie*. Milano: Società Editrice Libraria, 1932.

Pighini, Giacomo. 'Per la eliminazione dei degenerati psichici dell'esercito combattente', *Giornale di Medicina Militare* (1918): 977–94.

Pighini, Giacomo. *Vita di psichiatra*. Parma: Maccari, 1968.

Puca, Annibale. 'Conversazione con le mamme', *Annali del Manicomio Provinciale di Catanzaro in Girifalco* (1933): 230–50.

Puca, Annibale. 'Che cosa diventerà mio figlio (saggio critico di psicotecnica)', *Annali del Manicomio Provinciale di Catanzaro in Girifalco* (1934): 227–45.

Puca, Annibale. 'Il 50° Annale dell'Ospedale Provinciale', *Annali del Manicomio Provinciale di Catanzaro in Girifalco* (October–November 1931): 1–222.

Puca, Annibale. 'La Società di Sociologia psichiatrica', *Rassegna di Neuropsichiatria* (1949): 94–9.

Puca, Annibale. *L'Epilessia. Riferimenti ad alcune zone Calabresi. Nuove concezioni sulla patogenesi e sulla cura*. Nicastro: La Calabria, 1933.

Puca, Annibale. 'Sessualità e lesioni vertebrali', *Il Pisani* (January–June 1933): 65–108.

Raffalovich, Marc André. *Uranisme et Unisexualité*. Paris: Lyon et Masson, 1896. Version consulted: *L'Uranismo, inversione sessuale congenita. Osservazioni e consigli*. Torino: Bocca, 1896.

Ribeiro, Leonidio. *Homosexualismo y Endocrinologia*. Rio de Janeiro: F. Alves, 1938. Version consulted: *Omosessualità e endocrinologia*. Milano: Bocca, 1940.

Rizzatti, Emilio, and Giovanni Borgarello. 'La leucotomia prefrontale di Egas Moniz in 100 casi di psicopatie gravi', *Schizofrenie* (1938): 241–67.

Rondoni, Pietro. *Le Malattie ereditarie: istituzioni di eredopatologia generale*. Milano: Casa Ambrosiana, 1947.

Roux, Joanny. *Psicologia dell'istinto sessuale*. Roma: Capaccini, 1900.

Ruiz-Funes, Mariano. 'L'imputabilità parziale', *Archivio di Antropologia Criminale* (1930): 15–24.

Saint-Paul, Georges. *Tares et Poisons. Perversion et perversité sexuelles*. Paris: Carré, 1896. Reprinted: *Invertis et Homosexuels*. Paris: Vigot, 1930.

Santangelo, G. 'Le aberrazioni del carattere nel cocainismo cronico', *Archivio Generale di Neurologia, Psichiatria e Psicoanalisi* (1930): 296–306.

Scremin, Luigi. 'Problemi sessuali e morale cattolica', *Rassegna di Studi Sessuali* (January–June 1932): 1–24.

Sergi, Giuseppe. *Le Degenerazioni umane*. Milano: Dumolard, 1889.

Servadio, Emilio. 'Sessuologia'. In *Encliclopedia Italiana*. Roma: Treccani, 1936, 494–500.

Spotti, Luigi. 'Importanza della rilevazione grafologica nello studio del giudizio e condotta morale', *Archivio Generale di Neurologia, Psichiatria e Psicoanalisi* (1933): 12–26.

Steinach, Eugen, and Joseph Löbel. *Sex and Life: Forty Years of Medical Experiments*. London: Faber & Faber, 1940.

Tanzi, Eugenio. *Trattato delle malattie mentali*. Milano: Società Editrice Libraria, 1905.

Tirelli, Vitige. *Appunti di Psicopatologia Femminile*. Torino: Checchini, 1929.

Tobino, Mario. *Le libere donne di Magliano*. Firenze: Vallecchi, 1953. Version consulted: Milano: Mondadori, 1963.

Tomellini, Luigi. 'Alcuni casi di pazzia morale studiati in rapporto all'imputabilità secondo il nostro codice', *Bollettino dell'Accademia di Genova* (1906): 147–75.

Vanelli, Angelo. 'Un caso di Eunucoidismo', *Rassegna di Studi Psichiatrici* (1931): 949–58.

Ventra, Carmelo. 'Brevi considerazioni cliniche e medico-legali sopra un caso di reversione atavica dell'istinto sessuale in una giovane imbecille sotto forma di fregola periodica animalesca', *Annali del Manicomio Provinciale di Catanzaro in Girifalco* (1920): 4–17.

Venturi, Silvio. *Le degenerazioni psico-sessuali*. Torino: Bocca, 1892.

Vidoni, Giuseppe. *La Delinquenza dei minorenni*. Roma: Da Vinci, 1924.

Vidoni, Giuseppe. *Valori e Limiti dell'Endocrinologia nello studio del delinquente*. Torino: Bocca, 1923.

Visintini, Fabio. *Memorie di un cittadino psichiatra (1902–1982)*. Napoli: Edizioni Scientifiche Italiane, 1983.

Weygandt, Wilhelm. *Atlas und Grundriss der Psychiatrie*. München: Lehmann, 1902. Version consulted: *Psichiatria*. Milano: Società Editrice Libraria, 1908.

Published secondary sources

Aldrich, Robert. *The Seduction of the Mediterranean. Writing, Art and Homosexual Fantasy*. London: Routledge, 1993.

Antonelli, Quinto, and Felice Ficco, eds. *Memorie di un internato psichiatrico.* Trento: Museo Storico di Trento, 2003.

Arthurs, Joshua, Michael Ebner and Kate Ferris, eds. *The Politics of Everyday Life in Fascist Italy.* Basingstoke: Palgrave Macmillan, 2017.

Babini, Valeria. *La questione dei frenastenici, Alle origini della psicologia scientifica in Italia, 1870–1910.* Milano: F. Angeli, 1996.

Babini, Valeria. *Liberi Tutti. Manicomi e psichiatri in Italia. Una Storia del Novecento.* Bologna: Il Mulino, 2009.

Babini, Valeria, Chiara Beccalossi and Lucy Ryall, eds. *Italian Sexualities Uncovered, 1789–1914.* Basingstoke: Palgrave Macmillan, 2015.

Babini, Valeria, Fernanda Minuz and Annamaria Tagliavini. *La donna nelle scienze dell'uomo.* Milano: F. Angeli, 1986.

Barberis, Walter. *Storia senza perdono.* Torino: Einaudi, 2019.

Bartolucci, Chiara, and Giovanni Pietro Lombardo. 'Evolutionary monism in the study of mental phenomena: The clinical-differential psychopathology of Enrico Morselli, scientist and philosopher (1852–1929)', *History and Philosophy of Psychology* 14, no. 2 (2012): 11–21.

Beccalossi, Chiara. *Female Sexual Inversion: Same-sex Desire in Italian and British Sexology, c 1870–1920.* Basingstoke: Palgrave Macmillan, 2012.

Beccalossi, Chiara. 'Optimizing and normalizing the population through hormone therapies in Italian science, c. 1926–1950', *British Journal of History of Science* 53, no. 1 (2020): 1–22.

Bellassai, Sandro. 'The masculine mystique: Antimodernism and virility in fascist Italy', *Journal of Modern Italian Studies* 10, no. 3 (2005): 314–35.

Bellassai, Sandro, and Maria Malatesta, eds. *Genere e Mascolinità. Uno sguardo storico.* Roma: Bulzoni, 2000.

Benadiba, Laura. 'The persistence of silence after dictatorships', *Oral History Review* 39, no. 2 (2012): 287–97.

Benadusi, Lorenzo. *Il nemico dell'uomo nuovo. L'omosessualità nell'esperimento totalitario fascista.* Milano: Feltrinelli, 2005.

Benadusi, Lorenzo. 'La storia dell'omosessualità maschile. Linee di tendenza, spunti di riflessione e prospettive di ricerca', *Rivista di Sessuologia* 31, no. 1 (2007): 1–15.

Benvenuti, Paola, and Esther Diana, eds. *Il contributo della Toscana alla psichiatria.* Firenze: Polistampa, 2018.

Berenbaum, Michael, and Abraham J. Peck, eds. *The Holocaust and History: The Known, the Unknown, the Disputed and the Reexamined.* Bloomington: Indiana University Press, 1998.

Bernardi, Marco, and Fabio Milazzo, eds, *La devianza in Italia dall'Unità al fascismo. Discorsi e rappresentazioni.* Milano: Biblion, 2022.

Berrios, G. E., and N. Kennedy. 'Erotomania: A conceptual history', *History of Psychiatry* 52, no. 13 (2002): 381–400.

Bini, Elisabetta. 'La fotografia come fonte storica', paper presented at Seminar entitled 'Quale lente per lo storico?', Istituto Gramsci dell'Emilia Romagna, 20 October 2005, available on-line: www.sissco.it.

Bivins, Roberta, and V. John Pickstone, eds. *Medicine, Madness and Social History.* Basingstoke: Palgrave Macmillan, 2007.

Bonella, Anna Lia, and Franca Fedeli Bernardini, eds. *L'ospedale dei pazzi di Roma dai papi al '900. Fonti per la storia della follia: S. Maria della Pietà e il suo Archivio Storico (sec. XVI–XX)*, vol. I. Bari: Dedalo, 1994.

Bonsaver, Guido. *Mussolini censore. Storie di letteratura, dissenso e ipocrisia.* Bari: Laterza, 2013.

Borgna, Eugenio. 'La psichiatria negli anni del fascismo'. In *Novara fa da sé. Atti del Convegno di Belgirate–1993*, edited by Adolfo Mignemi, 285–7. Novara: Provincia di Novara, 1993.

Bourke, Joanna. *Fear, A Cultural History.* 2005. London: Virago, 2006.

Brady, Sean. *Masculinity and Male Homosexuality in Britain, 1861–1913.* 2005. Basingstoke: Palgrave Macmillan, 2009.

Brady, Sean, and John Seymour, eds. *From Sodomy Laws to Same-Sex Marriage.* Cergy: Université de Cergy-Pontoise Press, 2019.

Burgio, Giuseppe. 'Uomini senza orientamento: Genere maschile e comportamenti sessuali "mediterranei"', *Ag About Gender* 6, no. 11 (2016): 98–125.

Caglioti, Angelo Matteo. 'Race, statistics and Italian eugenics: Alfredo Niceforo's Trajectory from Lombroso to fascism (1876-1960)', *European History Quarterly* 47, no. 3 (2017): 461–89.

Canosa, Romano. *Storia del manicomio in Italia dall'Unità a oggi.* Milano: Feltrinelli, 1979.

Capogreco, Carlo Spartaco. *I campi del Duce.* Torino: Einaudi, 2004.

Carrino, Candida. *Luride, Agitate, Criminali. Un secolo di internamento femminile (1850–1950).* Roma: Carocci, 2018.

Cassata, Francesco. *Building the New Man: eugenics, racial science and genetics in XX century Italy.* 2006. Budapest: Central European University Press, 2011.

Cassata, Francesco, and Massimo Moraglio, eds. *Manicomio, società e politica: storia, memoria e cultura della devianza mentale dal Piemonte all'Italia.* Pisa: BFS, 2005.

Castronovo, Valerio, and Nicola Tranfaglia, eds. *La stampa italiana nell'età fascista.* Bari: Laterza, 1980.

Cavaglion, Alberto. *La filosofia del pressappoco. Weininger, sesso, carattere e la cultura del Novecento.* Napoli: L'Ancora del Mediterraneo, 2001.

Champagne, John Gerard. *Queer Ventennio: Italian Fascism, Homoerotic Art, and the Nonmodern in the Modern.* Pieterlen: Peter Lang, 2019.

Chiodi Nannini, Ivana, ed. *Abbiamo tutti un romanzo nella testa. Venti storie di donne ricoverate nelle case manicomiali di Torino*, vol. II. Collegno: no date, no publisher.

Circolo Pink, ed. *Le ragioni di un silenzio. La persecuzione degli omosessuali durante il nazismo e il fascismo.* Verona: Ombre Corte, 2002.

Cleminson, Richard, and Francisco Vasquez Garcia. *Los invisibles: A History of Male Homosexuality in Spain 1850–1940*. Cardiff: University of Wales Press, 2007.

Coccanari De' Fornari, Maria Antonietta, Andrea Piazzi, Gioia Piazzi and Luana Testa, 'La Rappresentazione della psichiatria italiana nell'Enciclopedia Italiana Treccani negli anni Trenta', *Medicina nei Secoli, Arte e Scienza* 25, no. 2 (2013): 541–64.

Coccanari De' Fornari, Maria Antonietta, and Angela Iannitelli and Massimo Biondi, 'Storia della Clinica Psichiatrica della Sapienza Università di Roma nel Policlinico Umberto I', *Rivista di Psichiatria* 52, no. 1 (2017): 1–8.

Consoli, Massimo. *Homocaust*. Milano: Kaos, 1991.

Corner, Paul. 'Dictatorship revisited: Consensus, coercion, and strategies for survival', *Modern Italy* 22, no. 4 (2017): 435–44.

Corner, Paul. 'Everyday fascism in the 1930s: Centre and periphery in the decline of Mussolini's dictatorship', *Contemporary European History* 15, no. 2 (2006): 195–222.

Corner, Paul. *The Fascist Party and Popular Opinion in Mussolini's Italy*. Oxford: Oxford University Press, 2012. Version consulted: *La dittatura fascista. Consenso e controllo durante il Ventennio*. Roma: Carocci, 2017.

Corritore, Renzo, and Enzo Laforgia. *La Provincia di Varese negli Anni Trenta. Istituzioni, società civile, economia*. Milano: F. Angeli, 2002.

Cosmacini, Giorgio. *Medici e Medicina durante il fascismo*. Milano: Pantarei, 2019.

Cosmacini, Giorgio. *Storia della medicina e della sanità in Italia*. Bari: Laterza, 2005.

Cossa, Diana. *Ospedali psichiatrici di Torino, Archivio Storico (1685–1987)*. www.cartedalegare.it, dated December 2012.

Dall'Acqua, Marzio, and Maristella Miglioli. 'I viaggi d'istruzione medica nel processo di formazione della psichiatria italiana', *Sanità, Scienza e Storia* 2 (1984): 173–97.

Dall'Orto, Giovanni. 'La "Tolleranza Repressiva" dell'Omosessualità', *Quaderni di Critica Omosessuale* 3 (1987): 37–57.

Dall'Orto, Giovanni. 'Ci furono femminelle che piangevano quando venimmo via dalle Tremiti!', *Babilonia*, no. 50 (October 1987): 26–8.

Dall'Orto, Giovanni. 'Credere, Obbedire, Non Battere', *Babilonia*, no. 36 (May 1986): 13–17.

Dall'Orto, Giovanni. 'Il concetto di degenerazione nel pensiero borghese dell'Ottocento', *Sodoma* 2, no. 2 (1985): 59–74.

Dall'Orto, Giovanni. 'Manicomi e Omosessualità in Italia (1880–1978)', www.wikipink. it, dated 20 December 2017.

Dall'Orto, Giovanni. 'Per il bene della Razza al Confino il Pederasta', *Babilonia*, no. 35 (April–May 1986): 14–17.

Dall'Orto, Giovanni. *Tutta un'altra storia. L'omosessualità dall'antichità al secondo dopoguerra*. Milano: Il Saggiatore, 2015.

Dario, Mariopaolo, Giovanni Del Missier, Ester Stocco, and Luana Testa. *Psichiatria e psicoterapia in Italia dall'unità a oggi*. Roma: L'Asino D'Oro, 2016.

De Bernardi, Alberto, ed. *Follia, Psichiatria, Società*. Milano: F. Angeli, 1982.

De Bernardi, Alberto. *Fascismo e Antifascismo. Storia, memoria e culture politiche.* Roma: Donzelli, 2018.

De Felice, Renzo. *Rosso e Nero.* Milano: Baldini & Castoldi, 1995.

De Grazia, Victoria. *How Fascism Ruled Women, 1922-1945.* Los Angeles: University of California Press, 1992. Italian Translation: *Le donne nel regime fascista.* Venezia: Marsilio, 1993.

De Leo, Maya. *Queer. Storia culturale della comunità LGBTQ+.* Torino: Einaudi, 2021.

De Peri, Francesco. 'Il Medico e il Folle: istituzione psichiatrica, sapere scientifico e pensiero medico tra Otto e Novecento'. In *Storia d'Italia, Malattia e Medicina*, Annali 7, edited by Franco della Peruta, 1057-1140. Torino: Einaudi, 1984.

De Rosa, Diana. *La carrozza di Treves. Storie di donne e della loro follia.* Dogliani: Sensibili alle Foglie, 2002.

Des Dorides, Luca. 'Scemi, derelitti e degenerati. Strategie di potere e contrattazione del sapere nell'ospedale dei matti di Roma (1918-1938)' (PhD diss., academic year 2009-10, La Sapienza, University of Rome).

Dickinson, Tommy. *Curing Queers. Mental Nurses and their Patients 1935-1974.* Manchester: Manchester University Press, 2015.

Donnelly, Michael. *The Politics of Mental Health in Italy.* London: Routledge, 1992.

Dörner, Klaus. *Burger und Irre. Zur Sozialgeschichte und Wissenschaftsoziologie der Psychiatrie.* Frankfuhrt Am Main: Europäische Verlagsanstalt, 1969. Version consulted: *Madness and the Bourgeoisie. A Social History of Insanity and Psychiatry.* London: Basil Blackwell, 1981.

Duggan, Christopher. *Fascist Voices. An Intimate History of Mussolini's Italy.* 2012. Oxford: Oxford University Press, 2013.

Dunnage, Jonathan. 'Policemen and "women of ill repute": A study of male sexual attitudes and behaviour in fascist Italy', *European History Quarterly* 46, no. 1 (2016): 72-91.

Durham, Martin. *Women and Fascism.* London: Routledge, 1998.

Ebner, Michael. *Ordinary Violence in Mussolini's Italy.* Cambridge: Cambridge University Press, 2011.

Eder, X. Franz, Leslie Hall, and Gert Hekma, eds. *Sexual Cultures in Europe. Themes in Sexuality.* Manchester: Manchester University Press, 1999.

Ferraro, Stefania. *La semimbecille e altre storie. Biografie di follia e miseria: per una topografia dell'inadeguato.* Milano: Meltemi, 2017.

Fiocchetto, Rosanna. *L'Amante Celeste. La Distruzione Scientifica della Lesbica.* 1987. Milano: Il Dito e la Luna, 2003.

Fiorani, Matteo. *Bibliografia della psichiatria italiana.* Firenze: Firenze University Press, 2010.

Fiorino, Vinzia. *Le Officine della Follia. Il frenocomio di Volterra (1888-1978).* Pisa: ETS, 2011.

Fiorino, Vinzia. *Matti, Indemoniati e Vagabondi.* Venezia: Marsilio, 2002.

Fiorino, Vinzia, and Alessandra Fussi eds. *Emozioni, Corpi, Conflitti*. Pisa: ETS, 2016.

Foot, John. *Divided Memory*. Basingstoke: Palgrave Macmillan, 2009.

Foucault, Michel. 'Des Espaces Autres', *Architecture, Mouvement, Continuité* (October 1984). Available on-line in English translation: https://web.mit.edu/ allanmc/ www/ foucault1.

Foucault, Michel. *Herculine Barbin dite Alexina B.* Paris: Gallimard, 1978. Version consulted: *Herculine Barbin, being the recently discovered memoirs of a nineteenth-century French Hermaphrodite*. New York: Pantheon Books, 1980.

Foucault, Michel. *Histoire de la Folie à l'âge classique*. Paris: Librairie Plon, 1961. Version consulted: *Madness and Civilisation*. London: Routledge, 1989.

Foucault, Michel. *Histoire de la Sexualité. La volonté de savoir*. Paris: Gallimard, 1976. Version consulted: *La volontà di sapere. Storia della sessualità*. Milano: ES, 2014.

Franzinelli, Mimmo, and Nicola Graziano. *Un'Odissea Partigiana. Dalla Resistenza al Manicomio*. Milano: Feltrinelli, 2015.

Frigessi, Delia. *Cesare Lombroso*. Torino: Einaudi, 2003.

Gentile, Emilio, ed. *Modernità totalitaria. Il fascismo italiano*. Bari: Laterza, 2008.

Giartosio, Tommaso, and Gian Franco Goretti. *La città e l'Isola*. Roma: Donzelli, 2006.

Ginsborg, Paul. *Family Politics. Domestic life, Devastation and Survival, 1900–1950*. 2013. London: Yale University Press, 2014.

Ginsborg, Paul. *Storia d'Italia 1943–1996. Famiglia, società, Stato*. 1989. Torino: Einaudi, 1998.

Giovannini, Paolo. *La psichiatria di guerra. Dal fascismo alla Seconda guerra mondiale*. Milano: Unicopli, 2015.

Giovannini, Paolo, and Marco Palla, eds. *Il fascismo dalle mani sporche. Dittatura, corruzione, affarismo*. Bari: Laterza, 2019.

Gnerre, Francesco. *L'Eroe negato. Omosessualità e letteratura nel Novecento italiano*. 1981. Roma: Rogas, 2018.

Goffman, Erving. *Asylums. Essays on the Social Situation of Mental Health Patients and Other Inmates*. 1961. New York: Anchor Books, 1968.

Götz, Helmut. *Der Freie Geist und Seine Widersacher: die Einverweigerer an den italienischen Universitäten im Jahre 1931*. Frankfuhrt am Main: Haag & Herchen, 1993. Version consulted: *Il giuramento rifiutato. I docenti universitari e il regime fascista*. Milano: La Nuova Italia, 2000.

Gordon, S. C. Robert. *The Holocaust in Italian Culture, 1944–2010*. Stanford, CA: Stanford University Press, 2012.

Grandi, Casimira, and Rodolfo Taiani, eds. *Alla ricerca delle menti perdute*. Trento: Museo Storico di Trento, 2002.

Grassi, Gaddamaria, and Chiara Bombardieri, eds. *Il Policlinico della Delinquenza. Storia degli ospedali psichiatrici giudiziari italiani*. Milano: F. Angeli, 2016.

Grassi, Umberto, Vincenzo Lagioia, and Gian Paolo Romagnani, eds. *Tribadi, sodomiti, invertite e invertiti, pederasti, femminelle, ermafroditi: per una storia*

dell'omosessualità, della bisessualità e delle trasgressioni di genere in Italia.
Pisa: Ets, 2017.

Graziosi, Marina. 'Disparità e diritto alle origini della disuguaglianza delle donne'. In *Diritto e genere. Analisi interdisciplinare e comparata*, edited by Stefania Scarponi, 7–50. Padova: Cedam, 2014.

Greco, Oscar. *I Demoni del Mezzogiorno. Follia, pregiudizio e marginalità nel Manicomio di Girifalco (1881–1921)*. Soveria Mannelli: Rubbettino, 2018.

Greenslade, William. *Degeneration, Culture and the Novel 1880–1940*. Cambridge: Cambridge University Press, 1994.

Guarnieri, Patrizia. 'The history of psychiatry in Italy', *History of Psychiatry* 7, no. 2 (1991): 288–301.

Guarnieri, Patrizia. *La Storia della Psichiatria. Un secolo di studi in Italia*. Firenze: Olschki, 1991.

Guarnieri, Patrizia. 'Madness in the Home: Family Care and Welfare Policies in Italy before Fascism'. In *Psychiatric Cultures Compared. Psychiatry and Mental Health Care in the Twentieth Century: comparisons and approaches*, edited by Marijke Gijswit-Hofstra, Harry Oosterhuis, Joost Vijselaar and Hugh Freeman, 312–28. Amsterdam: Amsterdam University Press, 2005.

Guazzo, Paola, Ines Rieder, and Vincenza Scuderi, eds, *R/esistenze lesbiche nell'Europa nazifascista*. Verona: Ombre Corte, 2010.

Hacking, Ian. *Mad Travelers: Reflections on the Reality of Transient Mental Illnesses*. Charlotteville: University of Virginia Press, 1998.

Herzog, Dagmar. *Sexuality in Europe. A Twentieth Century History*. Cambridge: Cambridge University Press, 2011.

Herzog, Dagmar. *Sexuality and German Fascism*. 2002. New York: Berghahn Books, 2005.

Herzog, Dagmar. 'Syncopated sex: Transforming European sexual cultures', *American Historical Review* 114, no. 5 (2009): 1287–1308.

Hide, Louise. *Gender and Class in English Asylums, 1890–1914*. Basingstoke: Palgrave Macmillan, 2014.

Iaria, Antonino, Tommaso Lo Savio and Pompeo Martelli. *L'Ospedale Santa Maria della Pietà*, vols. I, II, III. Roma: Dedalo, 2003.

Irwin-Zarecka, Iwona. *Frames of Remembrance: The Dynamics of Collective Memory*. New Brunswick: Tranaction, 1994.

Jones, David W. *Disordered Personalities and Crime: An Analysis of the History of Moral Insanity*. Oxon: Routledge, 2016.

Jones, David W. 'Moral insanity and psychological disorder: The hybrid root of psychiatry', *History of Psychiatry* 28, no. 3 (2017): 263–79.

Kotowicz, Zbigniew. 'Psychosurgery in Italy, 1936–1939', *History of Psychiatry* 19, no. 4 (2008): 476–89.

Kotowicz, Zbigniew. *Psychosurgery: The Birth of a New Scientific Paradigm. Egas Moniz and the Present Day*. Lisbon: Centre for Philosophy of Science, University of Lisbon, 2012.

Laqueur, Thomas W. *Solitary Sex: A Cultural History of Masturbation*. New York: Zone Books, 2003. Version consulted: *Sesso solitario. Storia culturale della masturbazione*. Milano: Il Saggiatore, 2007.

Leone De Andreis, Marcella. *Capri 1939. L'isola in bianco e nero*. Capri: La Conchiglia, 2002.

Lippi, Donatella. *San Salvi. Storia di un manicomio*. Firenze: Olschki, 1996.

Lombardo, Giovanni Pietro, and Giorgia Morgese. 'La comparsa della malattia mentale in età evolutiva tra freniatria e neuro-psichiatria: la *Dementia Praecocissima* di Sante De Santis', *Physis* 52 (2017): 221–46.

Lombardo, Giovanni Pietro, and Elisabetta Cicciola. 'The Clinical Differential Approach of Sante De Sanctis in Italian "Scientific" Psychology', *Physis* 43 (2006): 1–16.

Magherini, Graziella, Roberto Vigevani, Giovanna Gurrieri and Ivan Nicoletti. *Salute Mentale e Territorio. Rapporto del servizio di igiene mentale dal centro di Firenze*. Firenze: Le Monnier, 1977.

Magistro, Cristoforo. *Adelmo e gli altri. Confinati omosessuali in Lucania*. Verona: Ombre Corte, 2019.

Maiocchi, Roberto. 'Gli Istituti di ricerca scientifica in Italia durante il fascismo', in *Ricerca e Istituzioni Scientifiche in Italia*, edited by Raffaella Simili, 182–212. Bari: Laterza, 1998.

Malone, Hannah. 'Legacies of Fascism: architecture, heritage and memory in contemporary Italy', *Modern Italy* 22, no. 4 (2017): 445–70.

Manacorda, Alberto. *Il manicomio giudiziario. Cultura psichiatrica e scienza giuridica nella storia di un'istituzione totale*. Bari: De Donato, 1982.

Mantovani, Claudia. *Rigenerare la società. L'eugenetica in Italia dalle origini ottocentesche agli Anni Trenta*. Soveria Mannelli: Rubbettino, 2004.

Marcello, Domenico. *Un secolo di Manicomio: Storia del Manicomio di Girifalco*. Catanzaro: Ursini, 1995.

Marchitelli, Anna. *Tredici canti (12 + 1)*. Vicenza: Neri Pozza, 2018.

Masi, Lorenzo. 'Rassegna di Studi Sessuali, 1921–1932: Autonomia di un periodico' (BA diss., University of Pisa, academic year 2014–15).

Melis, Guido. *La Macchina Imperfetta*. Bologna: Il Mulino, 2018.

Micale, Mark. *Approaching Hysteria, Disease and its Interpretations*. Princeton: Princeton University Press, 2019.

Mignemi, Adolfo, ed. *Novara fa da sé. Atti del Convegno di Belgirate-1993*. Novara: Provincia di Novara, 1993.

Mignemi, Adolfo. *Lo sguardo e l'immagine*. Torino: Bollati Boringhieri, 2003.

Mignemi, Adolfo. 'Ruolo delle fonti fotografiche nel lavoro dello storico', *Rivista Scuola Ticinese* 242 (April–May 2001): 10–12.

Mildenberger, Florian. 'Kraepelin and the 'urnings': male homosexuality in psychiatric discourse', *History of Psychiatry* 18, no. 3 (2007): 321–35.

Mildenberger, Florian. *Kulturverfall und Umwandlungsmännnchen. Die Haltung der Psychiatrie gegenüber den Homosexuellen im Dritten Reich am Beispiel München.* München: Forum Homosexualität und Geschichte München e. V., 2000.

Milletti, Nerina. 'Analoghe sconcezze. Tribadi, saffiste, invertite e omosessuali: categorie e sistemi sesso/genere nella rivista di antropologia fondata da Cesare Lombroso (1848–1949)', *DWF* 24 (1994): 50–122.

Milletti, Nerina, and Luisa Passerini. *Fuori dalla Norma. Storie lesbiche nell'Italia del primo Novecento.* Torino: Rosenberg & Sellier, 2007.

Mondella, Felice. 'Il Concetto di malattia mentale nell'opera di Emil Kraepelin', *Sanità, Scienza e Storia* 1 (1986): 83–110.

Moraglio, Massimo. *Costruire il manicomio. Storia dell'ospedale psichiatrico di Grugliasco.* Milano: Unicopli, 2002.

Moraglio, Massimo. 'Dentro e fuori il manicomio. L'assistenza psichiatrica tra le due guerre', *Contemporanea* 9, no. 1 (2006): 15–34.

Moraglio, Massimo, ed. *Effimeri entusiasmi, quotidiane sofferenze. La fondazione del manicomio di Racconigi.* Boves: Araba Fenice, 2007.

Mosse, George. *The Image of Man. The Creation of Modern Masculinity.* Oxford: Oxford University Press, 1996.

Mottola, José. *Gente di razza. Così parlò Nicola Pende, tutore della stirpe e pupillo dei Gesuiti.* Foggia: Bastogi, 2010.

Parrini, Alberto, ed. *La Norma Infranta. Pratica e teoria di una équipe psichiatrica fra ospedale e territorio.* Firenze: Guaraldi, 1978.

Parrini, Alberto, ed. *Sansalviventanni. Dal Manicomio alla psichiatria nella riforma.* Firenze: Amministrazione Provinciale di Firenze, 1980.

Passalia, Ennio. 'Frammentari ricordi di esistenze scomparse. Storie del Manicomio di Girifalco (1881–1920)' (PhD diss., University of Genova, academic year 2009–10).

Passerini, Luisa. *Torino Operaia e Fascismo.* Bari: Laterza, 1984.

Peloso, Paolo Francesco. *La Guerra Dentro. La Psichiatria Italiana tra Fascismo e Resistenza 1922–1945.* Verona: Ombre Corte, 2008.

Peloso, Paolo Francesco. 'Psychiatry in Genoa', *History of Psychiatry* 15, no. 1 (2004): 27–43.

Petracci, Matteo. *I Matti del Duce.* Roma: Donzelli, 2014.

Petrosino, Dario. 'Traditori della Stirpe: il razzismo contro gli omosessuali nella stampa del fascismo'. In *Studi sul Razzismo Italiano*, 89–107, edited by Alberto Burgio and Luciano Casali. Bologna: Clueb, 1996.

Piazzi, Andrea, Giovanni Del Missier, Mariopaolo Dario, Ester Stocco and Luana Testa. 'The history of Italian psychiatry during Fascism', *History of Psychiatry* 22, no. 3 (2011): 251–67.

Pick, Daniel. *Faces of degeneration: A European Disorder, c. 1844–c. 1918.* Cambridge: Cambridge University Press, 1989.

Pisanty, Valentina. 'Saul e gli altri: il nuovo cinema sulla Shoah e i dibattiti sulla memoria', *Storica* 66 (2016): 7–44.

Pogliano, Claudio. 'Bachi, Polli e Grani. Appunti sulla ricezione della genetica in Italia', *Nuncius* 14 (1999): 133–68.

Pogliano, Claudio. *L'Ossessione della razza: antropologia e genetica nel ventesimo secolo*. Pisa: Edizioni Scuola Normale di Pisa, 2005.

Porter, Roy. *Madness: A Brief History*. Oxford: Oxford University Press, 2002.

Pozzi, Lucia. 'The regulation of public morality and eugenics: A productive alliance between the Catholic Church and Italian Fascism', *Modern Italy* 25, no. 3 (2020): 317–31.

Quazza, Guido, ed. *Fascismo e società italiana*. Torino: Einaudi, 1973.

Rieff, David. *In Praise of Forgetting*. New Haven: Yale University Press, 2016.

Robin, Régine. *I Fantasmi della Storia. Il passato europeo e le trappole della memoria*. Verona: Ombre Corte, 2005.

Roccatagliata, Giuseppe. *Riflessioni sulla decadenza dell'isteria*. Napoli: Liguori, 1992.

Rodulgina, Ira. 'Why are we the people we are? Early Soviet homosexuals from the first-person perspective', *Ab Imperio* 2 (2016): 183–216.

Romano, Gabriella. *The Pathologisation of Homosexuality in Fascist Italy: The Case of G.* Basingstoke: Palgrave Macmillan 2019.

Romano, Gabriella. *Talking about silence, EUI Working Papers HEC* 1 (2020): 1–16. Available online: http://hdl.handle.net/1814/66587.

Rossi Barilli, Gianni. *Il movimento gay in Italia*. Milano: Feltrinelli, 1999.

Salkovskis, Cora. "'They cannot reason, they can only feel". Positioning and experiencing the "insane body" and its perversions of feeling in Britain, c. 1840–1914' (PhD diss., Birkbeck College, University of London, academic year 2020–1).

Salvante, Martina. 'La prostituzione maschile nel discorso scientifico della prima metà del Novecento in Italia'. In *Nuove Frontiere per la Storia di genere*, vol. III, edited by Laura Guidi and Maria Rosaria Pelizzari, 533–40. Padova: Webster Press, 2013.

Scaramella, Tommaso. 'La storia dell'omosessualità nell'Italia moderna: un bilancio', *Storicamente.org* 12 (2016): 1–21.

Scartabellati, Andrea. *'La "questione follia" in Italia tra fine Ottocento e inizio Novecento e il caso del Manicomio Provinciale di Cremona*. Milano: F. Angeli, 2001.

Schettini, Laura. *Il gioco delle parti. Travestismo e paure sociali tra Otto e Novecento*. Firenze: Le Monnier, 2011.

Schettini, Laura. 'Un sesso che non è un sesso: medicina, ermafroditismo e intersessualità in Italia tra Otto e Novecento', *Genesis* 11, nos. 1–2 (2012): 19–40.

Schneck, M. Jerome. *A History of Psychiatry*. Springfield: Charles C. Thomas, 1960.

Scurti, Alessandro. 'Gli esordi della medicalizzazione degli omosessuali', *Società e Storia* 108 (2005): 283–317.

Sengoopta, Chandak. 'Glandular politics: Experimental biology, clinical medicine, and homosexual emancipation in fin-de-siècle Central Europe', *Isis* 89, no. 3 (September 1998): 445–73.

Sengoopta, Chandak. *The Most Secret Quintessence of Life. Sex, Glands and Hormones, 1850–1950*. Chicago: University of Chicago Press, 2006.

Setaro, Marica. 'Le belle addormentate in manicomio. Infanzia ed encefalite letargica', *Italie et Mediterranée modernes et contemporaines* 133, no. 1 (2021): 197–210.

Silvano, Franco. *Legislazione e politica sanitaria del fascismo*. Roma: APES, 2011.

Spackman, Barbara. *Fascist Virilities. Rhetoric, Ideology and Social Fantasy in Italy*. Minneapolis: University of Minnesota Press, 1996.

Stok, Fabio. 'Kraepelin in Italia', *Il Piccolo Hans* 46 (1985): 89–108.

Stok, Fabio. *La Formazione della psichiatria*. Roma: Il Pensiero Scientifico, 1981.

Tagliacozzi, Bruno, and Adriano Pallotta. *Scene da un manicomio. Storia e storie del Santa Maria della Pietà*. Roma: Edizioni Scientifiche Magi, 1998.

Tamagne, Florence. *Histoire de l'Homosexualité en Europe*, vol. I e II. Paris: Du Seuil, 2000. Version consulted: *A History of Homosexuality in Europe. Berlin, London, Paris 1919–1939*. New York: Algora, 2006.

Todorov, Tzvetan. *Le Abus de la Mémoire*. Paris: Arléa, 1998. Version consulted: *Gli Abusi della Memoria*. Milano: Meltemi, 2018.

Tornabene, Massimo. *La Guerra dei Matti. Il Manicomio di Racconigi tra fascismo e Liberazione*. Boves: Araba Fenice, 2007.

Tranfaglia, Nicola. *Dallo Stato Liberale al regime fascista. Problemi e ricerche*. Milano: Feltrinelli, 1973.

Valeriano, Annacarla. *Ammalò di testa. Storie del Manicomio di Teramo (1880–1931)*. Roma: Donzelli, 2014.

Valeriano, Annacarla. *Malacarne. Donne e manicomio nell'Italia fascista*. Roma: Donzelli, 2017.

Valeriano, Annacarla. 'Voci dalle cartelle. Alcune linee di ricerca dall'archivio storico del manicomio di Sant'Antonio abate di Teramo', *Mefisto* 3, no. 2 (2019): 61–72.

Vecchioni, Domenico. *Le spie del fascismo. Uomini, apparati e operazioni di intelligence nell'Italia del Duce*. Sesto Fiorentino: Editoriale Olimpia, 2005.

Venè, Gian Franco. *Mille Lire al mese. Vita quotidiana della famiglia nell'Italia fascista*. Milano: Mondadori, 1988.

Vergine, Lea, ed. *Capri 1905–1940. Frammenti postumi*. Milano: Il Saggiatore, 2018.

Vernon, A. Rosario, ed. *Science and Homosexuality*. New York: Routledge, 1997.

Villa, Renzo. *Il deviante e I suoi segni. Lombroso e la nascita dell'antropologia criminale in Italia*. Milano: F. Angeli 1985.

Villano, Raimondo. 'Farmaci di Sintesi: origini e sviluppo', *puntoeffe*, 61–2, https://www.researchgate.net/publication/332736022_Farmaci_di_sintesi_origine_e_sviluppo, consulted February 2021.

Volpato, Chiara. 'Mario Canella e la psicologia razziale. Un caso di conformismo al potere universitario', http://aipass.org, associazione italiana di psicologia, consulted January 2020.

Wanrooij, P. F. Bruno. *Storia del pudore. La questione sessuale in Italia 1860–1940*. Venezia: Marsilio, 1990.

Weston, Janet. *Medicine, the Penal System and Sexual Crimes in England, 1919–1960s*. London: Bloomsbury, 2017.

Wilson, Perry, ed. *Gender, Family and Sexuality: The Private Sphere in Italy 1860–1945*. Basingstoke: Palgrave Macmillan, 2004.

Zunino, Pier Giorgio. *Interpretazione e memoria del fascismo. Gli anni del regime*. Bari: Laterza, 1991.

Websites

www://aipass.org, Associazione Italiana di Psicologia.

www.aspi.unimib.it

www.cartedalegare.it. SIUSA, Sistema Informativo Unificato per le Soprintendenze Archivistiche, Direzione Generale Archivi, Ministero della Cultura.

www.leggeresansalvi.it

www.siusa.archivibeniculturali.it

www.treccani.it

www.wikipink.it

Index

www.ingramcontent.com/pod-product-compliance
Lightning Source LLC
Chambersburg PA
CBHW071852270326
41929CB00013B/2193